50 plus one

Tips for Handling Everyday Stress

by

Michael Carney, Ph.D
&
Heather Z. Hutchins

$24.95

GLOBAL
professional
publishing

Global Professional Publishing
Random Acres
Slip Mill Lane
Hawkhurst
Cranbrook
Kent TN18 5AD
Email: publishing@gppbooks.com

ISBN 978-1-933766-26-3

Printed by Good News Press

Contents

Introduction

Stress is now the number one cause of disease in the United States. Everything from heart disease to high blood pressure and excess weight can all be attributed to stress.

And stress is everywhere from work to home to personal life. In fact, many experts point to modern life as the cause of excess stress. Yet, no matter how much stress you have, you can learn to reduce, relieve or cope with the stress in your life.

That is why *50 Plus One Tips for Handling Everyday Stress* was written. Everyone deals with stress differently. In fact, no two people deal with the same stressors in the same way. For this reason, the answer to your partner's stress may not work for you.

The trick is to find out what your stressors are, how you typically deal with them and how you can reduce, relieve or cope with the stress in your life no matter where it comes from.

This book was written with the average person in mind. It explains what stress is, the causes of stress and how to assess your own personal stress level. In addition, it includes a whole host of antidotes for stress including:

- How to deal with a perfectionist boss, the know-it-all co-worker and other stressors on the job,
- How to create a work/life balance that will give you peace not stress,
- How to ask for help and create a support system that relieves your stress instead of adding to it,
- How to troubleshoot stress in your home life,
- How to know when to seek professional help to deal with your stress,
- How to know when to change the stressful situation or change your reactions to it,
- How to relax your body and your mind,
- How to monitor your stress level and
- How to help your spouse, partner and children deal with their stress.

50 Plus One Hot Tips for Handling Everyday Stress will help you reduce, relieve and cope with the stress in your life in a useful way.

Forms and checklists are illustrated in the book. All the forms are free to readers by going to www.encouragementpress.com and clicking on the forms tab.

If you want to find a way to successfully cope with your stress and your life, this is the book for you.

Part One:

What is Stress?

1

Definitions

Before you can deal with stress and its effects you must have a working knowledge of what stress is. This means understanding the definitions of stress and how they can apply to your situation. Once these definitions are clear, as in the case of many medical conditions, you can be better equipped to deal with the challenges of stress.

The Challenge

Many people believe they understand the concept of stress. It is a term that is used constantly around them in popular usage and medical diagnoses. But, what is stress? What led to its identification and classification as a mental and medical disorder? How can you better realize what you are dealing with? Answering these questions depends on knowing what the definition of the various types of stress and its manifestations are. You can find this information or acquire it from your physician, but you must be prepared to make the effort to apply the definitions to your own conditions. The challenge is to find the appropriate information on stress definitions, make sure these definitions are the most up-to-date, recognize what you understand and do not and be prepared to seek professional assistance to use the definitions to help your condition.

The Facts

There is an old line that someone may not be able to define obscene materials, but they know it when they see it. The same can be said for stress. Most people believe they can recognize stress when it is occurring to them, but are hard-pressed to define exactly what stress is. By knowing the nature of stress, you can be ready to deal with the stressful condition and separate it from other feelings that may not be stress-related.

One of the many problems in coming up with a definition of stress is that it is made up of many things. Different people experience different aspects and may identify with different definitions. Hans Selye, one of the founding fathers of stress research, stated in 1956 that some level of stress is beneficial and the biochemical effects of stress would be experienced no matter whether the situation that caused the stress was positive or negative.

According to the National Association of Occupational Safety and Health, NIOSH, stress is simply defined as the harmful physical and emotional responses that occur when the requirements of work or even life in general do not match the needs, capabilities or resources of the person suffering from the stress. Stress can lead to poor health and even on-the-job injury.

Different types of stress are generally described in general terms. Within these broad definitions are further delineations of what is stress:

- Task-related stress which usually includes a heavy workload, infrequent breaks, long hours, hectic lifestyles and routine tasks that seem without purpose and are seemingly outside of your control.
- Management stress where you are in a work environment that allows you little participation in the decision-making process that affects your work.
- Interpersonal relationship stress comes from a poor social environment and a feeling of a lack of support from friends, family and co-workers.
- Career stress where a feeling of job insecurity causes stress and there is a feeling of a lack of opportunity for growth, advancement or promotion.
- Environmental stress by being in an upsetting or unsafe workplace or living in a home environment that does not adequately meet your needs or expectations.
- Personal stress where relationships with your partner and family are causing you more stress than satisfaction, and there seem to be few, if any options to improve your situation.

According to the Mayo Clinic, just 10 minutes of watching the news can make your levels of stress soar. They bring on physical reactions that should be recognized as helping to define stress. These are sometimes referred to as defense mechanisms and are built into us. They were developed thousands of years ago to help deal with the threats of predators and aggressors. We no longer fear being attacked by carnivorous animals, but these well-adapted defenses against physical dangers may not be as effective at dealing with the modern causes of stress. These defense mechanisms, when constantly activated can make your body more vulnerable to life-threatening problems.

A definition of stress is that it is a prolonged response that can have a debilitating effect on your body. Much of the stress due to threats that use the body defense mechanisms is short-lived, but if the response goes on for days, weeks or months, you are probably experiencing some form of unhealthy stress.

The Solutions

The concept of stress is often confused with the daily challenges of work and life. But, these concepts are not the same. Challenges can be seen as a positive thing and, when dealt with properly, can energize us both psychologically and physically. Challenges can motivate us to learn new skills and master the factors in our lives. A challenge that is successfully met can help us feel relaxed and satisfied. Challenge is therefore an important ingredient for a healthy and productive life. The challenges in our work life is likely what people are referring to when they say a little bit of stress is good for you.

Separating stress from other feelings is essential in dealing with it. You must understand the definitions before you can talk to your physician or a therapist about your feelings. A good physician should be able to ask you the proper follow-up questions to determine if your condition is stress-related or coming from some other environmental, physical or psychological factor:

- Has anything changed in your work life or personal life recently?
- Do you feel like you have lost control of the factors that affect your life?
- Has there been any changes in your appetite or eating habits? Are you putting on weight or losing it without trying to?
- Are you consuming more alcohol than usual?
- Do you have trouble sleeping at night?
- Are you unable to communicate your problems with your family or friends?
- Do you feel anxiety that is hard to define but has been bothering you?
- Are any of these feelings brought about recently or have they been affecting you for some time?

A good definition of stress is the urge to constantly fight or take flight. This is your body's rapid and automatic switch into a higher gear. When you encounter a stressful threat, the hypothalamus, a tiny region at the base of your brain, sets off an alarm system in your body. It sends out nerve and hormonal signals that prompt your adrenal glands to release a surge of hormones. The adrenaline increases your heart rate, elevates your blood pressure and boosts energy supplies. The primary stress hormone is cortisol which increases glucose in the bloodstream and increases the availability of substances that repair tissues.

It is often possible to determine whether you are stressed and where it is coming from because of a major change in your life. This can be positive such as a promotion or a new baby, or it can be negative such as being laid off or going through a divorce or death in the family. Some types of stress are harder to determine and will take some extra effort on your part. One idea is to keep a Stress Journal where you get a notebook and write down when something makes you feel stressed. Note how you reacted and what the results were in how you dealt with the stress. Keeping and reviewing the stress journal can help you find out both what is causing your stress and what level you think it is at. It will help you focus any discussion you may have about your stress with a physician or therapist. The stress journal can help you plan on what steps you need to take to deal with the stress.

The Resources

The following Web sites offer more information about the definitions of stress:

National Institute of Occupational of Safety and Health, *www.niosh.gov*

The Mayo Clinic, *www.mayclinic.com*

Web MD, *www.webmd.com*

Mind Tools, *www.mindtools.com*

Medicine Net, *www.medicinenet.com/stress*

Health Line, *www.healthline.com*

Rand, *www.rand.org*

Many books can help you understand the definitions of stress such as:

Measuring Stress: A Guide for Health and Social Scientists (Oxford University Press, USA, 1997)

The Complete Idiot's Guide to Managing Stress (Alpha, 1999)

The Stress Management Handbook (McGraw-Hill, 1999)

Stress and Health: Biological and Psychological Interactions (Sage Publications, 2004)

Stress, Workload and Fatigue (CRC, 2000)

Structural and Residual Stress Analysis by Nondestructive Methods (Elsevier Science, 1999)

Adrenaline and Stress: The Exciting New Breakthrough That Helps You Overcome Stress Damage (W. Publishing Group, 1995)

2

Physical, Emotional and Behavioral Symptoms of Stress

Every diagnosis of a mental or physical condition starts with an evaluation of the symptoms that might indicate you are suffering from the condition. These symptoms, depending on the condition, can take on many forms and be deceptive in what they are indicating. This is never more true than evaluating your feelings of stress. You may be showing symptoms that are entirely stress-related or are stress based on how you are dealing with other medical conditions and their symptoms.

The Challenge

Very few medical conditions can affect such a variety of areas as stress. This all-encompassing condition can manifest itself in a variety of ways including physical disabilities, mental strain and the effect on your psyche and behavioral issues that can seriously impact the quality of your life and how you deal with the world around you. Researchers are continually trying to find and isolate recognizable symptoms of stress, but the challenge in doing so is to separate stress-based symptoms from other indications of a medical condition. The challenge to you is to thoroughly evaluate your feelings and behavior, consult with friends and family regarding how you are dealing with your life and properly communicating these symptoms to a physician. More so than most conditions, a physician's recognition of the stress in your life will depend on your interpretation of your condition rather than through quantifiable tests. Knowing these symptoms will also help you see how you are coming to grips with the stress in your life and limiting its negative effects.

The Facts

It is inevitable that modern life will present stress, especially job-related stress. A small amount of stress and our reaction to it is not necessarily a bad thing, but when stress becomes debilitating and seriously affects your quality of life, it becomes destructive. It can be difficult to determine, in broad terms, how stress is affecting you, but in most cases it is a feeling that goes for some length of time, can be difficult to define and leads to negative reactions to normal situations.

It is easy to confuse the symptoms of stress with the symptoms of other health and psychological conditions. Often, people think they are suffering health effects from certain physical conditions based on symptoms such as chest pain, digestive problems, headaches or an inability to concentrate. However, when the condition is carefully evaluated by a physician, it may turn out that the symptoms being experienced are caused by some type or combination of stress. This stress should not be seen as less destructive than a physical ailment. But it must be dealt with in different ways than you would to treat a specific physical condition that is curable from drugs or other types of treatment.

When it comes to the major cause of stress, job-related, stress, before the symptoms manifest themselves in debilitating ways, there are several early-warning signs that you may be experiencing job stress:

- Headaches of an increased level of frequency or intensity;
- sleep disturbances where you are not sleeping enough or too much;
- difficulty in concentrating over normal tasks;
- short temper;
- upset stomach;
- hard-to-define dissatisfaction with your job and
- overall low morale.

It is the sympathetic nervous system that is most often attacked by stress. This is also called the Autonomic Nervous System or ANS which contains two types of nerves: the parasympathetic nerves that conserve energy and keep the body systems in a relatively resting state and sympathetic nerves which prepare the body for action through the Fight-or-Flight reaction. The ANS can cause two types of major stress, emotional/behavioral and physical that have their own distinct symptoms.

Emotional/behavioral symptoms of stress include:

- Feelings of irritation;
- frustration to having to wait for something;
- restlessness;
- inability to concentrate;
- confusion;
- experiencing memory problems;
- thinking negative thoughts constantly;
- negative self-talk;
- marked mood swings;
- lack of energy;
- difficulty in making decisions;
- emotional and inappropriate outbursts and
- lack of a sense of humor.

Physical symptoms of stress include:

- Muscle tension;

- pain in the back, shoulders, neck or chest;
- stomach or abdominal pain;
- unexplained rashes or skin irritations;
- a pounding or racing heart;
- sweaty palms or sweating when not physically active;
- butterflies in the stomach;
- indigestion and diarrhea and
- shortness of breath or a feeling of holding your breath.

Understanding the Symptoms of Stress

Often dealing with stress means balancing the demands of work with the needs of a family or your personal life. When you feel that these relationships are out of balance, negative stress can result and you are saddled with a feeling of powerlessness over your life. This type of stress can also lead to inattention in your daily life or work that can lead to injury due to inattention to details because of an obsession over the larger, perceived, picture of your life being out of control.

Two of the most obvious symptoms of stress are sleep-alteration and mood. Sleep-altering means you are having trouble maintaining a normal sleep cycle because of worries that have turned into stress. This interruption is most frequently an inability to go to sleep at your usual time during the night, or waking up from sleep. This can cause a general feeling of fatigue that can affect us in a variety of ways and have long-ranging impacts. The flip side of this is sleeping too much with longer sleep needed at night or feeling the need for frequent naps. Mood altering stress means, in general, you tend to react more strongly or negatively to situations that did not bother you in the past. This mood change can lead to expressions of frustration or anger that are directed at your family, friends or co-workers and can lead to an escalating feeling of frustration.

Your symptoms of stress are based very much on your reaction to stress. Some people are able to take a variety of issues in stride. They have a naturally laid-back attitude that manifests itself in many situations. Other people react instantly and negatively to stress and can get anxious at the first sign of trouble. This can be brought on by a simple interruption or change in plans. Most people have stress responses that fall somewhere in the middle of these extremes.

One of the ways to recognize symptoms of stress is to be aware of a change in your coping mechanisms that often involve what might have been seen as destructive behavior pre-stress, but now seems logical and vital:

- You tense up with a clenched shoulder, neck, jaws or fists. This tension may also be manifested in an upset stomach, shortness of breath, back pain, headaches and other physical symptoms.
- Are you overeating with food providing comfort? You may eat when you are not really hungry or lose track of your meal and exercise program.

- You may get impatient and find yourself pacing the floor or twitching.
- You may be more prone to crying spells over situations that do not merit this type of reaction.
- If you feel your stress is too much to take, you may give up by denying the issue, avoiding the problem, calling in sick or just stopping trying.
- You may automatically expect the worst from a stressful situation.
- You may start smoking or begin smoking after you have previously given it up. Stress is often considered the leading cause of smoking relapses. Nicotine is not only bad for your general health, it is a stimulant that can actually increase stress.
- You may be turning to alcohol and other drugs as a stress relief.

The Resources

The following Web sites offer more information about the various symptoms of stress:

Changing Minds, *www.changingminds.org*

Stress About, *www.stress.about.com/library/symptoms*

Stress Focus, *www.stressfocus.com*

Mayo Clinic, *www.mayoclinic.com/print/stress-management*

National Institute of Occupational Safety and Health, *www.niosh.gov*

EMedicince Health, *www.emedicinehealth.com/stress*

Life Positive, *www.lifepositive.com*

The following books offer more information about the various symptoms of stress such as:

Dr. Susan Lark's Anxiety & Stress Self Help Book: Effective Solutions for Nervous Tension Emotional Distress, Anxiety & Panic (Celestial Arts, 1996)

The Stress Management Handbook (McGraw-Hill, 1999)

The Relaxation & Stress Reduction Workbook (New Harbinger Publications, 2000)

10 Simple Solutions to Stress: How to Tame Tension and Start Enjoying Your Life (New Harbinger Publications, 2007)

Eliminating Stress, Finding Inner Peace (Hay House, 2003)

Stress Free for Good: 10 Scientifically Proven Life Skills for Health and Happiness (Harper San Francisco, 2005)

The Little Book of Stress Relief (Firefly Books, 2004)

3

Two Types of Stress: Acute and Chronic

Just as there are a variety of differences in medical conditions, there is a fundamental difference in the type of stress you might be feeling. The type of stress will greatly influence your diagnosis and your method of treatment. There is no good type of too much stress, but you can recognize the difference between chronic and acute stress and deal with them accordingly.

The Challenge

Most people have a hard enough time determining whether they are suffering from some type of debilitating stress in their lives than to add to this evaluation as to whether the stress is chronic or acute. But, not all stress is created equally and the way we deal with it will vary depending on what type it is. You need to know the differences and what you can do to alleviate them. The challenge with chronic and acute stress is to recognize the differences, what contributes to each type of stress, the effects they will have on your mental and physical health and how to help combat each type. By knowing where your stress falls, you can take the first important steps in diagnosing and treating it, and help you and your healthcare professionals work through these conditions that each present their own difficulties.

The Facts

In general, as in other physical disorders the terms acute and chronic refer to the onset and duration of the illness. This means that acute stress is a temporary and rapidly developing condition that might be linked to specific triggers such as a job change, divorce, death in the family or other factors. Chronic stress means it is a condition that is ongoing and may not be linked to specific events, but rather to an overall feeling of stress and a problem in dealing with the normal aspects of life. Both can be physically caused.

As a rule, chronic stress is the most common type of stress according to stress experts such as the Wellness Center, the Mayo Clinic, the British Medical Journal and the American Psychological Society. It may be indicated by long-term psychological and physical symptoms. These physical symptoms might include aches and pains, always being hot, always being cold, poor nutrition, inadequate hydration and sleep disorders.

Acute stress can be difficult to determine. You can experience short-term stress for a variety of reasons, some genuinely life-threatening. That type of stress usually goes away when the situation eases. Most experts agree that genuine acute stress becomes a problem when it is experienced for at least two days and can cause a variety of mental and physical disorders. Acute stress may be caused by non-life-threatening problems such as work issues or dealing with a life situation, such as having relationship problems or difficulty with a child who may be displaying disturbing behaviors.

Long-term worriers are candidates for chronic stress. They cannot turn off the elements of the sympathetic system that help them handle acute stress. After dealing with the physical elements of stress, such as increased adrenaline and cortisol, these levels of body hormones may be depleted. This leads to a feeling of fatigue that is not in keeping with your ordinary feeling of tiredness. Over time this increased response can lead to cardiovascular disease, colitis, irritable bowel syndrome, ulcers or even cancerous tumors. This means the life-saving stress response system can be life-threatening when dealt with over time as a chronic stress syndrome.

The acute stress disorder can be brought on by a number of recognizable factors. Each or any combination can bring on acute stress:

- The person has been exposed to a traumatic event in which both these were present: the person experienced, witnessed or was confronted with an event that involved real death or serious injury or a threat to the safety of others; and the person's response involved intense fear, or feelings of helplessness and horror.
- While experiencing or after experiencing the distressing events, you have three or more of these dissociative syndromes: a subjective sense of numbing, detachment or absence of emotional response; a feeling of being in a daze; derealizing; depersonalization and an inability to recall an important part of the trauma.
- The traumatic event is reexperienced by recurrent images, thoughts, dreams, illusions and flashbacks or a sense of reliving the experience.
- Avoiding the stimuli that arouse recollection of the trauma.
- Experiencing symptoms of anxiety or increased arousal.
- The disturbance causes clinically significant distress or impairment in social, occupational or other important areas of functioning or impairs your ability to pursue some necessary task.
- The disturbance lasts for a minimum of two days and a maximum of four weeks and occurs within four weeks of the actual event.
- The disturbance is not due to the direct physiological effects of a substance, such as drugs or alcohol.

There are several key terms when discussing and understanding both acute and chronic stress:

- Depersonalization is a dissociative symptom in which the patient believes his or her body is unreal, is changing or dissolving.
- Derealization is a dissociative symptom where the external environment is seen to be unreal.

- Dissociation is a reaction to trauma in which the mind splits off certain aspects of the trauma from conscious awareness. This can affect your memory, sense of reality and sense of identity.
- Trauma, in the context of acute stress, is a disastrous or life-threatening event.

As opposed to acute stress, chronic stress is a state of ongoing physiological arousal. It occurs when the body experiences so many stressors that it does not have a chance to activate the stress-relief systems. It can be a frequent product of the modern lifestyle from work to family to things that should be relaxing. It is estimated that as much as 90 percent of visits to a physician's office are caused in some part by stress.

The Solutions

Your stress response is ingrained in you and was designed primarily to save your life in the event of an acute physical stress cause. It comes from a time when we survived by being hunter-gatherers and faced daily dangers in our lives. These dangers triggered what is known as the fight-or-flight response where adrenaline and hormones in the body prepare you to either flee a stressful situation or to fight against it.

Acute stress is recognizable by being relatively short-lived. After the stress factor has been successfully dealt with our body systems would return to their natural state. Some chronic stress factors, such as hunger, are no longer the causes of chronic stress when food is made available.

Unlike chronic stress, acute stress can be dealt with more easily medically if the person suffering from the stress visits a physician or therapist who is experienced in recognizing and treating acute stress. A diagnosis of acute stress is based on a combination of your honest history and a physical examination that can eliminate diseases that cause anxiety. The treatment for acute stress disorder usually involves a combination of antidepressant drugs and psychotherapy. Often these two are linked together as part of the plan of treatment. The prognosis for recovery from acute stress is influenced by the severity and duration of the trauma and the patient's previous level of functioning.

Traumatic events that can cause both acute stress and chronic stress cannot be usually foreseen and are very difficult to prevent. The key to prevention is to address the condition with a professional intervention as soon as possible after the trauma has occurred. You can sometimes recognize acute stress disorder by monitoring biochemical changes in the central nervous system, muscles and digestive tract.

One of the most important impacts of chronic stress is the debilitating effect it has on your immune system. This creates a cascading condition where your body is affected by diseases that may have nothing directly related to the stress. Rather these diseases are brought on by chronic stress causing the poor function of the immune system.

The Resources

The following Web sites offer more information about acute and chronic stress stress:

Wellness Tips, *www.wellnesstips.ca*

Mental Health, *www.mentalhealth.com*

Health A to Z, *www.healthatoz.com*

Psychnet, *www.psychnet-uk.com*

Psychology Today, *www.psychologytoday.com*

Stress About, *www.stress.about.com*

American Psychological Association, *www.apa.org*

The following books offer more information about acute and chronic stress such as:

Post-Traumatic and Acute Stress Disorders: The Latest Assessment and Treatment Strategies (Compact Clinicals, 2005)

Acute Stress Disorder: A Handbook of Theory, Assessment and Treatment (American Psychological Association, 2000)

Post-Traumatic Stress Disorders: Diagnosis, Management and Treatment (Informa Healthcare, 2000)

Does Stress Damage the Brain? Understanding Trauma-Related Disorders from a Mind-Body Perspective (W.W. Norton and Company, 2005)

Coping with Chronic Stress (Springer, 1997)

Miss Diagnosed: Unraveling Chronic Stress (iUniverse, Inc., 2005)

Rhodiola Rosea for Chronic Stress Disorder (Safe Goods Publishing, 2003)

4

Health Risks of Stress

Some stress can actually be fun, such as when we are competing in a sport or doing something for recreation such as skiing or surfing. But, the effects of acute or chronic stress are usually damaging to our health. This can manifest itself with psychological health effects such as an inability to focus or general feeling of anxiety. In some cases, stress can have a negative impact on our physical health and be very harmful.

The Challenge

It is often easy to discount or ignore the health effects of stress. We can experience physical effects and believe they are caused by measurable causes such as a disease or medical condition that can be treated with drugs or other therapies. It is not unusual for us to discount the health risks of stress because we know that stress is simply a part of everyday life and almost everyone experiences some type of stress. If those people are feeling okay, your logic will tell you, then it should not negatively affect your health. But, the truth is everyone has different reactions to stress, and what may not constitute a health risk for one person may be a very real threat to someone else. The challenge is to recognize the mental and physical health risks of stress as a concept, apply those concepts to your own feelings, discussing these health risks with your physician and discovering ways to lessen the stress or better deal with it to eliminate the bad effects of stress. Knowing what you are facing health-wise with stress can help you cope with the challenges of the stress and modern life in a positive way.

The Facts

The health effects and risks of stress are due to the fight-or-flight response to perceived dangerous situations. The term was based on the principle that ancient people needed a physical response to very real dangers, such as predators encountered during the course of normal life. The fight-or-flight response releases hormones such as adrenaline and cortisol. These speed the heart rate, slow digestion, shunts blood flow to major muscle groups and effects other autonomous nervous functions. Within normal parameters, these hormones return to a normal level after the stimulus has been dealt with. However, with stress, the hormones do not return to normal and can cause serious problems and damage to the body.

When dealing with chronic stress and, because of the stress, an overactivated autonomous nervous system, you will begin to see physical symptoms. These symptoms usually begin as mild risks such as headaches and an increased susceptibility to colds. More exposure to chronic stress, however, can trigger more serious health risks. The most often experienced of these are:

- Depression;
- diabetes;
- hair loss;
- heart disease;
- hyperthyroidism;
- obesity and eating disorders;
- obsessive-compulsive or other anxiety disorders;
- sexual dysfunction, usually erectile dysfunction;
- tooth and gum disease unrelated to poor dental care;
- ulcers and
- possibly cancer.

Substance abuse is a very real health risk of dealing with chronic stress. A patient who is trying to cope with stress may turn to self-medication that can cause more harm than the stress or react negatively with the stressful condition. Often it means using the substance to initially relieve the stress and then increasing the abuse of the substance as it has less and less effect on the stressful condition. These substances usually include the obvious suspects of alcohol or drugs, but might also involve prescription drugs such as pain killers or other behaviors such as a sex addiction, overeating or gambling.

While it may seem less problematical, there is a real relationship between stress and the health of your skin. Your skin health is vital to your overall good health and can also affect your appearance. Skin can be very reactive to strong emotions. For example, someone suffering from the often debilitating conditions of psoriasis or eczema may see the condition exacerbated by stress. In the past, physicians treated skin conditions with topical treatments or with hormones. Now, many physicians are combining traditional physical treatments for skin problems with relaxation techniques and other methods of relieving stress. Although the research is still in an early stage, it seems this combination of physical and emotional therapy can be very effective in dealing with chronic skin conditions.

The Solutions

Your physician can help you determine if you are suffering health effects of stress, but only if you are willing to be as honest and detailed as possible in explaining your symptoms and seeking help. This means supplying a complete history to your physician and to not discount any symptom without discussing it with your physician. It is ironic that often the act of visiting a physician because of health effects from stress can be a major cause of stress. There is a symptom called the white-coat reaction which is only a half-joking reference that some patients can experience stress from simply being in a physician's examination room. This can lead to irregular heartbeats and elevated blood pressure that has nothing to do with general health, but, instead are reactions to the stress of going to a physician, especially if the physician is one you have never visited before, or if it has been some time since you saw a physician for any reason.

As you work to understand the risks of stress there are probably going to be two different types of professionals you will consult.

- Therapists including psychologists, psychiatrists or therapists without PhD degrees can help you recognize when stress is presenting a risk to your general feelings of well-being. These feelings can certainly affect your physical health, but, are usually addressed in a stand-alone fashion where the mental effects are set apart from the physical effects of stress.
- Medical physicians, especially your primary care physician, can evaluate your physical symptoms and help you determine if they are caused by a specific and treatable condition or whether they may be a product of stress. This can be a difficult process and is not as measurable as testing for specific medical conditions. In some cases, stress can aggravate a medical condition even if it is not the only condition to deal with.

Dealing with the risks of stress and its debilitating health effects should not be put off any more than you would put off the risks and effects of other diseases. If you do not visit a physician or therapist and get your life back in balance, the effects will get worse and not better. This cumulative effect can move from minor effects to serious risks of exhaustion depression and anxiety disorders. Your health, your family and your career can be affected by these risks. You should not believe you can handle the effects of stress on your own, but seek the type of help you need to combat the effects.

There are three ways a physician will help you deal with the real health risks of stress. Sometimes these methods will stand alone, often they are combined into a variety of treatments. The challenge in this treatment is that dealing with stress is not as cause-and-effect as dealing with other conditions and may require more experimentation by a physician to find the type of treatments best suited to dealing with your health risks.

- Recommending therapists who can talk to the patient regarding his or her feelings of stress, their causes and how to place the stress into the context of daily life. Sometimes this may lead to a patient participating in a group that will include others dealing with stress and sharing their symptoms and approach to treating it.
- Prescribing psychoactive drugs such as anti-depressants to treat the psychological causes of the disease. These must be closely monitored and the physician may change the prescription and dosage depending on the drugs' impact and side effects.
- Treating the actual effects as much as possible, such as heart problems, diabetes or muscle pain. It is important that the physician looks beyond these immediate symptoms and links them to the risks of stress.

The Resources

The following Web sites offer more information about the health risks of stress:

Stress About, *www.stress.about.com*

Web MD, *www.webmd.com*

Website 101, *www.website101.com*

Stress Management, *www.stress-management.net*

Ladies Home Journal, *www.lhj.com*

Science Daily, *www.sciencedaily.com*

Obgyn, *www.obgyn.net*

The following books offer more information about the health effects of stress such as:

Stress, Risk, and Resilience in Children and Adolescents: Processes, Mechanisms, and Interventions (Cambridge University Press, 1996)

Effective Health Risk Messages: A Step-By-Step Guide (Sage Publications, 2001)

Communicating Health Risks to the Public: A Global Perspective (Gower Publishing Company, 2006)

Historical and Current Perspectives on Stress and Health (JAI Press, 2002)

Stress Management for Primary Health Care Professionals (Springer, 2002)

Measuring Stress: A Guide for Health and Social Scientists (Oxford University Press, USA, 1997)

Stress, Health, & Fitness: A Higher Perspective (BookSurge Publishing, 2006)

5

How Men and Women Handle Stress Differently

Each individual handles stress in a unique manner. For example, two people could be presented with the same stressful situation, and they could react to it differently. In fact, one or both people may not perceive the situation as stressful at all. One of the most interesting facts about stress is that everyone reacts to it differently. In addition, studies have shown that men and women tend to handle stress in opposite ways.

The Challenge

A landmark study in 2000 showed that women often handle stress in a totally different manner than men do. While men tend to evoke the fight-or-flight response that has always been associated with stress research, women tended toward a response called tend-and-befriend. Men fight or run away in relation to stress. Women more often spend time nurturing those around them or reaching out to a different community. Because of these opposite approaches, stress advice for men and women needs to be tailored to the gender and the individual.

For example, not every woman will exhibit tend-or-befriend tendencies. Some women and men will react with a typical fight-or-flight response. However, research shows that a majority of women exhibit some tendency towards the tend-and-befriend model.

The Facts

Stress Tips for Men

Many men react to stress by running away or turning to fight. In modern life, this response translates to men ignoring their stress and not talking about it or funneling the stress into helping them improve their performance at work or at something else they care about.

Because men react differently than women, their stress tips are geared to their tendency toward fight-or-flight responses.

- **Take some time for yourself.**
  When they are under stress, some men prefer to take some time for themselves. They may go and participate in a solo hobby or just go off to a movie by themselves. This is one good way to deal with stressful events.

- **Exercise**.
  Many men use exercise to help them relax their muscles and relieve their stress. Jogging, biking, hiking and weight training are common ways that men decompress. Any exercise that gets the heart rate up is a good option.
- **Spend time with others**.
  Many men like to get away with their male friends when they are stressed. Fishing, hunting and group sports are common ways that men use to rid themselves of stressful feelings. Although they may not discuss their stress with friends, most men feel better after hanging with the guys for a few hours.

Stress Tips for Women

Women often have their own unique reactions to stressful situations. Many women tend to nurture their family or friends or befriend others in order to combat stress. This tend-and-befriend reaction is a very common one for women even though not all women will fit into the pattern.

In modern life, this response means that women often want to vent their feelings and discuss their stress with friends. Since women react to stress so differently than men, the stress reduction tips for women will not usually work for men.

- **Talk to friends and family you trust**
  If you feel the inclination, spend time talking to family and friends about what stresses you out. Be sure that you are sharing your secrets with people you can trust. You need to talk about what is bothering you and try to make sense of it. However, do not go over and over the same points. This can get depressed for both you and your friends.

- **Say no to extra work or responsibilities**
  Women often tend to take on too many responsibilities, especially when they are stressed. Instead, cut down on your activities and the activities of your family. Running your children back and forth to play dates, sports activities and school events is not a good recipe to combat stress.

- **Take time for yourself**
  In many cases, women spend time nurturing everyone but themselves. When you are stressed, take time for yourself. Get away or find some me-time to do exactly what you would like to do: read a book, glance at a catalog, have coffee with a friend or watch all the movies you like. Taking a long, hot bath with music and candles can also be a good stress reliever.

The Solutions

Stress Tips That Work for Either Gender

Despite the differences between men and women, the stress response is unique to each person. For this reason, you can feel free to try to stress relievers that are suggested for men or for women. In addition, experts offer the following stress relief techniques that can work for someone of either gender.

- **Create a support system for stress**

  Whether you are male or female, you need a support system to help you deal with your stress. This can be a bunch of guys you play softball with or a book group that meets once a month. No matter what the group is, you need to find other people that you like and trust.

  Even if you do not talk about your problems with these people directly, you want to spend time with upbeat people who renew your energy and make you feel better. Stay away from relatives or anyone else who tends to drain you and make you feel bad.

- **Use pets as solace**

  Your pets can also be helpful in dealing with stress. You can go running with your dog, give it a walk or curl up on the couch with it. Cats are good for snuggling. They are also fun to play with because they love to chase everything from feathers to catnip mice. No matter what you inclination—couch potato or activities—your pets can contribute to your stress reduction.

- **Listen to music**

  Listening to music that you like is an excellent way to relieve stress, according to experts. You can exercise to the music or just listen while you relax. However you decide to use your tunes, they can help you decompress and get over your initial stress.

- **Find an absorbing hobby**

  Finding a hobby can seem like a silly way to combat stress. Nonetheless, people who find a hobby that engrosses them (they lose track of time while working on a project) find that they look up from their hobby project to see that hours have passed. In addition, they no longer feel stressed. In fact, the stress of their work or home life seems miles away.

  No matter what kind of hobby you choose, find something that appeals to you. Do not be put off by what you liked or did not like in the past. Even if you used to hate cooking class in high school, try it again. Many people find that cooking or baking calms the mind and the body.

- **Be healthy**

  People under stress often skip their usual healthy behaviors because of the stress. For example, those who exercise regularly may give it up because they are too busy at work. Those who normally eat a healthy salad at lunch suddenly opt for the biggest, greasiest hamburger they can find. No matter how busy you are, you have time to be healthy.

  When you are stressed is exactly the time that you need to keep up your healthy routines. Eat right. Try to ignore cravings for sweet or fatty snacks. Exercise. Get enough sleep. Keeping yourself healthy will help you combat stress in the long term.

The Resources

The following Web sites offer more information about the different ways that men and women deal with stress:

www.webmd.com

This Website has everything that you ever wanted to know about your health. Their section on stress and stress relief is excellent.

www.mayoclinic.com

This Website offers a huge amount of information about the various sources of stress along with research about the differences between the sexes when it comes to dealing with stress.

http://helping.apa.org

This Website from the American Psychological Association offers huge amounts of information about the mind/body connection including reactions to stress.

Part Two:

Causes of Stress

6

Work Stress

Stress can be caused by many factors, but most people will point at work or job factors as primary causes of stress. This stress can be brought on for a variety of reasons whether they involve your current workplace or your career in general. Unless you are one of the few who can survive on an independent income, you will probably have to work for a living. Indeed, most of us want to work for a living and welcome the opportunities and challenges it can present. But, when the stress of working piles up into negative feelings, work stress can be a problem that has to be dealt with.

The Challenge

There are many ways that job stress can alter our lives. We may find ourselves having to accept new responsibilities that are added to whatever we are doing. We may have to deal with a new supervisor who we may not mesh well with. We may be facing a work situation where our company is in real danger of going out of business. We may believe our neck is on the chopping block and do not understand how to get away. We may be looking at starting a new job or making a major career change. All of these challenges can bring on stress. But, they can be successfully dealt with, and, in some cases, can be used to improve our attitude and our ability to handle our jobs. The challenge is to recognize what about our work or job is causing stress, how to put it in context of the good things about our job and how to work with our supervisors or fellow workers to alleviate the stress. Job stress is almost always inevitable in some type of context, but it can be worked with and we can learn and grow from it.

The Facts

One of the agencies which have taken a special interest in work stress is the National Institute for Occupational Safety and Health, or NIOSH. Under the Occupational Safety and Health Administration, OSHA, NIOSH has been directed to study the psychological aspects of occupational safety and health, including the issue of stress at work. NIOSH recognizes that work stress can affect worker safety and health and seeks to find ways to reduce stress in the workplace.

Surveys about work stress are consistent in how they find employees reacting to their jobs:

- A survey by Northwestern National Life found that 40 percent of workers find their jobs to be very or extremely stressful.
- A survey by the Families and Work Institute found that 26 percent of workers report they are often or very often burned out or stressed by their work.
- A survey by Yale University found that 29 percent of workers report they feel quite a bit or extremely stressed at work.

The causes of job stress can vary by situation, but, in general there are several major causes of job stress:

- Worker characteristics which mean there are other factors in a worker's life that can contribute to a feeling of stress;
- Differences in worker characteristics such as personality and coping style—what is stressful for one person may not be for another;
- Excessive workload demands and conflicting expectations and
- Personality conflicts with supervisors or fellow workers.

OSHA has identified several different conditions that can be closely linked to job stress:

- Cardiovascular disease;
- musculoskeletal disorders including neck and back pain;
- psychological disorders such as burnout and depression;
- workplace injuries and
- suicide, cancers, ulcers and impaired immune functions.

Often times prevention of stress on the job can depend on interventions an employer can use. These interventions follow a set formula that has been found to be very beneficial in relieving stress:

- Identify the problem. Lack of productivity, loss of employees and poor job quality are symptoms, but not the actual problem. Once you have determined the real problem behind the destructive stress, it will be easier to deal with it.
- Design and implement interventions that target the actual problem. The intervention may be situational for a certain employee or company wide. Be sure your employees know what you plan on doing before starting the intervention. Sometimes a kick-off breakfast or lunch can be beneficial.
- Evaluate the intervention. You must determine whether the intervention has worked, and, if not, what can be done to change the intervention. This determination may be based on employee focus groups, surveys or simple observation.

The Solutions

To boost productivity and maintain a competitive edge in the world marketplace, American workers are being asked to do more on the job. Workers are being laid off to save money or are not replaced after leaving from attrition, which could be voluntary leaving for another position or retirement. The solution to many companies is to have workers do the jobs others were doing as well as their own. This type of increased workload can lead to tremendous job stress with workers thinking constantly about their work and trying to get as much done as before. It can lead to increased hours and the fatigue experienced may cause workers to make mistakes that could lead to their or their co-workers' injuries. The solution is to have companies looking to downsize to keep in mind the needs of their current workers and avoid the type of overwork that may temporarily boost productivity, but will ultimately lead to burnout. This means examining the company structure and looking at new systems or technologies that can help existing employees handle the job stress. It may involve bringing in consultants or doing training to help employees organize their time better and face job changes in a positive way.

Two creative ways to help remove stress from a job are to provide rewards and giving employees flexible time. The rewards, which do not have to be financial, can help keep your employees motivated. Flexible time helps employees balance their work time with their personal needs while still getting the job done.

Individual and situational factors can affect a worker on the job and increase feelings of stress. These can include changes in a person's life outside the workplace. NIOSH has found three main ways to deal with job stress contributed to by individual and situational factors:

- Finding a balance between work and family or personal life;
- using a support network of friends and co-workers and
- maintaining a relaxed and positive outlook.

The work organization is not carved in stone and can be changed to help workers deal with job stress. According to American Psychologist:

- Ensure the workload is in line with worker capabilities and resources.
- Design jobs to provide meaning, stimulation and opportunities for workers to use their skills.
- Clearly define worker roles and responsibilities.
- Give workers opportunities to participate in decisions and actions that affect their jobs.
- Improve communications.
- Provide opportunities for social interactions among workers.
- Establish work schedules compatible with demands and responsibilities outside the job.

Dealing with job stress is not just the responsibility of the employer. A worker needs to be proactive with the process.

- If overwork is seen as a problem, take a vacation, leave work on time and avoid taking work home.
- If layoffs are a possibility and you are worried about them, make sure you are prepared for them.
- If you believe you have made a bad career choice or it is no longer fulfilling, make a change.

- If you are experiencing conflicts with your boss or co-workers, try to work them out and get along better.
- If your stress is adversely affecting your life, seek professional help.
- Reduce the clutter of your job and get organized.
- Find humor in your job situation. Stress is not the end of the world and work should not be the be-all of our existence. Keeping a positive attitude can help cope with job stress.
- Maintain realistic expectations about what you can accomplish during the day.
- Realize you are not perfect. Do your best and learn from your mistakes.

The Resources

The following Web sites offer more information about work stress:

National Institute of Occupational and Health Safety, *www.niosh.gov*

Career Planning About, *www.careerplanning.about.com*

Quintessential Careers, *www.quintcareers.com*

Malone Counseling and Consulting, *www.canville.net/malone/jobstress*

Health Guidance, *www.healthguidance.org*

Mindtools, *www.mindtools.com*

ERIC Digest, *www.ericdigest.org*

The following books offer more information about work stress such as:

Surviving Stress at Work: Understand It, Overcome It (Trafford Publishing, 206)

Stress at Work: Management and Prevention (Butterworth-Heinemann, 2005)

Toxic Work: How to Overcome Stress, Overload and Burnout and Revitalize Your Career (Plume, 1997)

Resilience at Work: How to Succeed No Matter What Life Throws at You (AMACOM/ American Management Association, 2005)

Work Stress and Social Support (Addison Wesley Longman Publishing, 1981)

Don't Sweat the Small Stuff at Work: Simple Ways to Minimize Stress and Conflict While Bringing Out the Best in Yourself and Others (Hyperion, 1999)

Anxious 9 to 5: How to Beat Worry, Stop Second Guessing Yourself, And Work With Confidence (New Harbinger Publications, 2006)

7

Personal Stress

Most people believe stress is common at work, and, indeed workplace stress can be a pervasive problem. But, work is not the only cause of common stress. Often personal issues we deal with can be stressors to us. Most people look for their homes to be havens from the craziness of everyday living, but due to a variety of factors, personal life can be very stressful in ways that are hard to recognize. A mixture of personal and work stress can cause significant health and psychological problems.

The Challenge

Personal stress can take many forms and depend on temporary conditions as well as ongoing issues. It is often difficult to recognize personal stress, assuming that everyone goes through some type of stress in their daily lives outside the workplace. But, personal stress is a very real issue that can have just as debilitating effects as work stress. In some ways, it can be more difficult to recognize and deal with personal stress due to issues that impact you in ways that work stress would not. The challenge is to understand the nature of personal stress, identify what is causing stress in your personal life, communicating these stress factors to professionals as needed and finding ways to successfully deal with both the symptoms of the stress and lessen the causes. Personal stress is a difficult issue to deal with for most people, but when properly addressed can be dealt with and lessened.

The Facts

Personal stress can take on many forms, but, in general, personal stress is caused by some event or situation in your personal life that no longer seems manageable. Personal stress can be a stand-alone event, such as a divorce or death in the family. It can be ongoing as in dealing with destructive family issues and behaviors that may be manageable in the short run but seem insurmountable in the long run. Whether the stress is caused by a single event or pattern, personal stress can be very harmful.

Personal stress factors are different for everyone and totally depend on their life situations. But, there are personal stress factors that are very common and need to be recognized:

- Long-range illness for yourself or a family member;
- death in the family, especially someone in the immediate family;
- money issues including dealing with debt;
- moving to a new home or buying or selling a home;
- dealing with a natural disaster such as fire or flood that causes extensive property damage;
- crime against you or your property such as robbery, burglary or vandalism;
- handling personal conflict with a spouse or partner including dealing with the psychological aspects of a divorce or permanent break-up;
- being drawn into a family conflict outside your immediate family;
- planning and executing a major event such as a wedding or large social event;
- working with children who are not functioning properly at school or engaging in other potentially destructive behavior and
- fixating on the natural aging process and the feeling that our lives have not gone the way we had planned.

Personal stress that is not properly addressed can cause worry to become destructive anxiety. Some anxiety should be recognized as a normal reaction to stress. But, when anxiety becomes an irrational and excessive dread of everyday life it can lead to problematic behaviors such as phobias out of proportion to the situation. Knowing when you are suffering debilitating anxiety is often a matter of discussing your feelings with a physician or therapist.

Stress research shows that personal stress is a worldwide problem and usually affects women more than men. According to a recent survey of people between the ages of 13 and 65 in 30 countries conducted by Roper Starch Worldwide:

- Women who work full-time and have children under the age of 13 report the greatest stress worldwide.
- Nearly one in four mothers who work full-time and have children under the age of 13 feel stress almost every day.
- Globally, 23 percent of women executives and professionals, and 19 percent of their male peers, say they feel super-stressed.

The Solutions

An issue of personal stress that has to be handled separately in most cases is stress based on other health or medical issues. This stress may be caused by concerns over a medical condition, either diagnosed or not diagnosed, having to go through testing to determine the condition, understanding the full scope of how the condition will affect your life and dealing with the stress of undergoing long-term treatments or surgeries. Even visits to the dentist can cause stress based on your feelings about dental procedures and any pain they may cause. A good physician will help provide you with as much information as possible to lessen health-oriented stress, but, often this type of stress simply has to be dealt with by putting it into a context of what you are dealing with and what your prognosis is. Knowledge is the key to handling medical stress, although it is not a cure all.

Taking action to combat personal stress can be just as challenging, if not more so, than dealing with work stress. With personal stress you are dealing with feelings and histories that are not as transient as those based on work. Personal stress may feel like it hits much closer to you than work stress. The key is to take action against the stress when you recognize its existence. This means keeping the lines of communication open with your family and using therapists for not only yourself but also for your family.

Substance abuse is a very important aspect of personal stress. Often we may have a reliance on alcohol or illegal drugs that is destructive to our health, expensive and having a bad effect on our personal relations. Sometimes it means dealing with family members who are experiencing substance abuse issues. There are several rehabilitation centers that can help you deal with the effects of substance abuse and correct this behavior. Support groups such as Alcoholics Anonymous can help you deal with abuse of alcohol or drugs. Groups such as Al-Anon can be beneficial in helping you find ways to deal with a loved one who has a destructive substance abuse problem. Nowadays, there is no reason to feel alone in dealing with substance abuse, even if the treatments involved can take time and tinkering.

Dealing with personal stress can depend on the type of stress being experienced, but there are several common methods of addressing personal stress:

- Discussing honestly with your family the nature of what you believe the stress is and trying to find ways to relieve it;
- visiting a therapist, in some cases a couples or family therapist, to discuss the issues involved in the stress;
- going through relaxation efforts such as yoga, therapeutic massage and acupuncture;
- monitoring the use of alcohol or tobacco;
- getting plenty of sleep at night or discussing sleep disruption with your physician;
- vigorously exercising on a regular basis;
- eating healthy and drinking plenty of water and
- asking friends to listen to your concerns and, if requested, give you their own perspective on the stress and ideas on how to handle it.

A vacation can be vital in relieving personal stress, but, if not handled properly can add to the stress. Here are some ideas in properly using a vacation to combat stress:

- Take at least seven days for a vacation.
- Make a list of what you must leave behind including your electronics or work-related material.
- Leave your cell phone behind or give it to someone you can trust.
- Make it clear you cannot be contacted.
- Try to avoid traveling too far.
- Choose a vacation that includes lots of places to go, things to see and do and fresh experiences to keep you engaged.
- Stay in the moment and ignore the past or speculating about the future.

- Let go of worries, fears, hopes, expectations and anxieties.
- Get plenty of sleep.
- Accept the vacation for what it is and do not strive for the perfect vacation. It does not exist.
- Keep the television off.
- Read books or magazines, but make sure they are not work-related.
- Fill your days with music.
- If you find yourself feeling bored, go for a walk or swimming.

The Resources

The following Web sites offer more information about personal stress:

Mayo Clinic, *www.mayoclinic.com*

Stress Directions, *www.stressdirections.com*

North Carolina State University, *www.ces.ncsu.edu*

Geocities, *www.geocities.com/beyond_stretched*

Lie Hack, *www.lifehack.org*

City University of London, *www.city.ac.uk/hr/policies/stress*

Wellteacher, *www.wellteacher.pbwiki.com*

The following books offer more information about personal stress such as:

Your Personal Stress Profile and Activity Workbook (McGraw Hill Humanities/Social Sciences/Languages, 2005)

The Truth About Burnout: How Organizations Cause Personal Stress and What to Do About It, (Jossey-Bass, 1997)

Post-Trauma Stress: A Personal Guide to Reduce the Long-Term Effects and Hidden Emotional Damage Caused By Violence and Disaster (Fisher Books, 2000)

Coming to Terms with Mediocrity: One Life Lesson at a Time (BookSurge Publishing, 2007)

Stress Busting Through Personal Empowerment (Routledge, 1994)

Getting Things Done: The Art of Stress-Free Productivity (Penguin, 2002)

Personal Stress and Well-Being Assessment (HRD Press, Inc., 2002)

8

Stresses of Modern Life

Life has always been stressful. Thousands of years ago, simply surviving could be stressful. This included being invaded or being a victim of disease, famine or drought. Later on, the stress of life included making a basic living and trying to survive a world of poor hygiene and aristocracy that could affect your life. Slowly, but surely these stresses have changed into the 20th and 21st centuries with stress that can still affect you on a daily basis. Those stresses can now include dealing with the threat of terrorism, global warming, overpopulation and a society that is heavy on technology, but sometimes light on people skills.

The Challenge

Unless we are willing to live in a cave, we are going to be affected by the stresses of modern life. These stresses have changed throughout the centuries, but have always manifested themselves as challenges to dealing in a positive way to everyday life. Sometimes we allow these stresses, most of which are completely out of our control, to overwhelm us and cause stress that is difficult to alleviate. For example, there is little most of us can do about terrorism or world diplomacy, and yet the stresses from these can sometimes feel as if we have lost control of our lives. Our reliance on the convenience of electronics, the computer and the Internet have vastly improved our lives, but also have left us open to having our identity misappropriated, making us feel suspicious of everyone around us. Modern life will always have stresses we must deal with. The challenge is to recognize the nature of modern stresses, placing them in a historical context that can help us cope more effectively with them, see how those stresses affect our lives and coming up with systems and coping measures that allow us to conduct our lives without feeling crushed by modern stresses. There is no reason we cannot enjoy and thrive in our times, once we realize the stress modern life presents will always be there and, often, is easier to deal with than we imagine.

The Facts

The stress of modern life will vary depending on your socio-economic position. For example, someone who is dealing with a lack of money or uncertain job will face different types of stress from modern life than those of us who are successful business people or professionals. Each type of stress is valid and must be recognized as such. However, in general, modern life will present certain types of stress we must all deal with no matter what we do and how much we have:

- The ability to pay the bills, keeping in mind that many people with high incomes tend to overspend;
- dissatisfaction with the technology we are using and wanting to upgrade your computers or cell phones;
- pressures on the family including juvenile delinquency and drug use;
- marital and relationship problems;
- worries over the world situation;
- concern about the environmental impact we are having and worrying that the world we are passing to our children will not be as good as what we have;
- worry about diseases including antibiotic resistant diseases and pandemics such as HIV/AIDS and
- concern over crime whether it is something we must deal with personally or have become aware of in the world around us.

Chronic stress, combined with chemical changes in the brain, can cause depression. Depression is a debilitating disease that can be hard to diagnose or understand. Maintaining good mental health and avoiding depression caused by the stresses of modern life can be treated with getting enough sleep, eating sensibly, exercising appropriately and avoiding the harmful use of substances such as alcohol or drugs. Beyond that, you should consider visiting a physician or therapist for the use of counseling and drugs to help with depression.

Sleep can be a wonderful cure-all for stressful situations. Think about how well you are sleeping and how you felt when you had a good night's sleep. Suddenly, your problems do not seem quite so overwhelming and you may wake up with new ideas on how to handle modern stress or how to address the problems you are stressing over.

According to Dr. Jacky Bolvin at Cardiff University, modern life stress is contributing to infertility through body and lifestyle changes. If you are contemplating having a baby, but are having trouble getting pregnant, you may want to consult your physician about the level of stress in your life and how it is contributing to your inability to conceive, which can also be due to reduced men's sperm counts because of stress.

The Solutions

Sometimes you can feel stressed by modern life, but are truly unaware of what these stresses might be. There are online sites that can help you identify and rate your stressors, but the table below is a plan to track your stress. It is called the Holmes-Rahe Scale and is frequently used and interpreted by professional therapists to understand your stress. Check the event which has occurred in your life over the last two years and add your score together to see how much stress you might be under and from what source.

Life Events	Life Crisis Points	Check if Yes
Death of a spouse	100	
Divorce	73	
Marital Separation	65	
Jail Term	63	
Death of a Close Family Member	63	
Personal Injury or Illness	53	
Marriage	50	
Fired At Work	47	
Marital Reconciliation	45	
Retirement	45	
Change in Health of a Family Member	44	
Pregnancy	40	
Sex Difficulty	39	
Gain of New Family Member	39	
Business Readjustment	39	
Change in Financial State	38	
Death of A Close Friend	37	
Change to Different Line of Work	36	
Change in Number of Arguments with Spouse	35	
Mortgage Over $100,000	31	
Foreclosure of Mortgage or Loan	30	
Change in Responsibilities at Work	29	
Son or Daughter Leaving Home	29	
Trouble with In-Laws	29	
Outstanding Personal Achievement	28	
Wife Begins or Stops Work	26	
Begin or End School	26	
Change in Living Conditions	25	
Revision in Personal Habits	24	
Trouble With Boss	23	
Change in Work Hours or Conditions	20	
Change in Residence	20	
Change in Schools	20	
Change in Recreation	19	

Life Events	Life Crisis Points	Check if Yes
Change in Church Activities	19	
Change in Social Activities	18	
Mortgage or Loan Less Than $30,000	17	
Change in Sleeping Habits	16	
Change in Number of Family Get-Togethers	15	
Vacation	15	
Christmas Alone	12	
Minor Violations of the Law	11	
Total		

Our bodies still have the ability to go into high alert, even though the stress factors of having to face a threatening situation have mostly dissipated. This is evident when you go to a scary movie or get on a thrill ride. In ancient man, the stress reaction was vital to survival, when our ancestors had to mobilize enough energy to deal with a threat by either fight or flight. This type of stress reaction may still be vital, for example if we are caught in a fire, but is inappropriate to modern life. Sometimes rush hour traffic, rude customers and misbehaving technology can activate this type of stress to no good. We have to recognize that most of our stressors are not life-threatening. Modern day life also means that ongoing stress can be experienced in ways that ancient man never had to handle. This can result in unpleasant and also unhealthy wear and tear on our bodies.

Recognizing you are the victim of work holism can help you cope with modern stresses. Often, we are spending more time at work than we are even aware of, believing this is helping us get the work done and making us look good to our bosses. However, workaholism usually means developing a feeling of dissatisfaction with your life and wondering how you are really spending your time. It is okay to back off the workload a little and realize you are not a super person who can get anything done simply by working more hours.

You can use meditation and to-do lists to help put your stress in context and deal with it in a positive manner. Visualize the source of your stress and mentally eliminate it. Write down all your tasks and rate them as to what needs to be done immediately. Organizing your life can be very helpful in dealing with the stress of modern life.

The Resources

The following Web sites offer more information about the stresses of modern life:

Mayo Clinic, *www.mayoclinic.com*

Making the Modern World, *www.makingthemodernworld.net*

Ezine Articles, *www.ezinearticles.com/?Stress*

Shrink Stress, *www.shringkstress.com*

Uplift Program, *www.upliftprogram.com*

Goal Setting Guide, *www.goal-setting-guide.com/articles/stressmanagement*

Red Orbit, *www.redorbit.com/news/health*

The following books offer more information about the stresses of modern life such as:

No Time: Stress and the Crisis of Modern Life (Douglas and McIntyre, 2005)

Life Without Stress: The Far Eastern Antidote to Tension and Anxiety (Broadway, 1997)

Beyond Prozac: Antidotes for Modern Times (Regan Books, 1996)

Stone Age Present: How Evolution Has Shaped Modern Life—From Sex, Violence and Language to Emotions, Morals and Communities (Touchstone, 1995)

Cold New World: Growing Up in Harder Country (Modern Life, 1999)

How to Deal With Stress (Kogan Page, 2007)

Principles and Practices of Stress Management (The Guilford Press, 1993)

9

Perfectionism

There is certainly nothing wrong with wanting to get the job done right. Most people do not want to do sloppy work. But, when this desire turns into an obsession, it can become perfectionism, which is an often crippling cause of stress. Perfectionists feel the job is never right and cannot get anything done. This begins a cascading effect where the perfectionism expands into even greater obsession and is now coupled with a feeling of hopelessness. The stress from this can be as destructive as being in a situation where life is spiraling out of control.

The Challenge

Not too long ago perfectionism was seen as a good condition. Perfectionists were sought after because it was believed they would spend the extra time and effort to get the job done right. Bosses and teachers now recognize more and more that, instead of helping get the job done, perfectionism can stand in the way of getting the job done at all. Work is left unfinished or turned in past deadline because the worker or student is never satisfied with it. This feeling of dissatisfaction can lead to tremendous stress because the perfectionist can not only not finish a project, the pile up of work due to their perfectionism leads to more stress and more obsession with doing everything perfectly. This type of behavior is particularly hard to deal with because aspects of it seem to be positive and most employers or teachers want people to work as hard as possible. But, a good employer or teacher must recognize the debilitating effects of perfectionism and work with the employee or student to get past the perfectionism. For the people suffering from perfectionism, the condition can be hard to understand because it seems like a positive thing at first and may have worked in the past. The challenge is to recognize what perfectionism is, when it can stand in the way of getting projects done, what type of stress it can cause in your life and how to deal with perfectionism so that aspects of it remain positive while the negatives are put aside or dealt with in context. A perfectionist will probably never completely lose this impulse, but can deal with it and use it to help in life rather than suffering from the negative aspects of it.

The Facts

Perfectionism can affect us in several areas:

- Home life where projects or family issues seemingly need the touch of a perfectionist;
- school where assignments and long-term projects take on a level of perfectionism that is inappropriate to the importance of the assignment and
- work where daily and larger projects seem so daunting that perfectionism is the only approach and prevents the worker from ever satisfactorily, to their own mind, finish the project or task.

Perfectionism refers to a set of self-defeating thoughts and behaviors aimed at reaching excessively high and unrealistic goals. In general, there are three questions to ask yourself if you believe you are a perfectionist:

- Do you feel like what you accomplish is never quite good enough?
- Do you often put off turning in papers or projects, wanting to get them just right?
- Do you feel you must give more than 100 percent on everything you do or else you will be doomed to mediocrity or even failure?

Perfectionism is not a condition we are born with. It is a learned behavior and evolves over time and experience. If you are suffering from perfectionism, it is likely you believed early in your life that you were valued because of how much you accomplished. This can result in your learning to value yourself based mainly on your perception of other people's approval. Your self-esteem may have come to be based mostly on external standards that may not be true. This can lead you to be excessively sensitive to the opinions and criticism, perceived or real, of others. You may want to protect yourself from this criticism and this can lead to erecting the defense of perfectionism.

There are a number of negative feelings, thoughts and beliefs that may be associated with perfectionism:

- Fear of failure where perfectionists equate failure to achieve their goals with a lack of personal worth or value.
- Fear of making mistakes where perfectionists equate mistakes with failure. They orient their lives around avoiding mistakes and miss opportunities to use mistakes to learn and grow.
- Fear of disapproval where perfectionists believe if they let others see their flaws they will not be accepted. Striving to be perfect is one way of trying to protect themselves from criticism, rejection and disapproval.
- All-or-none thinking where perfectionists believe they are worthless if their accomplishments are not perfect. They have difficulty in seeing situations in perspective.
- Overemphasis on a *should* attitude where perfectionists' lives are often structured by an endless list of *shoulds* that serve as rigid rules. This reliance means perfectionists rarely take into account their own wants and desires.

- A belief that others are easily successful with a minimum of effort, few errors, little emotional stress and great self confidence. Perfectionists view their own efforts as unending and never adequate.

Perfectionism often sets in motion a vicious cycle where perfectionists first set unreachable goals, then fail to meet these goals and suffer from constant pressure to achieve perfection with the inevitable chronic failure reducing productivity and effectiveness. This cycle leads perfectionists to be overly self-critical and self-blaming and results in lower self-esteem. This cycle can make perfectionists react defensively to criticism, apply unrealistically high standards to others and avoid letting others see their legitimate mistakes. Perfectionism, based on this cycle, can go beyond school and work and lead to an inability to be close to people and generate a feeling of isolation.

The Solutions

You must recognize that perfectionism is not normally a desirable thing. Recent academic studies have shown that a perfectionist attitude actually can interfere with success in the home, school or workplace. An unrealistic desire to be perfect can rob you of a sense of personal satisfaction and contribute to you failing to achieve as much as people who have more realistic expectations and strivings.

There is a distinct difference between perfectionism and healthy goal striving. Healthy strivers tend to set goals based on their own wants and desires than just in response to external expectations. The goals grow on what has already been accomplished. Healthy strivers take pleasure in the process of pursuing the task at hand rather than focusing only at the end result. When they experience failure, their reactions are generally limited to specific situations rather than their total self-worth.

One of the major steps in defeating perfectionism is to challenge the thoughts and behaviors that fuel perfectionism. Some specific strategies can be helpful in dealing with perfectionism.

- Set realistic and achievable goals based on what you have accomplished in the past. This will help you succeed and generate a sense of self-esteem.
- Set subsequent goals in a sequential manner. Set each goal one step higher than the one you have just achieved.
- Experiment with your standards for success. Instead of aiming for 100 percent success, try for 90 percent, 80 percent or even 60 percent. You can come to realize the world will survive if you are not perfect.
- Use your feelings of anxiety or depression to ask yourself if you have set impossible expectations for yourself.
- Realize that perfectionism can be based on fear and confront those fears by imagining the worst thing that can happen and how you would deal with it.
- Know that making mistakes can be a positive thing and show you how to do things better the next time.
- Rank your tasks by how important they are and try not to do everything at once. Put forth the most effort to the most important task and save the others for less effort.

If you are experiencing the following symptoms, you may be suffering from stress caused by perfectionism:

- Depression;
- performance anxiety;
- test anxiety;
- social anxiety;
- writer's block;
- obsessive behaviors;
- compulsive behaviors;
- suicidal thoughts;
- loneliness;
- impatience;
- frustration and
- unreasonable anger turned at yourself, your family, your boss or your colleagues.

The Resources

The following Web sites offer more information about perfectionism:

University of Illinois at Chicago, *www.couns.uiuc.edu*

Psychology Today, *www.psychologytoday.com*

The Health Center, *www.thehealthcenter.info/emotions/perfectionism/causes*

BBC Science and Nature, *www.bbc.co.uk/science*

University of Texas, *www.utexas.edu*

Sandy Maynard, *www.sandymaynard.com*

Grace Tree Counseling, *www.gracetreecounseling.com*

The following books offer more information on perfectionism such as:

When Perfect Isn't Good Enough: Strategies for Coping with Perfectionism (New Harbinger Publications, 1998)

Perfectionism: What's Bad About Being Too Good (Free Spirit Publishing, 1999)

Overcoming Perfectionism: The Key to a Balanced Recovery (HCI, 1990)

Perfectionism: Theory, Research and Treatment (American Psychological Association, 2002)

Freeing Our Families from Perfectionism (Free Spirit Publishing, 2001)

Perfecting Ourselves to Death: The Pursuit of Excellence and The Perils of Perfectionism (InterVarsity Press, 2005)

Never Good Enough: Freeing Yourself from the Chains of Perfectionism (Free Press, 1999)

10

Lack of Work/Life Balance

Our lives consist of many important elements. Certainly we must work for a living, but we also must have a personal life to maintain an important balance. When these elements are in conflict or when one element seems to be more important than another we are suffering from an imbalance that can cause stress in our lives. We need to recognize this balance and address it to maintain a healthy lifestyle.

The Challenge

Although there are many aspects to our lives, for the most part they can be broken down between work and life. Work is what we do to earn a living and achieve a sense of self worth. Life is more complicated and can take into account your social life, family and friends. It is important to your general mental health to maintain the proper balance between work and life. This balance is highly subjective but must be addressed. When work and life are unbalanced, we can feel a sense of unease and a higher level of stress in our lives. The challenge is to understand the nature of your work and your life, how the two interact, what the consequences are of an improper balance between the two and what you can do to get back this balance. Once we have achieved a successful balance, we can get the most out of our lives and find a deep satisfaction. The process can take some time, effort, communication and even therapy, but is well worth pursuing and can lead to positive results that will influence the rest of your life.

The Facts

Although the factors of work and life can vary depending on your current situation there are several aspects that are applicable to almost all of us and must be considered as we try to determine if we are finding the right balance between work and life.

Work demands usually include:

- Dealing with changes at the workplace;
- handling managers;
- managing employees;
- setting goals and objectives;

- taking care of marketing work and training and
- coping with changes including the sale or merger of a company or lay-offs that increase workloads.

Life demands usually include:

- Marital concerns or issues involving close relationships;
- dealing with friends and family;
- selling a home or moving to a new location, especially one that is far away from your current location;
- sending a child to college;
- having a new baby;
- dealing with a death in the family and
- caring for family members who may be in a situation that means they cannot help themselves.

The stress of a lack of balance between work and life can lead to specific results. These symptoms can be put into large groupings:

- Physical symptoms such as headaches and general fatigue;
- mental symptoms such as poor concentration or irritability;
- emotional symptoms such as depression and
- social symptoms such as isolation and resentment.

Both the work organization and the individual can benefit from better work and life balance. The benefits for the organization include measurable increases in individual productivity, better teamwork and communication, improved morale and less negative organizational stress. The benefits for the individual include more value and balance in daily life, better understanding of what your best individual work/life balance is, increased productivity and the satisfaction that brings, improved relationships both on and off the job and reduced stress at work and home.

Establishing a good work and life balance is a problem for many people. A recent study of more than 50,000 employees from manufacturing and service jobs discovered that two out of every five employees are not satisfied with the balance between their work and life. You can get a glimpse of the balance between work and life by taking this simple true false quiz.

	I find myself spending more and more time on work-related projects.
	I often feel I do not have time for myself or for my family and friends.
	No matter what I do, it seems that every minute of the day is always scheduled for something.
	Sometimes I feel as though I have lost sight of who I am and why I chose this job.
	I cannot remember the last time I was able to find the time to take a day off.

	I feel stressed out most of the time.
	It sometimes feels like I barely have time to catch my breath before moving to the next project.
	I cannot remember the last time I finished a book that I read strictly for pleasure.
	I wish I had more time for outside interests and hobbies, but I do not.
	I often feel exhausted—even early in the week.
	I cannot remember the last time I went to a move or attended some other cultural event.
	I do what I do because so many people depend on me.
	I have missed many important family events because of work-related responsibilities.
	I almost always bring work home with me.

The Solutions

Everyone's balance between work and life is a subjective thing and depends very much on their attitudes about their lives. Some people find tremendous satisfaction and a sense of identity from their work. Others depend more on the other aspects of their lives to provide them with what they need to cope. There is no such thing as a perfect balance between work and life and what type of balance you need may be a matter of experience and trial and error rather than a quantifiable figure.

You must understand that a lack of proper balance between work and life can lead to stressors that are both external and internal. External stressors include:

- Major life changes, which can be positive but are still items to be dealt with;
- environment such as a noise or light disturbance;
- unpredictable events such as an increase in expenditures or cut in pay;
- family disputes;
- workplace stress usually caused by an overwhelming workload or impossible boss and
- social stressors such as a blind date or having to make a speech.

Internal irritations usually include:

- Fears such as fear of flying, heights or more subtle fears such as dealing with a social situation;
- uncertainty, stemming from work changes or medical diagnoses;
- attitude which means having a negative view of the world and
- unrealistic expectations often tied in to perfectionism or need to control.

If you own a business that employs others or are a supervisor, you need to recognize that employee productivity can be dependent on making sure your employees are maintaining a proper balance between work and life. If you detect an employee is acting in a stressed manner, it may be time to talk to him or her about how much time is being spent on the job and how that is impacting life in general. If you work for yourself, you must keep an eye on your own behavior and make sure you are finding the right balance between work and life. This can be especially challenging if you are working out of your home.

If you are looking to achieve a better balance between work and life, you may wish to visit a consultant, coach or therapist. But, there are some ideas you can incorporate immediately into your life.

- Try to work fewer hours and spend more time with your family.
- Take on a different job role or title, typically with less pressure and often for less monetary award.
- Decide to give up working entirely and become a stay-at-home mom or dad.
- Work less, but make lifestyle changes that means your life will require less money.
- Decide what really matters to you in life and pursue that accordingly.
- Drop unnecessary activities both at work and in your personal life.
- Do not overschedule yourself.
- Prioritize ruthlessly everything in your life and stay with the plan.
- Learn how to say no at work and at home.
- Organize your work space and your home.
- Let technology such as computers and PDA's help you achieve your goals, but use technology that is proven and you are comfortable with.
- Understand your life will never be perfect.

The Resources

The following Web sites offer more information about work and life balance:

Mayo Clinic, *www.mayoclinic.org*

Work Life Balance, *www.worklifebalance.com*

Quint Careers, *www.quintcareers.com/work_life_balance*

Quality of Life Research Center, *www.qlrc.cgu.edu*

Web MD, *www.webmd.com/balance*

Microsoft, *www.microsoft.com/smallbusiness/resources/management/leadership_training/work_and_life_balance*

iVillage, *www.ivillage.co.uk*

The following books offer more information on work and life balance such as:

Harvard Business Review on Work and Life Balance (Harvard Business School Press, 2000)

The Integration of Employee Assistance, Work/Life, and Wellness Services (Haworth Press, 2006)

Stop Living Your Job, Start Living Your Life; 85 Simple Strategies to Achieve Work/Life Balance (Ulysses Press, 2005)

Work + Life (Riverhead Trade, 2004)

Work-Life Balance (Overcoming Common Problems) (Sheldon Press, 2003)

Essential Managers: Balancing Work and Life (DK ADULT, 2002)

Striking a Balance: Work, Family, Life (Dollars and Sense, 2007)

Part Three:

Assessing Your Personal Stress Level

11

Stress Intake Form

You may have been feeling stressed for so long that an abnormal amount of stress seems normal to you. The physical conditions the stress has engendered are just something you have to deal with. But, you do not. By evaluating where your stress is coming from, you can begin coming up with coping strategies and changes to better deal with it.

The Challenge

It is easy to simply say that you feel stressed out. But, where is that feeling coming from and what combination of factors are making you feel like the stress has become hard to deal with? By carefully listing out the causes of your stress on a simple stress intake form, you can identify the sources of stress and what has changed in your life. You must take an honest look at your life and focus your thinking on your sources of stress and by taking a few minutes to complete this form you may be better able to do this. The sources of your stress may surprise you and lead you to new ways to deal with them. The challenge is to find a workable form, honestly complete it, review it and change it as your life changes. The form below includes the stressors you may have experienced in the last six months and those you expect to arise to better help you plan on coping with them.

Work Changes and Pressures

Our work life is usually one of the top stressors we must deal with. There is a perceived lack of control over what is happening on the job and that can affect us in many ways. Here are some of the most common stressors involved with work changes and pressures.

STRESSOR	EXPERIENCED IN LAST SIX MONTHS	EXPECT TO EXPERIENCE
Too many responsibilities		
Unreasonable or over demanding deadlines		
Conflicts or unclear expectations from superiors or management		
Difficult customers		
Difficult co-workers		
Lack of control over workload or decisions affecting the job		
Office politics		
Job insecurity because of layoffs, downsizing or reorganization		
Limited opportunities for advancement or perceived lack of adequate compensation		
Reduction or changes in benefits, especially health insurance		
Lack of needed resources		
Too much or too little contact with people		
Too many interruptions and meetings		
Other:		

Personal and Homelife

Right behind workplace stress is the stress we feel in our personal and homelife. This stress can come from our relationships, finances or physical demands and can be especially challenging to deal with due to the baggage we carry through our personal lives. We still must recognize them completely and by evaluating these issues, we can better understand the nature of personal or homelife stress and what changes we can make to better them.

STRESSOR	EXPERIENCED IN LAST SIX MONTHS	EXPECT TO EXPERIENCE
Death of a significant other such as a spouse, friend or family member		
Separation or divorce		
Remarriage and dealing with blended family		
Beginning a new relationship		
Moving to a new location, especially in another part of the country		

STRESSOR	EXPERIENCED IN LAST SIX MONTHS	EXPECT TO EXPERIENCE
Planning and taking an elaborate vacation		
Dealing with a catastrophic occurrence such as a flood or fire		
Having to plan major repairs or improvements		
Sending a child to college or private school		
Returning to school for extended training or an advanced degree		
Substance abuse such as alcohol or drugs		
Dealing with psychological illnesses for yourself or others		
Moving a parent to a long-term care facility		
Dealing with serious illness or injury to ourselves or to significant others		
Not having enough money to run our lives or incurring a heavy debt load		
Ongoing conflicts with spouses, in-laws, family or friends		
Planning a major social event such as a significant party for graduation, birthday or other commemoration		
Dealing with the stresses of the holidays		
Sexual difficulties or other similar problems		
A perception of a child showing unacceptable behavior or having bad friends		
Difficulties in maintaining effective child care such as ongoing day care		
Conflicts or doubts with spiritual, moral or ethical values		
Other:		

The Solutions

Now that you have some idea of what may be causing your stress, you must take the next logical steps in evaluating the physical and mental effects of your stress and how to cope with them, relieve or reduce them. Completing this form is not an end in itself, but a logical starting point in the process of dealing with stress. Keep moving through it and you will find your stress is easier to deal with and, no matter how many stressors you are experiencing, you will be better able to handle them.

The Resources

The following Web sites offer more information about evaluating your stress intake:

Stress Less, *www.stressless.com/stressquiz.cfm?*

Stress Clinic, *www.stressclinic.com*

Web MD, *www.webmd.com*

Homeopathic Cures, *www.homeopathiccures.net/homeopathicintakeform.doc*

Form Router, *www.formrouter.net*

The following books offer more information on evaluating your stress intake such as:

Stress and Burnout Among Providers Caring for the Terminally Ill and Their Families (Haworth Press, 1988)

Stress Management for Dummies (For Dummies, 1999)

The Stress Management Handbook (McGraw-Hill, 1999)

10 Simple Solutions to Stress: How to Tame Tension and Start Enjoying Your Life (New Harbinger Publications, 2007)

Stress Management: A Comprehensive Guide to Wellness (Ballantine Books, 2004)

Guide to Stress Reduction (Celestial Arts, 2001)

Principles and Practice of Stress Management, Second Edition (The Guilford Press, 1993)

12

Stress Quiz

Stress comes in many forms, but the two most common designations are acute and chronic stress. Acute stress is usually caused by some individual event that may have been unexpected and could be short-lived. Chronic stress is long-term stress caused by ongoing elements in our lives and may have been affecting us for some time. To help evaluate whether we are suffering from acute or chronic stress we can take a simple quiz to determine what we are feeling.

The Challenge

Stress effects can involve a variety of physical and mental factors. They are symptoms of acute or chronic stress. How we deal with stressors in our lives depends on determining not only the causes of stress, but what effects they are having on us. Sometimes it is difficult to logically examine the effects of stress, but by taking a simple quiz and evaluating the results, we can determine what stress is doing to us and begin to lessen those effects. The challenge is to find a good form that is comprehensive without being burdensome, honestly answering the quiz and then reviewing it by ourselves or with a professional to see how valid our responses are and what they mean. Writing it down can do wonders to help us conquer disabling stress in our lives. Here are some ways to identify what the acute or chronic effects of stress are on our mental and physical health and relationships.

Physical Effects of Stress

Quite often the physical effects of stress can be confused with physical effects based on other medical conditions. If the stress is effectively dealt with, the physical effects should dissipate and eventually go away. While you should always have any physical condition checked out by a physician, it may be helpful to recognize what you are feeling and its severity.

SYMPTOM	SEVERE = 1	MODERATE = 2	MILD = 3	LOW OR NONE = 0
Chest Pain				
Headaches (Tension Migraine)				
Back Pain				
Tense Neck and Jaw				
Throat Constriction, Difficulty Swallowing				
Muscle Cramps				
Sleeplessness				
Sexual Difficulties, Loss of Sexual Interest				
Dizziness				
Cold Hands/Feet				
Fatigue, Low Energy, Tired				
Bloating				
Diarrhea				
Nail Biting				
Reduced Immunity (Frequent Colds/Flu, Allergies, Infections)				
Heart Racing/Rapid Pulse				
High Blood Pressure				
Shortness of Breath				
Overeating				
Loss of Appetite				
Ulcers				
Colon Problems				
Shaky Voice, Stuttering, Strained				
Tight Muscles or Muscle Aches				
Bruxism (Grinding or Teeth Clenching)				
Gas Pains or Cramping				
Acid Stomach, Heartburn				
Constipation				
Nausea				

Mental Effects of Stress

Most of us experience stress affecting our mental processes. This does not mean we will start acting in a bizarre way, but exhibit some subtle forms of mental problems that are brought on by stress. Recognizing when we are having mental difficulties and whether they may be caused by stress, we must first recognize what we are feeling.

SYMPTOM	SEVERE = 1	MODERATE = 2	MILD = 3	LOW OR NONE=0
Forgetfulness				
Negating Own Ideas				
Disorganized Thinking				
Mental Chatter				
Mind Racing				
Lack of Concentration or Attention				
Obsessive Thinking				
Worry				
Unable to Prioritize				
Decision Making Difficulties				
Automatic Thoughts or Images				
Irrational Beliefs and Self Talk				

Emotional Effects of Stress

Emotional stress is different than mental stress and can be harder to evaluate. For emotional problems, you should probably visit a therapist and discuss your feelings in some detail. A good therapist can help you discover if any symptoms you are feeling are more stress related than because of other, more deep-seated problems and help you deal with the stress for your emotional health.

SYMPTOM	SEVERE = 1	MODERATE =2	MILD =3	LOW OR NONE=0
Anger, Irritability				
Anxiety, Panic, Fearfulness				
Depressed, Sad, Downhearted, Blue				
Feeling Strongly Needed				
Helplessness				
Hopelessness				

SYMPTOM	SEVERE = 1	MODERATE =2	MILD =3	LOW OR NONE=0
Lonely				
Pessimism				
Unworthy				
Flattened Affect				
Blaming				
Guilt				
Impatience				
Frustration				
Feeling Inadequate				

Personal Behavioral Signs of Stress

Stress can manifest itself in a variety of personal changes or new behavior patterns. Our behavior may change periodically depending on what is going on in our lives, but when the behavior patterns are unusually prolonged or severe, they can mean definite signs of stress. Often, our behavior changes are invisible to us and will be pointed out by family or friends. We must listen to them and know when the observations are valid.

SYMPTOM	SEVERE = 1	MODERATE =2	MILD =3	LOW OR NONE=0
Lack of Close Relationships				
Low Trust				
Non-assertive				
Will Not Take Risks				
Avoid Challenges				
Dull & Boring				
Avoid Change				
Poor Love Relationships				
Withdrawal from Social Life				
Lack of Control Over Life				
Poor Self-Esteem				
Fear of Commitments				
Lack of Self-Forgiveness				
Indecisive				
Make Unrealistic Demands				

SYMPTOM	SEVERE =1	MODERATE =2	MILD =3	LOW OR NONE=0
Coercive				
Unmotivated, Lack Drive				
Over Reacting				
Passive, Dependent, Controlled by Others				
Poor Family Harmony				
Domineering				
Inability to Reach Out to Others				
Critical				
Marital Problems				
Alienation				
Poor Communications				
Making Mountain out of Molehills				
Lack of Compassion				
Jealousy				
Inability to Relax				
Inability to Express True Feelings				

Work Behavior Signs

Some of the signs of stress we may manifest are just in our work environment. They may be causing us problems relating to our co-workers and getting our jobs done. A good boss or trusted co-worker can recognize these symptoms and bring them to your attention. If left unattended too long, poor work behaviors based on stress can severely affect our job performance and career.

SYMPTOM	SEVERE = 1	MODERATE =2	MILD =3	LOW OR NONE=0
Over eating				
Lack of Response to Challenges				
Making Choices Related to Self-Image Rather Than Reality				
Loss of Creativity				

SYMPTOM	SEVERE = 1	MODERATE =2	MILD =3	LOW OR NONE=0
Hostile and Oppositional				
Rigidity By Doing Everything By the Book				
Poor Performance				
Low Motivation				
Lack of Self-Initiative				
Absenteeism				
Low Aspirations				
Accepting Low Status				
Trying to Over Please Others				
Avoid Responsibility				
Avoid Risks				
Inability to Work Well with Others				
Poor Time Management				
Too Controlling				
Creating Tension in Others				
Poor Communications				
Wasting Time, Procrastination				
Poor Skill Development				
Unable to Complete Tasks				
Crisis Oriented				
Lack of Respect for Others				
Low Delegation				
Lack of Interpersonal Skills				
Overwork				
Loss of Clarity of Goals				

The Solutions

Total each section separately, and, if appropriate, add the sections together. The lower the number, the less stress you are feeling in those broad areas. What may be more useful is to see what specific areas you are rating moderate to severe stress and concentrate on working on those symptoms and the stress they represent. Take this test at regular intervals and see what may have changed in the stressors in your life. Hopefully, the numbers will be going down.

The Resources

The following Web sites offer more information about your stress:

Stress Less, *www.stressless.com/stressquiz.cfm?*

Stress Clinic, *www.stressclinic.com*

Web MD, *www.webmd.com*

Mayo Clinic, *www.mayoclinic.com*

EMedicine Health, *www.emedicinehealth.com*

Health Scout, *www.healthscout.com*

The following books offer more information on stress symptoms such as:

Stress and Burnout Among Providers Caring for the Terminally Ill and Their Families (Haworth Press, 1988)

Stress Management for Dummies (For Dummies, 1999)

The Stress Management Handbook (McGraw-Hill, 1999)

Stress and Job Performance: Theory, Research and Implications for Managerial Practice (Sage Publications, 1998)

Family Stress Management (Ballantine Books, 2004)

Changing Addictive Behavior (Amapedia, 2006)

Principles and Practice of Stress Management, Second Edition (Sage Publications, Inc., 2001)

13

Major Life Changes List

To keep growing throughout our lives, we must face the prospect of major life changes. These changes may be consciously selected by us or thrust upon us due to circumstances we encounter on the job or in our personal lives. These changes will profoundly affect how we deal with the world around us and the decision to accept them and the effort involved in dealing with them can be a major cause of stress. We need to accept the necessity and inevitability of major life changes and recognize them for the positive things they can be.

The Challenge

Our lives are constantly going through changes. Most of these are minor and transitory such as dealing with repairs, changes in schedules or health issues that are not life-threatening. We deal very well with these changes and adapt accordingly without too much stress. The stress enters our lives when we have to deal with major life changes. The term major can mean many different things to different people, but, in general they are things that literally shake up our world and invite or force us into interacting with our lives in new ways. To deal with major life changes we need to change our belief systems to allow for new levels of thinking and performance. Luckily, most of us will not experience major life changes on a regular basis, but when they come, we must recognize their ability to cause us great stress. The challenge is to recognize when a life change is a major change, decide if the change is for the good, consider how to deal with the major life change and evaluate its ultimate effect on us. To not experience major life changes is to live life without possibility of growth, and, while this can feel safe, it does not allow us to live our lives to the utmost. Here are some ideas on major life changes, what might constitute them and what thinking or coping devices we use to deal with them.

Major Life Changes: A List of Choices

Below are some possible major life changes you are either experiencing or expect to experience in the near future. Choose yes for the changes that intuitively seem to you to represent major life changes, then logically choose seven to 10 of them that resonate with you the most and will most deserve your attention. This will help you focus on the change and your feelings about it.

PERSONAL LIFE CHANGE	YES	NO
Addictions to alcohol, drugs, gambling, sex		
Bankruptcy		
Career change		
New children		
Children leaving home		
Chronic pain		
Confrontation with authority		
Connecting with symbolic, universal realities		
Crime—perpetrator or victim		
Death of one or more people close to you		
Depression of yourself or someone close to you		
Different cultures and customs		
Divorce		
Emotional to cognitive processing		
Environmental shifts		
Falling in love		
Fame		
Financial windfall		
Illness		
Injury		
Left to right brain processing		
Loss of job or income		
Major change in income		
Major dietary changes		
Marriage		
Menopause		
Mid-life crisis		
Natural and man-made disasters		
Puberty		
Negative to positive thinking		
Overcoming victimhood and being accountable for everything		
Progressively sensing experiences, lessons, meaning and purpose of all events and encounters		
Loss of purpose		

PERSONAL LIFE CHANGE	YES	NO
Relocation		
Retirement		
Suicide of someone close to you		
War or physical conflict		

BUSINESS AND TECHNOLOGY CHANGES

	YES	NO
Become an entrepreneur		
Become an employer		
Become a leader rather than a follower		
Move office out of or into home		
Globalization		
Major expansion or downsizing		
Computer upgrade		
Decentralization		
Team work		
Virtual workplace		
Internet commerce		
Mergers and takeovers		

MASLOW'S HIERARCHY OF NEEDS (PROGRESSIVE)

	YES	NO
Physiological needs		
Security and safety needs		
Love and affection needs		
Self-esteem needs		
Self-actualization needs		
Self-transcendence needs		

CONSCIOUSNESS LEVELS (PROGRESSIVE)

	YES	NO
Follow the masses		
Individuality		
Independent, accountable		
Intuitive, spiritual		
Other—conscious		
Contributor, server		

Major Life Changes Tips and Pitfalls

You must keep in mind some tips and potential stumbling blocks in deciding on making major life changes and then accepting what is required to make the change work for you. Mark yes for any tips or pitfalls below that seem valid to you and keep them in mind as you face your next major life change. Keep in mind these tips and pitfalls may change depending on the exact nature of the major life change.

SIGNIFICANT LIFE CHANGE TIP OR PITFALL	YES	NO
Fail to recognize you are part of a vital network that will impact the change.		
Believe that everything will work because you deserve it to.		
Recognize the balance in your life and how it will be affected by a major life change.		
Recognize change is an affirmation that you are doing significant work on your life.		
Be clear about where you are heading and why.		
Identify the payoffs and price of staying where you are.		
Begin developing a reserve of everything.		
Develop a vision of what is possible to get you through this transition.		
Recognize and uncover your self-judgments.		
Stop playing the victim.		
Give up analysis that breeds paralysis.		
Risk failure.		
Access your inner warrior.		
Do not get to the end of life wondering what would have happened if…		
Get support to help you prepare and navigate through the transition.		
Be adverse to possible loss.		
Be true to yourself regarding how you deal with the change.		
Try to place the fear of hurting others into context.		
Give yourself credit for making a change.		
Get adequate sleep and exercise.		
Pray or meditate on the future and its possibilities.		

Using the Internet for Major Life Changes

According to a recent study by the Pew Organization, 91 percent of all Americans have made one of the major life changes shown below and the use of the Internet was instrumental in acquiring the information and advice needed to make the change. Of those making a major life change, 96 percent of Internet users have done so and 83 percent of non-Internet users have done the change. Those who have used the Internet for at least three years are the most comfortable in using the Internet to make a major life change. There was no evidence that younger Americans benefited more from using the Internet for a major life change than older Americans. Below are the most common uses of the Internet for major life changes. Mark each one you have used or plan on using as a yes and recognize when there is an area you are missing where you might use the Internet more effectively.

USING INTERNET FOR A SIGNIFICANT LIFE CHANGE	YES	NO
Choosing a school, especially college or university		
Starting or working on a hobby		
Getting additional education or career training		
Buying a car		
Treating illnesses—for yourself and for helping others		
Changing jobs		
Making a major investment or financial decision		
Finding a new place to live		
Falling in and out of love		
Getting involved with the law		
Gaining promotions and raises		

The Solutions

Use these lists as a guide to help you decide on and get through major life changes. There are no hard and fast rules in successfully negotiating a major life change, but if you trust your research, your judgment and the advice from others you value, you can help make sure you are making a positive change. Keep in mind that no change is written in stone and do not let the fear of failure hinder you from taking a chance. Taking chances is part of being a success in life, and when they are taken intelligently we can grow into a rich life that is worth living.

The Resources

The following Web sites offer more information about making major life changes:

Pew Organization, *www.pewinternet.org*

Evan Carmichael, *www.evancarmichael.com*

Higher Awareness, *www.higherawareness.com/listsm/major-life-changes*

Virginia State, *www.dhrm.state.va.us/training/change/Top10StepstoMakingMajorLifeChanges*

Nehemiah Gospel Com, *www.nehemiagospelcom.net/turning2*

Family.Org, *www.family.org/lifechallenges*

The following books offer more information on making major life changes such as:

Making Crucial Choices and Major Life Changes (Media Psychology Associates, 2006)

In Transition: Navigating Major Life Changes (Morehouse Publishing, 2002)

When Life Changes or You Wish it Would: A Guide to Finding Your Next Step Despite Fear, Obstacles or Confusion (Harper Books, 2003)

Rites of Passage: Celebrating Life's Changes (Beyond Words Publishing, 1998)

Change Your Thinking, Change Your Life: How to Unlock Your Full Potential for Success and Achievement (Wiley, 2003)

The Power of A Single Thought: how to Initiate Major Life Changes from the Quiet of Your Mind (Hay House, 2006)

When Life Changes or Your Wish It Would: How to Survive and Thrive in Uncertain Times (William Morrow and Company, 2002)

14

Stress Coping Strategies Assessment

Being stressed by modern life is a given and depends on our situation at work and in our personal lives. However, many people choose to accept the stress without working out ways to cope with them. This lack of coping mechanisms can lead to stress being more debilitating than it has to be. We must evaluate the strategies of our coping with stress and look for mechanisms that help us deal with it.

The Challenge

By adapting the quiz in Chapter 11, we can add in responses that help us evaluate the coping levels we must look at in evaluating our stress. These coping levels can give us a good idea of what areas need particular attention, what is working in coping with stress and what is not working as well as we would like. We can then add on a simple assessment of what coping mechanisms we are employing and their level of success. This information will let us know what we have developed that works well in coping with our stress and what elements are being ignored that might be very useful. Coping with stress does not mean we are hiding from it, but rather that we recognize what is stressing us and dealing with the issues and symptoms in a proactive and positive way. The challenge is to honestly assess our coping levels and mechanisms and changing our attitudes and lifestyles to better cope with the often-overwhelming feeling of stress in our lives.

Work Changes and Pressures

It is difficult, if not impossible to walk away from work stress. We need to work to maintain our lifestyle and pay our bills. But, workplace stress can often be some of the most debilitating we face and set up unique coping challenges. Mark how you feel about the stressor and how you think you are coping with it without additional help.

STRESSOR	STRESSED OUT	STRAINED	BALANCED	HIGHLY EFFECTIVE
Too many responsibilities				
Unreasonable or over demanding deadlines				
Conflicts or unclear expectations from superiors or management				
Difficult customers				
Difficult co-workers				
Lack of control over workload or decisions affecting the job				
Office politics				
Job insecurity because of layoffs, downsizing or reorganization				
Limited opportunities for advancement or perceived lack of adequate compensation				
Reduction or changes in benefits, especially health insurance				
Lack of needed resources				
Too much or too little contact with people				
Too many interruptions and meetings				
Other:				

Personal and Homelife

It may seem easier to cope with personal stress. But, often personal stress can present challenges that are every bit as daunting as workplace stress and our coping mechanisms are now being filtered through our personal feelings and relationships. Similar to workplace stress, we must define our coping levels to various aspects of personal stress by seeing which ones are affecting us and to what extent. The results may be startling, but are a starting point to developing coping mechanisms.

STRESSOR	STRESSED OUT	STRAINED	BALANCED	HIGHLY EFFECTIVE
Death of a significant other such as a spouse, friend or family member				
Separation or divorce				
Remarriage and dealing with blended family				
Beginning a new relationship				
Moving to a new location				
Taking an elaborate vacation				
Dealing with a catastrophic occurrence				
Having to plan major repairs or improvement				
Sending a child to college				
Returning to school for extended training				
Substance abuse such as alcohol or drugs				
Dealing with psychological illnesses				
Moving a parent to a long-term care facility				
Dealing with serious illness or injury to ourselves to significant others				
Not having enough money to run our lives or incurring a heavy debt load				
Ongoing conflicts with spouses, in-laws, family or friends				
Planning a major social event such as a significant party for graduation, birthday or other commemoration				
Dealing with the stresses of the holidays				
Sexual difficulties or other similar problems				
A perception of a child doing unacceptable behavior or having bad friends				
Difficulties in maintaining effective child care such as ongoing day care				

STRESSOR	STRESSED OUT	STRAINED	BALANCED	HIGHLY EFFECTIVE
Conflicts or doubts with spiritual, moral or ethical values				
Other:				

The Solutions

Now that you have some idea of what are the common stressors in your work and personal lives, you need to take the next step by identifying what you are currently doing to cope with the stress and what options are available to you that you have not explored. Use the simple assessment below to identify common coping mechanisms to stress and apply the findings to what you are or are not doing properly in your own lives. Take this assessment in a few months after you have made some changes and see what has changed in your approach to coping with stress. The lower the total, the less effective is your coping with stress.

COPING MECHANISM	VERY POOR =1	LOW OR MODERATE =2	GOOD =3	VERY GOOD =4
Diet and Nutrition— I eat a balanced diet, take appropriate nutritional supplements and limit intake of caffeine, sugar and fat.				
Relaxation— I am aware when stress builds up in my body and use relaxation techniques to reduce body tension.				
Physical Exercise— I am physically fit and exercise regularly to combat and prevent stress.				
Social Support— I am able to ask for and accept support from friends, family members or professionals as a buffer against stress.				

COPING MECHANISM	VERY POOR =1	LOW OR MODERATE =2	GOOD =3	VERY GOOD =4
Communication— I effectively listen to others and am comfortable expressing my own thoughts, feelings and opinions.				
Assertiveness— I am able to speak up for myself, honestly express my opinions, feelings and wishes, give constructive criticism and refuse unrealistic demands.				
Financial— I manage money well, do not needlessly worry about financial issues and have enough money to meet my needs and use to reduce stress.				
Time Management— I efficiently manage my time.				
Taking Action— I can establish priorities, work on my plans and goals and set limits, schedule effectively, avoid procrastination and pace my work.				
Problem Solving— I am skilled at defining problems and approach them in a timely and logical way.				

COPING MECHANISM	VERY POOR =1	LOW OR MODERATE =2	GOOD =3	VERY GOOD =4
Challenging Stressful Thinking— I can consciously monitor, challenge and change negative thought patterns, placing problems into proper perspective, relaxing and mentally rehearsing coping mechanisms.				
Functional Beliefs— I can change rigid and absolute stress inducing beliefs with more functional beliefs.				
Humor— I do not take myself or my stress too seriously and use humor to meet life's frustrations.				
Spiritual— I have faith in a higher power and feel a spiritual connection to life.				

The Resources

The following Web sites offer more information about assessing your stress coping:

Stress Less, *www.stressless.com/stressquiz.cfm?*

Stress Clinic, *www.stressclinic.com*

Health Resource Network, *www.stresscure.org*

American Institute of Stress, *www.stress.org*

Stress Reduction Techniques, *www.mindtools.com/stress*

Changing Minds, *www.changingminds.org/explanations/behaviors/coping/coping*

Web MD, *www.webmd.com/mental-health/caregiver-advice-cope*

The following books offer more information on assessing your stress coping such as:

Stress and Burnout Among Providers Caring for the Terminally Ill and Their Families (Haworth Press, 1988)

Stress Management for Dummies (For Dummies, 1999)

Attention Deficit Disorder: Practical Coping Mechanisms (Informa Healthcare, 2006)

Stress. Coping and Development in Children (The Johns Hopkins University Press, 1988)

Hypnosis: Trance as a Coping Mechanism (Springer, 1976)

Stress in Modern Motherhood and Coping Mechanisms (Personal Growth Service Center, 1985)

Coping With Your Difficult Older Parent: A Guide for Stressed-Out Children (Harper Paperbacks, 1999)

Families and Change: Coping With Stressful Events and Transitions (Sage Publications, Inc., 2005)

Coping: The Psychology of What Works (Oxford University Press, USA, 1999)

15

Job Burnout Quiz

Every type of job may offer stressful situations that can make us feel like we have had enough, we are burned out at the workplace or with the type of career we are pursuing. This happens to many people at any point of their worklife and can be troubling as well as causing great stress. However, often the burn out is the result of a temporary condition, such as dealing with a rise in workload rather than the more severe signs of complete burnout. We need to evaluate how we are reacting to the natural pressures of a job before deciding whether we are burning out or just feeling stress to a certain situation.

The Challenge

The stress effects of burnout on the job are different than the effects of being stressed over a particular job situation. We may be dealing with a temporary lack of resources, having to do more with less or being handed an unclear project with a seemingly impossible deadline. This type of stress is different from burnout, and, in some cases, can actually help us perform under pressure. Job burnout, however, is a much more debilitating form of stress that can cause us real mental and physical effects and lead to a dissatisfaction that does not allow us to adequately perform our job. Burnout can make us feel like we have failed in some ways and that we made a mistake in our choice of career. This type of self-doubt merely adds to the stress and makes change that much more difficult. The challenge is to recognize when we are genuinely experiencing job burnout symptoms and not just symptoms that will go away when the job inevitably changes. Here are several quizzes designed to help you discover whether you are burnt out on the job and to what extent this burn out is affecting you at work and in your personal life.

What is True Job Burnout Quiz

Sometimes when we are asked what is troubling us on the job, we can lay out a lot of elements that may or may not be true. Our responses are colored by our current reactions to a stressful situation and not a thorough and honest assessment of what is bothering us and to what extent By taking a simple true quiz, we can better see where our feelings of burnout are coming from.

SYMPTOM	ALWAYS TRUE	OFTEN TRUE	SOMETIMES TRUE	NOT TRUE
I feel increased anger at my coworkers and detachment from the people around me.				
I feel overwhelmed and suffer a loss of control on my job.				
I find myself feeling completely fatigued or exhausted when I come home from my job.				
I seem to be more susceptible to colds and other illnesses recently.				
I feel besieged at work as if nothing I do is right anymore.				
I find myself exploding in anger over small things.				
My weight and eating habits have changed recently resulting in weight gain or loss.				
I have noticed a definite change in my sleep pattern leading to insomnia or the need to sleep too much.				
I have been using more excuses to miss work by calling in sick.				
I am finding it harder to concentrate on my job.				
I feel like I am just not doing a very good job anymore.				
I have a sense of being isolated or alone.				
I have become much more negative and cynical about my job and employer.				
I cannot remember the last time I felt enthusiastic about my job.				
I am having problems with my family such as conflicts and fights.				
I feel that things are spinning out of my control.				

SYMPTOM	ALWAYS TRUE	OFTEN TRUE	SOMETIMES TRUE	NOT TRUE
I am finding comfort in increased use of food, alcohol or drugs.				
I am experiencing more physical ailments such as headaches, stomach problems or ulcers.				
It seems like I have lost interest for the things I used to value, that I am emotionally empty.				
I feel sad for no reason.				
I wake up in the morning and wonder why I even bother showing up for work.				
Television has become my haven and I am watching much more of it than I used to.				
I am taking more risks without thinking about the consequences.				
I have experienced panic attacks with chest pain and shortness of breath at work or when I think of work.				
I live for Friday afternoons and dread Sunday evenings the most.				
I am forgetful.				
I avoid people at work and in my private life.				
My attitude to work is why bother.				
It is a strain to communicate with others.				
I work hard but accomplish little.				
I simply do not like going to work.				
Social activities are draining instead of fun.				
Sex is not worth the effort.				
My work seems pointless.				
I am trapped in my job with little or no options.				

SYMPTOM	ALWAYS TRUE	OFTEN TRUE	SOMETIMES TRUE	NOT TRUE
I am unable to influence decisions that affect me.				
I may be laid off and there is nothing I can do.				
I do not have the information I need to do my job.				
Co-workers undermine me.				
People compete in office politics rather than cooperate.				
I frequently must work on my own time.				
I have too little to do.				
The majority of my time is spent on routine tasks.				
My supervisor is overcritical.				
Someone else gets credit for my work.				
I avoid telling people where I work or what I do.				
There is no relationship between performance and success.				
My career progress is not what I had hoped.				
I must compromise my values.				
I do not believe in the company.				
My heart is not in my work.				

Agreement Quiz—The Burnout Inventory

One good way to pinpoint the exact cause of your burn out is to take a test where you rate your agreement to various statements. This quiz allows you to place your burnout in context and honestly assess exactly what is bothering you and to what extent.

SYMPTOM	DISAGREE AGREE									
RATING	1	2	3	4	5	6	7	8	9	10
My work is characterized by intense pressure and deadlines.										
No matter what I do, things just do not seem to get done.										
I feel emotionally drained.										
I feel defeated, like I am up against a brick wall.										
I feel I give more than I get in return.										
I feel a sense of isolation from my co-workers.										
I do not have sufficient time or resources.										
I frequently experience conflicting demands.										
Efforts to make progress are fruitless.										
I am tired of trying										
I no longer have enough personal time.										
I have limited options to express and share job dissatisfaction.										
My workload is impossible to catch up with.										
I can affect little change in my situation.										
I do not trust my colleagues.										
I get no recognition for work well done.										
I have too much or too little contact with people.										
I worry about losing my job.										
I have not been as healthy as usual.										
Temporarily removing myself from the job seems to help my feelings.										

Are You at Risk for Job Burnout

A simple yes-or-no quiz can give you a snapshot of your susceptibility to job burnout. The results can lead to further examination of your situation and takes little time to complete. Be as honest as possible and do not rush through it.

SYMPTOM	YES	NO
Do you find yourself dreading to go to work in the morning?		
Are you regularly experiencing fatigue and low energy levels at your job?		
Are you easily bored with your job?		
Do work activities you used to enjoy now seem like drudgery?		
Are you depressed on Sunday afternoons, thinking about Monday and the coming work week?		
Have you become more cynical or bitter about your job, your boss or the company? Are you easily annoyed by your co-workers?		
Are personal relationships affected by your work feelings?		
Do you find yourself envious of individuals who are happy in their work?		
Do you now care less than you used to about doing a good job?		

The Solutions

Examine each quiz separately, and, if appropriate, blend the quizzes together. You should be able to see what specific areas you are rating moderate to severe burnout on the job and concentrate on working on those symptoms and the stress they represent. Take these quizzes at regular intervals and see if they may have changed with changes on the job. The results may prompt you to make small attitude adjustments or take major action by leaving a job, even if you have nothing else to go to yet. Your mental and physical health are more important, and you will always find work.

The Resources

The following Web sites offer more information about job burnout:

Quintessential Careers, *www.quintcareers.com/job_burnout_quiz*

My Prime Time, *www.myprimetime.com/health/burnout/burnout*

Secretan, *www.secretan.com/freetools_assessment_burnout*

MSNBC, *www.msnbc.msn.com/id/1584163*

Doc Potter. *www.docpotter.com/bo_quiz/bo-ami*

Career Builder, *www.careerbuilder.com*

Mindtools, *www.mindtools.com/stress/Brn/BurnountSelfTest*

The following books offer more information on job burnout such as:

Overcoming Job Burnout: How to Renew Enthusiasm for Work (Ronin Publishing, 2005)

Beating Job Burnout: How to Transform Work Pressure into Productivity (Ronin Pub, 1993)

The Garden at Night: Burnout and Breakdown in the Teaching Life (Heinemann, 2005)

Banishing Burnout: Six Strategies for Improving Your Relationship with Work (Jossey-Bass, 2005)

The Truth About Burnout: How Organizations Cause Personal Stress and What to Do About It (Jossey-Bass, 1997)

Work Overload!: Redesigning Jobs to Minimize Stress and Burnout (ASQ Quality Press, 2004)

Beating Job Burnout: How to Turn Your Work into Your Passion (Vgm Career Horizons, 1995)

Part Four:

The Basic Methods to Deal with Stress

16

Reduce Stress

Stress in our lives is inevitable whether it is from our personal life, work or concern about the world around us. Many researchers believe a manageable amount of stress is a good thing. It keeps us alert to events around us and can motivate us to take action. Stress has been with us since we first stood upright to face the world, based around the physical reaction to danger called fight-or-flight. It is when stress becomes a debilitating factor in our lives and prevents us from enjoying life that we need to look at ways to reduce stress to more manageable levels.

The Challenge

Stress will always be with us. The key to handling stress is to bring it under control by reducing it to a level we can successfully deal with, or, in some cases a level that can help us get the jobs done. You can never totally eliminate stress, nor should you, but you can work to reduce the stress to a point where it is not running your life, but rather helping keep you on top of things. Stress can be reduced either externally by addressing the stressors in our lives and trying to eliminate them or bring them into focus, or internally by developing techniques that help you better cope with the stress that cannot be eliminated. The challenge is to recognize when stress has become a problem for you, analyzing the source of the stress and then using techniques to reduce the stress. Once you can master these techniques, you can better function in a world that is becoming ever more stressful.

The Facts

Reducing stress usually revolves around gaining control of the normal stressors in your life. When these stressors become overwhelming, we start feeling as if we no longer have control over our lives. Most stressors come from family demands or from the responsibilities of work. In some cases, the stressors are temporary and based on an event that is short-lived, such as social occasion, death in the family, new duties at work or rumors of layoffs. Some stressors are more long-term such as dealing with marital difficulties, suffering from destructive debt, handling children with problems, coming to terms with substance abuse issues, having to cope with a difficult boss or co-workers or being asked to take on additional work because of a downsizing of the company.

There are professionals who can help you deal with debilitating stress, or at the very least, allow you to place the stressors into the context of normal life. You can get help from physicians, therapists including psychologists and psychiatrists and spiritual advisors. Some people have some success in reducing stress by using holistic methods such as therapeutic massage, aroma therapy, yoga, herbal supplements and hypnosis. When it comes to reducing stress, the key is to find methods that are effective for you, which may rely on some trial and error, and sticking with them.

Students, usually high school or college students, face their own type of stress. This stress must be reduced to experience academic success. Here are some ways students can handle the increasing demands of education:

- Manage your study time wisely.
- Organize your class work and prioritize projects.
- Create a soothing study environment that may mean using the library or a quiet study hall.
- Understand how you learn best and stick with that system.
- Use visualization and imagery to see yourself succeed.
- Be optimistic about doing well. You did not get to college by not being a good student.
- Get plenty of sleep and make sure your roommate does not bother you.
- Hone your study skills by using printed materials, a tutor or working closely with an advisor.

The Solutions

There are many ways to reduce stress. Some can be used by themselves, most of them are most effective when used in some type of combination and are designed to address overall stress:

- Get out of bed at least 15 minutes earlier in the morning. You will not really notice this and the extra time will help you plan your day.
- Prepare for the morning the evening before by making lunches and preparing your clothes.
- Use some method to write down appointments and other deadlines in your life.
- Duplicate your house keys and hide one set in a secret spot or carry a duplicate car key in your wallet.
- Practice preventive maintenance with your car or major appliances to avoid stressful surprises.
- Waiting is part of modern life. Enjoy the time by bringing a paperback book or magazine with you to a waiting room.
- Do not procrastinate. Whatever you need to do, do it now.
- Plan ahead by keeping your gas tank at least one-quarter full, having an emergency supply of food or water or not waiting until you are down to your last stamp.
- If something is not working right, get rid of it or have it fixed.
- Give yourself plenty of time to get to an appointment or to the airport.

- Reduce or eliminate the caffeine in your diet.
- Use contingency plans for social and business activities in case something comes up unexpectedly.
- Ease up on your standards and expectations for what you have to get done.
- Pollyanna's Glad Game was not such a bad idea. Remember, for everything that goes wrong for you there are plenty of blessings you can count.
- Clarify what you have been told. Repeat instructions and make sure you understand what you have to do.
- Say no to projects you cannot reasonably handle. You need some quiet time during your day to relax and recharge and saying no will not make you unpopular.
- Unplug your phone and turn off your cell for a while. You do not need to be in touch 24/7.
- Simplify your life wherever possible.
- Choose friends who do not fixate on the negative or who are chronic worriers.
- Get up and move around when you are on the job. Take a few minutes to stretch or just stare into space.
- Use earplugs or headphones to block out the world for some time, as long as it is safe to do so.
- Get plenty of sleep and do not stay up too late.
- Organize order out of the chaos of your home or work. Put things away or throw them away if you do not need them.
- Relax and take deep breaths. A simple yoga technique is to breathe in slowly through the nose than take at least 16 seconds to breathe out. Many people, when stressed, take shallow breaths that do not properly oxygenate their blood.
- Keep a journal and write down your thoughts or feelings. Review the journal later and be amazed at how these things worked out.
- Talk over your problems with a sympathetic listener. In some cases this might be a professional or part of a support group.
- Take your life one day at a time.
- Do something you really enjoy every day.
- Take warm baths or showers to relieve tension and review your day.
- Help other people, either one-on-one or as part of an organized group.
- Do something that you believe will improve your appearance such as redoing your makeup, getting a new haircut or buying some newer clothes.
- Do not overschedule your day.
- Be flexible in what you can or cannot do. Schedule a realistic day and give yourself periodic breaks between appointments.
- Eliminate destructive thoughts and self-talk.
- Make your weekends a time when you do things you would not during the week. You might want to take on a job on the weekend you would not have time to do in the week.
- Concentrate on today and yesterday will be in context and tomorrow will take care of itself.
- Do unpleasant tasks early in the day and get them over with. The rest of your day will be more free of anxiety.

- Delegate some responsibilities to others.
- Eat lunch and take a real break where you physically get away from your job or close your office door.
- Accept the fact that all of us live in an imperfect world and take on a forgiving view of events and people.
- Be optimistic and accept that most people are doing the best they can and are not here just to irritate you.

The Resources

The following Web sites offer more information about reducing stress:

Texas Women's University, *www.twu.edu*

Stress About, *www.stress.about.com/od/studentstress*

Stress EHow, *www.ehow.com*

Mayo Clinic, *www.mayoclinic.com/health/time-management*

Cleveland Clinic, *www.clevelandclinic.org*

Health.Com, *www.health.com*

Reduce Stress, *www.reduce.StressTips.org*

The following books offer more information on reducing stress such as:

Reducing Stress (DK ADULT, 1999)

Learn to Relax: Proven Techniques for Reducing Stress, Tension, and Anxiety—and Promoting Peak Performance (John Wiley & Sons, 2001)

Rainbow Stress Reduction: Play Your Stress Away With Colorful Healing Art and Stress Reducing Games (Newcastle Publishing Company, 1991)

Herbs for Reducing Stress and Anxiety (Storey Publishing, 1999)

Walk Don't Run: Tips for Reducing Stress (Peter Pauper Press, 1998)

Break the Stress Cycle: 10 Steps for Reducing Stress for Women (Diane Pub Co, 1998)

1001 Ways to Relax: An Illustrated Guide to Reducing Stress (Amazon Remainders)

17

Relieve Stress

When stress has become unmanageable and we have lost the ability to successfully reduce it, we must look at ways to relieve it. Relieving stress is different since it means eliminating the stress, rather than managing it. It depends on a vital awareness of what is stressing us and bringing that stress to non-existence. It is not easy, but it has to be done if stress is now ruling your life. How you relieve the stress and keep it away is the important part of this process.

The Challenge

Some stress in our lives is good, but too much, or stress from bad sources can lead to depression, anxiety and a variety of physical ailments. If the stress in your life has reached this level, you no longer have the option to reduce it. You must look for ways to relieve it, whether that involves removing the stressors from your life or coming up with coping mechanisms that, in a sense, make the stress go away. When the harmful stress is no longer present, you will be better able to handle the demands of everyday life and live a better quality of life with less harmful impact to your psyche, physical health, family and workplace. The challenge is to understand the concept of stress relief, where your bad stress has come from and why it is different than good stress, listing the stressors and their impact and then working with professionals to relieve the stress so that you can move on. Relieving stress is not an easy process, but may be absolutely vital and you must be prepared to take on the work necessary to do this coping mechanism.

The Facts

Relieving your stress is different than reducing your stress. Relieving your stress is geared towards alleviating it either by changing the causes of the stress or altering how you deal with it. Once stress is relieved it is theoretically gone from our lives, or at least put into a position where it can be managed much more easier. This does not have to be a harder process than reducing stress, and it can make our lives very much better.

We know we are stressed into uncomfortable positions when we become obsessed with the stress or it is having a debilitating effect on our bodies. These effects may manifest themselves as aches and pains, increased heart rates, shallow breathing, lack of sleep, sleeping too much and having a general sense of unease. You can relieve your stress in almost any environment from your office to your home to even your car as you are stuck in traffic, which is a major sources of temporary stress. They key is to find ways to relieve the stress that work well for you.

A mild degree of stress is actually beneficial, but you need to know what your limits are for stress and how to balance the stress with a healthy attitude towards your life. It means relaxing and not obsessing with stressors.

Music, humor and scents are good ways to regulate your sense of stress and relieve it. You can listen to music or sing tunes or tones by yourself. Augment the music with mental images that can help relieve stress. Keeping a sense of humor about our situations adds a balance to our lives. Aromas are some of the strongest sense memories we possess and aromatherapy is growing as a way to relieve stress through pleasant scents.

Massage can not only make your body feel better, it can relieve stress by affecting your feelings. Your mind and muscles are connected with the central and peripheral nervous systems being linked together. Massage can release endorphins that can calm your emotions. It increases circulation, speeds up removal of toxins from the body and reduces levels of stress hormones. Massage therapy can improve sleep and reduce a woman's post partum depression. Just make sure you are visiting a thoroughly trained and certified massage therapist.

Yoga is a series of personal exercises and can take on many forms. All forms of yoga are designed to bring together your physical, mental and spiritual selves. The term yoga is a Sanskrit word meaning to unite. Yoga teaches you a series of stationary and moving poses called asanas and a form of breath control called pranayama. Yoga slows down your physical activity and lets you stretch your body in ways that massage your internal organs. The benefits of yoga for body and mind include:

- Improved flexibility and joint mobility;
- strengthened and toned muscles;
- increased stamina;
- better digestion;
- lowered cholesterol and blood sugar levels;
- improved circulation;
- boosted immune response;
- increased positive body awareness;
- relief of chronic stress patterns;
- relaxed mind and body;
- centered attention;
- sharpened concentration and
- a freed spirit.

The Solutions

Most stress is in your mind and you need to find relaxing thoughts that can help you deal with stress. This can incorporate a variety of techniques to get in touch with relaxing thoughts such s seeing problems as opportunities, avoiding taking stressors personally, realizing that nothing is perfect not overgeneralizing and being yourself.

Besides getting inside your head there are certain activities you can do to relieve stress. These include exercise, meditation, napping, getting a massage, listening to soothing music, using guided imagery through tapes, taking anything from a short walk to a long vacation and getting away from the bad news of the world.

One of the techniques in relieving stress that is gaining in popularity is biofeedback coupled with hypnotherapy. Biofeedback uses electronic devices to see what is happening to your body and what progress you are making in calming down. Hypnotherapy uses a specialist to induce a trance that helps you relax and can give you post hypnotic suggestions on ways to trigger a stress relief response.

If you are stuck in your car or at your desk or find yourself having trouble sleeping you can relieve the stress through progressive relaxation techniques. Tense, then release, different muscles in your body in a set pattern. The technique is easy to learn and simple to do. Better yet, the technique works with a study finding that chronic headache sufferers experience a 50 percent reduction in pain and frequency using this approach.

One of the simplest forms of stress relief is through an involuntary activity: breathing. You can consciously control your breathing to relieve your stress. Try bringing your breathing under control by exhaling completely, slowly breathing in through your nose, expanding your diaphragm to take air into the lower part of your body, expanding your chest, lifting your shoulders for a last bit of volume, briefly pausing your breathing and finally relaxing and letting the air flow smoothly and fully out through your mouth.

Some stress relief can simply take time to learn and execute. There are ways, however, you can relieve stress very quickly and effectively:

- Practice breathing techniques.
- Use some music.
- Do an enjoyable activity, such as a hobby.
- Read a novel or poetry and avoid contemporary non-fiction.
- Take 10 minutes to meditate or pray.
- Plan and take a vacation.
- Learn how to separate your work life and your home life.
- Develop a support system with your friends, family or co-workers.

One of the most effective ways to relieve stress is one of the simplest and most intuitive: counting to 10. Think of your life as a tape recorder where you can press pause for a few seconds and then play again to restart your life activity. Take your time counting to 10 and remember it can help you step away from stress: a form of relief that is very effective. You can combine counting, by taking a brief walk or stretching.

The Resources

The following Web sites offer more information about relieving stress:

Franklin Institute, *www.fi.edu/brain/relieve*

Time Thoughts, *www.timethoughts,com/stress/stress-relief*

Help Guide, *www.helpguide.org/mental/stress_relief*

Ask Men, *www.askmen.com*

Stress Busting, *www.stressbusting.co.uk*

All About Life Challenges, *www.allaboutlifechanges.org/stress-relief*

Holistic Med, *www.holisticmed.com/stress/free*

The following books offer more information on relieving stress such as:

Transforming Stress: The Heartmath Solution For Relieving Worry, Fatigue, And Tension (New Harbinger Publications, 2005)

Smart Guide to Relieving Stress (Wiley, 1999)

The Brain Chemistry Diet: The Personalized Prescription for Balancing Mood, Relieving Stress and Conquering Depression, Based on Your Personality Profile (Putnam Adult, 2001)

The One-Minute Meditator: Relieving Stress and Finding Meaning in Everyday Life (De Capo, 2001)

The Big Book of Stress Relief Games: Quick, Fun Activities for Feeling Better (McGraw-Hill, 2000)

Yoga for Stress Relief: A Simple and Unique Three-Month Program for De-Stressing and Stress Prevention (Random House, 1998)

The Manager's Guide to Relieving Internal Stress (Anger Clinic, 2004)

18

Coping Mechanisms

We tend to build defenses against stressors and find ways to fight against the stress. In some cases these defenses were specifically designed to handle the pressure of acute or chronic stress. In other cases they are meant to deal with life in general. These are usually called coping mechanisms. They allow us to use methods and attitudes to deal with the stress of modern life and live happier lives. They are absolutely vital to surviving the real world, but must be used wisely and understood for what they are.

The Challenge

Coping mechanisms are a way for our minds and bodies to take a vacation internally from stress. These mechanisms are in place to help us deal with the pressures of daily life and are different for all of us. Whether we consciously use coping mechanisms or employ them without our active knowledge, they can be very helpful in allowing us to navigate modern life and remain productive and happy with our situations. They can also be negative and allow us to hide from the actual cause of stress and consciously dealing with it. Most experts believe it is acceptable to use some form of coping mechanisms, as long as we do not rely too heavily on them. The challenge is to understand the nature of general coping mechanisms, which ones we might be employing, how to separate the good coping mechanisms from what could be negatives and to use them effectively in dealing with our stress.

The Facts

We are complex mechanisms facing a challenging world. Sometimes we are not able to face the that world head on and must resort to coping mechanisms. Some of these are good and help us constructively deal with stress. Others are more negative and prompt us to hide from the root causes of stress, constructing a wall of coping mechanisms that obscure what is really stressing us out in our lives. Experts believe that all of us rely on some type of coping mechanisms and these are not necessarily bad, but the danger is to rely too heavily on the mechanisms and not recognize how we are using them. In some cases, a variety of coping mechanisms might be at work within us.

Although there are a variety of coping mechanisms, almost all of them fall into one or more of three large categories that are either action-based or emotion-based coping. Understanding these categories help us understand our coping mechanisms. These categories are :

- **Biological/physical**; the body uses internal systems to help cope with stress. This often triggers the fight-or-flight reaction to stress.
- **Cognitive**; based on the mental process of how you approach the stress. Cognitive reactions are based on primary and secondary appraisals of the situation. The primary appraisal is when you make a conscious evaluation of the matter at hand. A secondary appraisal is when you ask what you can do by evaluating the coping mechanisms available to you. A cognitive approach is usually based on your perception of how much control you have over a circumstance.
- **Learning**; which assumes much of your motivation and behavior are the results of what is learned through your volume of life experience.

Sometimes we can experience significant stress if we are thrust into the role of caregiver. This means we have become responsible for the well-being of a family member or close friend who needs special attention, usually due to a medical condition. We have to balance the demands of giving care to what we have to do in our daily lives. This can lead to tremendous stress which we can hide from by using coping mechanisms that separate us from the concern. In ways similar to dealing with normal stress, caregivers must move beyond coping mechanisms and find positive ways to deal with this unique stress:

- Creating a workable schedule that allows you to give care and maintain the elements of your life;
- communicating with the person you are providing care that there may be times you are not readily available but will make sure you have created a back-up plan and way for you to be contacted;
- setting boundaries where you let the person you are caring for know when you may not be easily available and what needs to be done in your absence;
- working closely with the medical staff, including visiting nurses, to make sure you are providing a good level of care without inflicting too much burden on yourself;
- keeping a positive attitude that this will pass;
- finding ways to relax when you are not part of the caregiving environment;
- exercising regularly, limiting alcohol intake and stopping smoking;
- making sure you get plenty of rest and sleep, you will not be a good caregiver if you are suffering from exhaustion and
- using deep breathing and guided imagery to get past the caregiving stress.

The Solutions

Most of us cannot easily recognize when we are relying on coping mechanisms and what the effect might be on us. The mechanism may be so ingrained in our lives that its existence is no longer obvious to us. This is when a trained and effective therapist can discover, usually through conversation, how you are dealing with stress and whether these coping mechanisms are doing more harm than good. The therapist can then help you get beyond that reliance on coping mechanisms and honestly face your problems.

Coping mechanisms will vary depending on your psyche and experience in dealing with stress. In some cases they may stand alone, other times they might be used together in some type of combination. Although you can be creative in your creation and use of coping mechanisms, there are several that are common for most of us:

- Acting out where we are not coping, but rather giving in to the pressure to misbehave due to the stressors in our lives.
- Aim inhibition when we lower our sights to accept what seems more achievable.
- Attack response which tells us to try to beat down anything that is threatening.
- Avoidance which can be both mentally or physically avoiding something that causes stress.
- Compartmentalization that separates conflicting thoughts and situations into separated compartments we deal with as we need to.
- Compensation that makes up for a perceived weakness in one area of your life by gaining strength in another.
- Conversion where stress is converted into physical symptoms by your subconscious mind.
- Denial which means you refuse to acknowledge that an event has occurred or it has had a negative effect on you.
- Displacement, a shifting of intended action to what is perceived as a safer target.
- Dissociation where you separate yourself from parts of your life that are stressing.
- Fantasy which replaces real life with an imagined world of possibility you can escape to as needed.
- Idealization where you highlight the good points of a situation and ignore the limitations of other things you may desire.
- Identification is when you copy others to take on what you believe are beneficial characteristics.
- Intellectualization that helps you avoid frightening emotions by focusing only on the facts and logic of a situation.
- Introjection where outer stimuli are brought into the mind.
- Passive aggression where you avoid angering anyone or refuse to deal with a stressful situation by passive avoidance techniques.
- Projection is when you see your own unwanted feelings in other people and can comment on them.
- Rationalization which creates logical reasons for inappropriate behaviors.
- Reaction Formation which allows you to avoid some type of situation by taking the exact opposite position, no matter what the situation is.
- Regression which allows you to return to a child-like state to avoid adult problems.
- Repression where you subconsciously bury and hide uncomfortable thoughts.
- Somatization which is another term for turning psychological problems into physical conditions.
- Sublimation where you channel psychic energy into acceptable activities.

- Suppression that allows you to consciously hold back unwanted urges.
- Symbolization that turns unwanted thoughts into metaphoric symbols that are seemingly easier to deal with.
- Trivializing where we take large, important events and see them as small or not really mattering.
- Undoing which are actions that psychologically undo the wrongdoings of the offender.

The Resources

The following Web sites offer more information about coping mechanisms:

Changing Minds, *www.changingminds.org/explanations/behaviors/coping/coping*

Web MD, *www.webmd.com/mental-health/caregiver-advice-cope*

California State University Northridge, *www.csun.edu*

Human Capital Initiative, *www.psychologicalscience.org*

Health Resource Network, *www.stresscure.org*

American Institute of Stress, *www.stress.org*

Stress Reduction Techniques, *www.mindtools.com/stress*

The following books offer more information on coping mechanisms such as:

Attention Deficit Disorder: Practical Coping Mechanisms (Informa Healthcare, 2006)

Stress. Coping and Development in Children (The Johns Hopkins University Press, 1988)

Hypnosis: Trance as a Coping Mechanism (Springer, 1976)

Stress in Modern Motherhood and Coping Mechanisms (Personal Growth Service Center, 1985)

Coping With Your Difficult Older Parent: A Guide for Stressed-Out Children (Harper Paperbacks, 1999)

Families and Change: Coping With Stressful Events and Transitions (Sage Publications, Inc., 2005)

Coping: The Psychology of What Works (Oxford University Press, USA, 1999)

19

Letting Go

Stress frequently means we cannot see any way out of a situation that is causing us distress. This means we can feel trapped in the situation and add to the stress in tremendous ways. There are a variety of techniques we can use to relieve or reduce the stress, but sometimes the most important method of finally dealing with a stressful situation is to let go of the situation and accept our limitations in what we can reasonably expect to change.

The Challenge

Some people experiencing major stress in their lives see letting go as giving up or giving in to the stress. It is perceived as a sign of weakness that we cannot adequately cope with the stress in an adult fashion. But, often letting go is the best way to start coping with stressors. Letting go does not necessarily mean you are admitting defeat, but, rather you are coming to terms with the stress by taking a first logical step. This is especially true when we are facing situations we have little or no control over, such as an unpleasant work atmosphere or troublesome family. The challenge is to recognize the true nature of letting go, knowing when this is the right step to take, how to successfully combine letting go with other methods of dealing with stress and seeing how this process can benefit us. We can often take the most positive action in dealing with stress by admitting we cannot control it and can only put it aside. This is letting go and it can be a very vital aspect of our life when it is not overused.

The Facts

You may feel bad about letting go, but you should understand that experts in the treatment of stress believe letting go is simply making a decision to no longer allow something from your past influence your present life or to reduce your inner sense of peace and well-being. Letting go allows you to live in the here and now, but can be complicated since we have so many beliefs that prevent us from enjoying the present.

The most important aspect of letting go is not to hold on to anything any longer than it actually lasted. That means what happened five minutes ago is over and should be discarded, while still learned from. You must abandon the attitude that things happen to you, but, rather, they happen from you. You should accept responsibility for your actions but then be ready to move on.

Making a judgment on someone else's actions and personally taking offense from it means you are adding your own anger to an uncomfortable situation. It is better to stay neutral and know that what is happening is happening to someone else, no matter how traumatic.

Although many people have reservations about using techniques to let go of stressors and put judgments aside in their lives, there are several major benefits in letting go that make the practice well worthwhile:

- We acquire a greater sense of being in the present and our needs are actually being met.
- Letting go of unreasonable expectations and harsh judgments helps us find a sense of calm and inner peace because we have eliminated the conflict with what we think things should be. Remember how frightened you were before or immediately after a stressful situation? But, during the actual situation, usually those fears were put aside and you were able to handle the experience.
- We gain a greater acceptance of others and so make a greater contribution to raising their awareness, developing a better sense of going with the flow.
- We find a better sense of fun in freedom of all we do. Letting go helps us rediscover the fun in our lives.

Letting go does not mean you simply check out of your life. It often involves the art of refocusing your energies. This is especially true if you find you have been putting too much energy into something that is not worth it and that you have too few things in your life to really recharge your batteries.

The Solutions

Letting go does not mean conceding defeat to the pressures of stress. Many times we are tempted to fight against stressors by taking action in real life or finding ways to build up coping mechanisms. While it is important to acknowledge the stressors of our lives and be willing to work with them, it is possible that these stressors cannot be adequately dealt with and our only option to regain some sense of health is to put them aside and address the issues we can reasonably control.

Deciding to let go is an important decision and should be arrived at in consultation with a physician or qualified therapist. These professionals can help you analyze the course of your reaction to stress, what, in their opinion, can reasonably be done to fight them and when your best bet on regaining your balance is to let go. The final decision will be yours, but professional consultation can help you make that decision.

You can learn from the intellectual aspect of something that has occurred in your life and use that learning to help you in the future, but you should not hold on to the emotional reaction. This is the key element of a past event that you should let go of. This learning from experience allows you to grow without being haunted by the emotions a sometimes traumatic event can trigger.

We are judgmental beings and, sometimes, we reserve the harshest judgments for our own actions. We all make mistakes or take choices that may not work out. This is part of living and growing. Letting go means not being bound by values, judgments, strict views of morality, criticisms and ideas of what should or should not be.

Sometimes letting go does not mean just letting go of personal feelings, it can mean letting go of people in our lives. In no other forum is this more evident than when you send your children to college and allow them to make their own way and their own mistakes. Some parents, who have been dubbed Helicopter Parents, find it hard to give up the coddling that got their children through high school and step in more than before to make sure their children are being treated fairly and doing their work. You want your children to succeed on their own, and you must learn to let them go to make their own way and hit the same snags you did. If you are asked for your advice and help, you can certainly give it, but you should not try to hold your children tight to you. You can keep up through phone calls and email, but you have to avoid the urge to step in unless the situation absolutely warrants it.

There are three basic ways to let go of stressors in our lives:

- Relax physically. A good exercise is to sit in a chair with your back straight, your knees over your ankles and your feet flat on the floor. Keep your eyes open and focus on your nostrils as you breathe deeply. Allow your shoulders to rise naturally and release any sense of holding on to tension as they relax.
- Falling still is a variation of the sitting and breathing exercise but is designed to last longer. In this exercise, you should gaze toward the horizon with your eyes closed. Take a few minutes and try to reconnect with your senses. Take in the sounds around you until you find the silence underneath.
- Besides relaxing, cut down on your busywork. Being productive is not a matter of rushing to get everything done as if you were going on vacation. Productivity is about the journey, not the destination. This requires you to live in the present and actually enjoy the tasks at hand. Establishing your true priorities allows busywork to slip away and finding time for the things that matter more.

The Resources

The following Web sites offer more information about letting go:

Positive Health, *www.positivehealth.com*

MSNBC, *www.msnbc.msn.com*

Health, *www.health.com*

Stress Doctor, *www.stressdoc.com*

Farmline, *www.members.farmline.com/stress/management/etgo*

Wellness Councils of America, *www.welcoa.org*

Soulful Living, www.soulfillliving.com

The following books offer more information on coping letting go such as:

Letting Go: A Parent's Guide to Understanding the College Years (Harper Paperbacks, 2003)

Secret of Letting Go (Llewellyn Publications, 2002)

The Language of Letting Go (MJF Books, 1998)

The Little Book of Letting Go (Vermillion, 2001)

Letting Go of Shame: Understanding How Shame Affects You (Harper Collins Publishers, 1990)

Letting Go of the Person You Used to Be: Lessons on Change, Loss, and Spiritual Transformation (Broadway, 2004)

The Power of Letting Go: 10 Simple Steps to Reclaiming Your Life (Multnomah, 2006)

Part Five:

Dealing with Workplace Stress

20

Stress and the Intergenerational Workplace

Stress in the workplace can be caused by misunderstandings. Some misunderstandings can be caused by generational issues. Each generation looks at the world in vastly different ways depending on their social, economic and educational background. In addition, people are shaped by how the world looked when they were young.

For this reason, older workers may not understand the working methods of younger workers or their ability to multi-task. In fact, some older workers may perceive this multi-tasking as a disrespectful lack of attention. On the other hand, younger workers may see their older counterparts as being stuck in their ways or too tied up in their work life to have a real life outside of the workplace.

No matter the differences, a multi-generational workforce can be a huge advantage to corporations and not-for-profits. Each generation has a unique skill set that can help companies succeed and prosper.

The Challenge

The challenge of the multi-generational workplace is that people of different generations have a tendency to rely on stereotypes of each other. Instead of finding out the personalities of their co-workers, many people opt for easy answers such as referring to those twenty-somethings and their non-existent work ethic or those fossils and their ideas that were out of date 20 years ago.

The key to developing teamwork in this environment is trying to understand the specifics and not the stereotypes. Not all Baby Boomers are married to their jobs, and not all Gen-Xers are slackers. Working together to find the inherent strengths in each co-worker is the only method to bridge the current generation gap.

The Facts

Four Generations in One Workforce

Issues involving the generation gap may seem quaint in the new millennium. However, if you have not yet begun to work with those of other generations, you soon will. The younger generations do not have the same work/life values as their older counterparts. These differences can cause stress on the work front.

Be aware that not everyone born in specific years will have the exact same attitudes about work. The descriptions below are offered as a general guideline.

- **The Great Generation**

  Often called the Greatest Generation, those born from 1900 to 1945 have gone through two world wars in their lifetime. These workers tend to be traditional in their values. They value institutions and believe in working hard and staying loyal to the same company. Many of them are also financially and socially conservative.

- **Baby Boomers**

  So much as been written about the Baby Boom generation—born 1946 to 1964— that little needs to be said here. They changed the world for the better and fought for what they believed in. In addition, they became used to fighting for every job or promotion because there were so many of them all in the workforce at the same time. Because of their experience with so many co-workers, many Boomers are good at navigating difficult political minefields at work.

- **Generation X**

  Also called Generation Next, those born from 1965 to 1980, are very different from their Boomer parents. Many of them were raised in single-parent households, and they grew up with video games and personal computers. For this reason, Gen-Xers are completely comfortable with technology and do not feel loyalty to large institutions such as corporations. Many of them have a good idea of work/life balance. They do not mind working, but they do not identify with their work as much as Baby Boomers do. Do not expect these folks to put in 60-hour weeks.

- **Generation Z**

  The youngest generation, also called Millennials, were born from 1981 to 1999. Many of them are just now joining the workforce. This generation grew up with advanced technology and teamwork since grade school. They have a good opinion of themselves and their abilities. For this reason, they tend to question everything. While the Gen-Xers often switch jobs, their Gen-Z brethren may decide to switch their whole career or worldview.

- **On the Cusp**

  Not everyone born in a particular year will comfortably fit into one of the above categories. These workers are often on the cusp between one generation and another. These workers are very helpful because they understand the issues involved with more than one generation. Those born on the cusp can be valuable peacemakers and mediators in your company.

The Solutions

How to Get Along With Older and Younger Colleagues

With workers that span four generations, workplace stress and tensions can be difficult to deal with. Different generations often look at such issues as working hours, work/life balance and advancement in unique ways.

- **Acknowledge differences in perception and experience.**

  Your colleagues will not view the world the same as you do. Some will find it silly to work 60 hours a week just to get ahead. Some will ignore the idea of paying dues to be promoted. Some will even wish for the good old days when everything made sense.

  No matter how your colleagues view the world, it is important for you to acknowledge that you all think of the world in different ways. Your experience and background is not superior to theirs. Theirs is not inferior to yours. Your worldviews are just different.

  Instead of judging, ask questions. Find out how your colleagues, both older and younger, look at the world—especially the working world. What are their experiences? What are their hopes? What do they want from the job? What are they willing to give in terms of hard work and hours?

- **Recognize the strengths of different colleagues.**

  No matter what their age, your colleagues have different strengths than you do. Find out what your colleagues are good at in the workplace. Let the Gen-X and Gen-Z workers handle the technology. Allow the Baby Boomers to negotiate the political landscape. Let the Greatest Generation use their experience in the organization to help you navigate issues with senior management.

  No matter what their skills, your colleagues can be joined together to make an effective team if you all can begin to trust and value one another. Moreover, your job as a manager will be easier if you can build bridges between the different generations.

- **Look for win-win opportunities.**

  Build on what your colleagues are good at to create opportunities for them (and you) to shine. If you can manage to get buy-in from all your co-workers, you can create an unbeatable team. In addition, upper management will notice that you have impressive management skills. Before long, other managers will be coming to you for advice about working with their intergenerational forces.

  Be sure to acknowledge the contributions of your younger colleagues and give credit where credit is due. In addition, younger workers often require more frequent feedback on their work or progress. Older colleagues may not want too much feedback. Choose your style based on the generation and personality of those you supervise or work with.

The Resources

The following Web sites offer more information about the different ways that men and women deal with stress:

www.cdc.gov/niosh

The National Institute for Occupational Safety and Health (NIOSH) has a wealth of information about workplace stress and how to deal with it.

www.stress.org

The American Institute of Stress has a Website with a monthly newsletter about stress issues. They also provide a wide variety of information on stress-related issues.

www.mayoclinic.com

This Website offers a huge amount of information about the various sources of stress along with research about the differences between the sexes when it comes to dealing with stress.

21

Stress and the Bad Boss

Work stress is one of the most pervasive sources of stress we will have to deal with. Frequently this stress is because we have to work under what we perceive as a bad boss. The demands and quirks of a boss who is not good at the job can add layers of stress to our lives. It is difficult to change the boss, but we can choose to adapt to the behavior and find ways to cope with the stress that the boss is putting into our lives.

The Challenge

Unless we own the business we are working at, we will have to deal with a boss or supervisor. That person, in a smaller company, may be the founder and sole owner of the operation who controls a small staff. In a larger company with a more complicated corporate structure, we may have to report to a middle manager who is responsible for certain aspects of the operation and will supervise their own division or department. In almost all cases, we will have to be responsible to this person, take direction from him or her and undergo yearly reviews with them. As in personal relationships, not all bosses will fit us. We may find the boss to have demands and personality traits that make it difficult or sometimes impossible to do a proper job. Often, we may encounter a change in the ownership or corporate structure that suddenly has us reporting to a boss we are not familiar with. The concept of a bad boss does not mean the boss is seen as doing a bad job by his or her supervisor or the company directors. It is a description of the complex relationship we have with the boss and how we perceive the boss. The challenge is to recognize when we are working with a bad boss, what types of behaviors or expectations are not working for us, how we can possibly work within the situation and, ultimately, deciding to make a change from the stress by accepting a new position within the company or moving to a different company. We can work with a bad boss successfully and endure the stress, but we must weigh the benefits of the job to the stresses we are experiencing and decide for ourselves if they are worth the effort.

The Facts

Back in the 1970's a popular business book came out called *The Peter Principle*. The book attempted to explain why companies sometimes fail or experience significant problems. One of the concepts in the book is that people in a company rise to the level of their own incompetence. This means an employee will, because of doing a good job, be promoted up the ladder until eventually he or she is filling a role they cannot adequately do. This can be frequently cited with a supervisor who has been promoted from worker to manager. The promotion is often based on the employee's good work, but does not take into account that managing people involves a special set of skills having little or nothing to do with previous job performance. It is ironic that many supervisors who have done good work are not good bosses because they cannot communicate or motivate their staff and believe can do the job better, leading to micromanagement and second guessing that can be very stressful. This situation is similar to the frequent failure of a major sports star to be able to manage a team because he or she knows how to do compete, but cannot tell someone else how. Good companies will recognize the special demands of being a manager and have new managers undergo some type of management training, but, unfortunately this is rare and many new managers are simply given the promotion without necessary training.

There are many aspects of what makes for a bad boss relationship depending on your particular company and duties, but, in general a relationship with a bad boss means:

- Unrealistic expectations for what needs to be done, sometimes based on directions being received from above;
- making frequent changes in requirements and work assignments;
- poor communication in explaining what needs to be done and what is expected;
- creating undoable deadlines requiring frequent long hours;
- using more criticism than praise to promote a good work environment;
- showing favoritism towards certain staff members at the expense of others;
- micromanagement and second guessing of projects so that nothing gets done;
- using personal criticism that has nothing to do with work performance and
- not properly executing yearly reviews that can help pinpoint problems or other areas that need to be addressed.

The small company which was founded and is still operated by the same person may be a cult of personality. This means the boss' word is law and no one will try to respectfully challenge instructions or company direction that appear to be wrong. The boss may have little interest in listening to employees since he or she is used to running the show and believes it is their way or the highway. Work demands can change rapidly and there may be a feeling that no matter what you are doing, it simply is not good enough.

A good personal coach or business coach can help you in dealing with a bad boss, but you must make sure the advice you are hearing and the person giving it has some real relevance to your particular situation. The coach should have some background as a boss or has worked in your particular type of business. You should seek direction from your coach in how to improve your relationship with a bad boss and then filter it into your particular situation. Like consulting with other professionals, such as physicians or lawyers, the information and help you receive will depend a lot on what you can relate to and how well you can separate facts from personal feelings. If you choose to accept a suggestion, tell your coach how it worked for you and make further adjustments as needed.

The Solutions

When at all possible, work with your existing boss through the review process and avoid going over his or her head. Hopefully, you are working with a review process that allows you to express your concerns or difficulties and not just hear what you need to do to make the job work better. Your company should recognize that your opinion matters and a good boss will listen to your concerns without taking it personally. Reacting negatively to any suggestions from you is a good sign you may be working with a bad boss. You can always try to improve the process to include your input, but that can be very difficult.

You must be careful in venting about your boss to your co-workers. Even if you believe you have good friends as co-workers, you must recognize that they are probably operating under their own agenda and have their own needs. It is unfortunate, but many of your co-workers will take your concern to your boss to make themselves look more like team players. There may be other more complicated office politics that can get involved in this process. Unless you are absolutely sure of the discretion of a fellow employee, vent your concerns to your family or non-work friends or see a professional coach to discuss what is bothering you.

There are several specific ways you can try to deal with a bad boss:

- Assume no bad intentions and recognize the behavior has nothing to do with you personally.
- Determine if your boss does not know he or she is bad, wants to improve and does not want to know or does not care about their relationships.
- Communicate clearly with your boss on how your relationship can work better.
- If you have a bad relationship, deal with it as soon as possible.
- Find the right time to talk when you can have your boss' attention.
- Explain the effects of your relationship on you and your work.
- Suggest ideas or alternatives to improve the relationship.
- Make a plan to follow-up.
- Praise your boss just as you would expect to be praised.
- Leave the company or ask for a new position if it is obvious nothing is going to improve.

If you believe you must go over your boss' head to express your concern over the way the boss is managing you or your department, make sure you have records and paperwork to back you up. Remember, the owner has made an investment in time, money and faith in appointing this boss and, unless you can back it up, may end up taking his or her side no matter what you say. You cannot rely on feelings or anecdotal evidence. You need records such as notes from conversations, memos, emails or copies of your reviews to indicate the problems you are having and know what these records say about your relationship.

The Resources

The following Web sites offer more information about dealing with a bad boss:

Psychology Today, *www.psychologytoday.com*

Positive Sharing, *www.positivesharing.com*

Health, *www.health.com*

Bad Bossology, *www.badbossology.com*

Ezine Articles, *www.exinearticles.com/?What-Makes-a-Manager-a-Bad-Boss:-Survey-Results*

Working America, *www.workingamerica.org*

Quint Careers, *www.quintcareers.com/bad_bosses*

The following books offer more information on dealing with bad bosses such as:

A Survival Guide for Working With Bad Bosses: Dealing with Bullies, Idiots, Back-stabbers, And Other Managers from Hell (AMACOM, American Management Association, 2005)

Dealing with the Boss from Hell (Kogan Page, Ltd., 2005)

Was Your Boss Raised By Wolves?: Surviving The Organizational Food Chain (Career Press, 2005)

Dealing with Difficult People (Kogan Page, 2006)

Retiring the Generation Gap: How Employees Young and Old Can Find Common Ground (Jossey-Bass, 2006)

The New Supervisor: How to Thrive in Your First Year As a Manager (Perseus Book Group, 1998)

Who's Afraid of the Big Bad Boss?13 Types and How to Survive Them (Infinity Publishing, 2005)

22

Stress and the Impossible Schedule

Much of the stress we experience in our lives is due to a schedule of tasks that we believe is undoable or impossible. This can be the result of several factors, but ultimately it makes us think we cannot possibly complete the tasks given to us within required deadlines without long hours or taking our work home, combined with the schedule of our personal lives. The impossible schedule may cause tremendous stress based life and, if we do not deal with it properly, can have significant effects on our mental health, physical health and healthy relationships with our family and personal life. In this chapter we will concentrate on the impossible work schedule.

The Challenge

Schedules in our lives are absolutely essential. They lay out expected deadlines, a timeline for completing the task and should be flexible enough to include aspects of our job such as appointments, phone calls or sales visits. The job schedules ideally should be created by both the employee and the supervisor, but, often, are imposed upon the employee in a process that filters the demands of the schedule from the top down. If you are a responsible employee, you want to make every effort to maintain your adherence to a schedule, but, if the schedule is truly impossible, this conscientiousness can lead to job frustration and a feeling of despair that nothing will get done within the time allotted. This can lead to poor job performance which will further add to our stress levels. Impossible schedules may be based on specific projects and will not last forever, but may also be involved with systemic changes that have no end in sight. The challenge is to recognize when a schedule is truly impossible, what we can do to try to streamline the work requirements, communicating our concerns without sounding like defeatists, and arriving at alternatives that can help get the job done without piling too much false expectations on us and our performance.

The Facts

A systemic increase in your workload and schedule may mean you are being asked to do the work of employees who are no longer with the company, either by lay-offs or by attrition. Many companies, in an effort to increase productivity, are asking existing employees to do more work with less resources and take on the duties of employees who are no longer working with the company. If your work schedule permits these extra tasks, these extra duties might be doable and will enhance your image as being willing to step up to accepting extra tasks and have the skills and ability to carry them out. The downside to showing this success is that you may be asked to do additional chores because you are perceived to be a miracle worker.

There are several significant effects on us when dealing with an impossible schedule:

- Physical effects such as muscle or joint pain, shortness of breath and digestive difficulties;
- a feeling of frustration that can lead to not being able to get anything done;
- sleep disruptions, usually being a lack of sleep;
- reliance on overeating or alcohol to provide relief from the stress;
- deteriorating relationships with your family due to your own frustrations and lack of time to spend with them;
- headaches;
- despair over meeting the schedule demands and
- lack of attention to details that can lead to mistakes or on-the-job accidents.

There are several elements that go into making a schedule impossible or setting up deadlines that cannot be met in the timeframe designed for them:

- The schedule is overly ambitious. Reducing the timeline and just adding resources to a project will only delay the project completion. No amount of money can compensate you for working around the clock. Performance penalties for not making a deadline can be extremely painful.
- The planning is inadequate. You must understand what you are doing and how you work. Leave room in your schedule for changes.
- The information is insufficient. You need to know exactly what is required of you and what is needed with each deliverable.
- The resources are inadequate or unavailable. You do not have what you need on a consistent basis to meet your deadlines.
- The requirements keep changing. Impossible schedules sometimes mean the playing field is constantly changing.
- Missing problems. As you accept a schedule, keep in mind any elements that could delay the project and express these possibilities at the beginning.

The Solutions

Much of workaholism is based on trying to meet an impossible schedule. We obsess over work, put in very long hours on a consistent basis and take work home. While this may be acceptable in a short-lived adjustment of our schedule, over the long run, these practices can be destructive. Even if we believe we identify strongly with our jobs and thrive under impossible schedules, the fact is that we need time to ourselves occasionally to cope with schedule demands. Advertising pioneer David Ogilvy wrote that he put in very long hours in growing and running his agency, but would make up for that by scheduling one or more long vacations to get away from the job and recharge his batteries. You need to find time away from work where you cannot be reached, whether these are daily activities with friends, family or hobbies or taking vacations that get you away from the office for a substantial period. Taking work home only helps isolate you from your family and makes you feel like your job is controlling your life.

Communication is key when dealing with an impossible schedule. When you are assigned new tasks, clarify exactly what is being required from you and if the deadlines are written in stone. Establish check points to determine if you are maintaining the schedule and to avoid unpleasant surprises. If the schedule shows itself to be unworkable, tell your boss about your feelings and why you believe the schedule is problematic. Be sure to include workable alternatives in this communication and do not just make it a chance to whine or admit defeat. If you can get help from somebody else in your company, ask for it, and let your boss know you are sharing the workload and why. When at all possible, make notes on these communications and your boss' response and keep them on file for later reference. Email responses are excellent ways to keep communication records.

Organization and prioritization are critical elements in gaining control over a seemingly impossible schedule. A desk full of paper and folders and an email inbox jammed with messages is going to be daunting for anyone. Go through the paper, be ruthless in tossing or filing what you no longer need and make to-do piles out of the rest of the work. This will help you more easily access your work and avoid wasting time in trying to find paperwork. Keep in mind that if every job is top priority then no job is top priority. Make sure you make lists of tasks to be done and list or rate them in order of what has to be done immediately, what can be done later and what can wait until you have time to address them.

You must keep an impossible schedule in perspective. If the project is finite it is easier to deal with. If the impossible schedule appears to have no end to it, or is getting worse, this is where the danger of stress lies. You have to be able to separate the two and keep each type of schedule in perspective. When at all possible, reward yourself for making a tough deadline by having a nice lunch or dinner or purchasing some small item such as a new book or CD.

You have to learn how to say no to outside commitments if you are facing strict work deadlines. Part of the stress of having an impossible schedule is balancing that schedule with outside duties. If you are under the gun at work, you have to be able to say no to helping out with an event or attending a family social function. You may have to ask your partner to take on some of these duties while you are working on this project, knowing there will be an end in sight. You should not make yourself a hermit, but you must avoid spreading yourself too thin in maintaining a work and life balance.

The Resources

The following Web sites offer more information about dealing with an impossible schedule:

Rothman Management Development, www.jrothman.com

Assembla, www.assembla.com

Tech Republic, www.articles.techrepublic.com.com

Transcender, www.certmag.com/itissues

Able Work Schedule, www.uos.harvard.edu

Guidebook, www.guidebook.dcma.mil

Springer Link, www.springerlink.com

The following books offer more information on dealing with an impossible schedule such as:

Manager's Guide to Alternative Work Schedules (Institute of Police Technology and Management, 1998)

Alternative Work Schedules: Integrating Individual and Organizational Needs (Addison-Wesley, 1978)

Using Flextime to Create a Competitive Workplace (Institute of Industrial Engineers, 2005)

Alternative Work Schedules (Allyn & Bacon, 1998)

Alternative Work Schedules: Selecting, Implementing, and Evaluating (Irwin Professional Pub, 1984)

The Impact of Work Schedules on the Family (Institute for Social Research, 1983)

Theory of Scheduling (Dover Publications, 2003)

23

Are You a Perfectionist?

Perfectionism is so endemic in many of our lives that we do not recognize when we are striving for perfection either on the job or in our personal lives. We may feel stressed because of these efforts and the frustrations they incur, but we do not translate that into identifying our own perfectionist tendencies. Through a simple process of self-examination we can determine our tendency to perfection and how that may be adversely affecting us.

The Challenge

Most of us would not identify perfectionism as a negative thing. We have been raised to believe that we should always strive to do our very best on any project we take on. We believe that nothing less than our best invites failure. But, when this desire turns into perfectionism, we can feel frozen in place. We are afraid to finish a task because we do not think it is just right. This can cause tremendous stress that can manifest in a variety of ways: work performance issues, mental disorders, behavioral problems, lack of social interaction and even physical symptoms. Perfectionism is insidious and can manifest itself slowly and in such a way that we have trouble consciously realizing we are working too hard to achieve the unachievable. A solution is to take a simple quiz to determine our behaviors and how they relate to perfectionism. We can fill this out based on our own feelings and self-knowledge or seek help from others in giving us feedback. The challenge is to locate a suitable quiz and be as honest as possible in filling it out. And, by all means, do not think it has to be perfect.

Rating Your Stress Quiz

If you feel like your life is full of thinking I must and I should, you are probably exhibiting some form of perfectionism. The quiz bellows allows you to acknowledge what behaviors you are displaying and to what extent they are dominating your life. The more times you answer Often, the more the perfectionism is taking control of your life and causing you stress.

SYMPTOM	NEVER	RARELY	SOMETIMES	OFTEN
If I do not set the highest standards for myself, I am likely to end up a second rate person.				
People will probably think less of me if I make a mistake.				
If I cannot do something really well, there is little or no point in doing it at all.				
I should be upset if I make a mistake.				
If I try hard enough, I should be able to excel at anything I attempt.				
It is shameful for me to display weaknesses or foolish behaviors.				
I should not have to repeat the same mistake many times.				
An average performance will certainly seem unsatisfactory to me.				
Failing at something I perceive important will make me less of a person.				
If I scold myself for failing to live up to my expectations, it will help me do better in the future.				
I feel like I am just not doing a very good job anymore.				

Another way to rate your perfectionism is to use statements you either agree with or disagree with logical differentiation in between. This will help you isolate your feelings needing to be a perfection and, like the quiz above, will allow you to put the perfectionist behaviors in some type of context. You may want to give this quiz to a trusted friend, co-worker or supervisor on the job to help you take an outside look at your possible perfectionism. The more you strongly agree or agree, the more you may be a perfectionist.

SYMPTOM	STRONGLY AGREE	AGREE	NOT SURE	DO NOT AGREE	STRONGLY DISAGREE
Being average at something is like failure to you.					
Your parents set unrealistically high standards for you when you were growing up.					
You are a neat freak and obsessed with organization.					
In public, you never let it show if you are upset, angry or hurt. Saving face is important.					
Mistakes, even small ones, make you very upset.					
It is hard for your friends or co-workers to live up to your standards. You are often disappointed by them.					
Even when your life seems to be going well, you can always find things that worry or bother you.					
You secretly feel inferior to other people. You believe you know many people who are more attractive, more popular and more successful than you.					
You want to be best at everything.					
You second guess yourself constantly and never feel like you are doing things right.					
The prospect of making a mistake angers you.					

SYMPTOM	STRONGLY AGREE	AGREE	NOT SURE	DO NOT AGREE	STRONGLY DISAGREE
You get impatient with people around you—they always seem to screw up.					
It always seems your mate/partner falls short of satisfying you and always misses the little details, doing nothing just right.					
If you make a mistake, others will think you are incompetent.					
You believe if you do things badly, others will reject you.					
Your partner is likely to reject you at some point unless you are better than any other potential mate.					
With most tasks, you feel there is a right way and a wrong way to do them and you are not comfortable with alternative ways to get them done.					
You would rather work harder and do things yourself than delegate tasks to others.					
Being average is a terrible thing for you.					
When things do not go as planned, you get extremely stressed out.					

Teenage/Student Perfectionist Quiz

Perfectionist behaviors often start in the teenage or student years. There is great pressure to succeed in school these days and, when those pressures are mixed with the confusion of growing up, the results can be a feeling of not measuring up and not fitting in. This will only get stronger as the teen moves into adult life and work pressures. Circle each item that applies to the statement about you.

BEHAVIOR	CONCLUSIONS			
After the track meet, your coach tells you ran the mile just three seconds over the record. You…	take your friends out for pizza and celebrate.	cannot stop thinking you could have beat the record if you had only pushed harder.	are happy about your accomplish-ment and make plans to train harder for the next race.	
Your friends would be most likely to say…	you never give up.	you usually try your best.	you usually do not try at all.	
You are ready to leave for school when your little sister spills corn flakes all over you. You…	wipe yourself off with a paper towel on your way to the bus stop.	are an hour late for school because you take another shower.	change clothes as fast as you can and cover your hair with a baseball cap.	
Your piano recital is next week, but you cannot seem to perform a difficult piece. You…	ask for something easier and work on the hard piece for your next recital.	skip the recital and go to the movies instead.	work on the hard piece until your fingers hurt.	
Who expects the most from you?	Your parents.	Yourself.	Nobody expects much from you.	
The new girl in class is nasty to you for no apparent reason. You…	treat her nicely, but do not let it bother you.	completely ignore her.	go out of your way to make her like you.	
How do you handle criticism?	I hate it when someone thinks I have made a mistake.	I try to listen to it and learn from it.	I am so used to it, I do not even notice.	

BEHAVIOR	CONCLUSIONS			
How do you react when you get a B on a test?	I am very disappointed with myself.	I am shocked. I never do that well.	An A would be better, but I did my best and I am happy with a B.	
The teacher assigns a class project for groups. Your first thought is…	It will be fun to work with other people.	I hate working in groups because no one works as hard as me.	How can I get into a group that will do the work for me?	
When you make a mistake, how much time do you spend worrying about it?	None, I just move on.	A little. I think about what I will do different next time.	A lot. It takes me a long time to get over something if I have messed up.	
Would you let someone else clean your room?	Yes.	No.	Depends on who it is.	
Does it bother you when people touch your stuff?	Yes.	No.	Depends on the stuff.	
Do you argue with people over the validity of their opinions?	All the time.	Often.	Rarely.	Never.
Do you like surprises?	Never.	Sometimes depending on the circum-stances.	I love surprises!	
How do you feel when you see someone else wearing the same outfit as you?	Extremely happy, we will be good friends.	Disturbed, what is he or she doing wearing my outfit?	Fine. I hardly notice.	Amused.

BEHAVIOR	CONCLUSIONS			
When someone's hair is out of place you…	hardly notice.	have urges to fix it.	quietly suggest they fix their hair.	think they look cute when they are a little
If someone you do not know sits in a place that is not their usual spot you, you feel…	like something is wrong, but you cannot put your finger on it.	you do not know them, why would you notice where they sit.	it feels totally wrong and it is going to mess up your day.	
In a group project you assume the position of…	helpful bystander.	leader.	the person who does what you are told to do.	try to contribute, but your ideas are crushed by others.
Do you edit books as you read?	Yes, in pen.	No, I would not do that.	That never occurred to me.	
How long does it take you write an essay?	Not that long, but it seems like forever.	It literally takes forever.	I do not time myself.	
What kind of tests do you do the worst on?	Multiple choice, I always second guess myself.	Essay questions.	Timed tests.	Fill in the blanks.
Would you rather hear someone speak fast, medium or slow?	It does not matter.	Fast, I am impatient.	Slow, I like to really read into what they are saying.	Medium, I have never really thought about it.
Does it take you a while to get used to a new sleeping arrangement?	I can sleep wherever whenever.	It would depend on the position, but usually no.	Yes, I am a very light sleeper.	

BEHAVIOR	CONCLUSIONS			
When someone else is driving you…	sit back and relax.	watch the road intensely and scrutinize the driver's actions.	I never drive, it is too much pressure.	None of these.

Are You at Risk for Perfectionism?

A simple true or false quiz can give you an idea if you are a perfectionist or displaying behaviors that might mean you will strive for perfection.. The quiz is simple and takes little time to complete. Be honest and interpret the results carefully. Not all trues or falses indicate perfectionism.

SYMPTOM	TRUE	FALSE
When you make an error, you rarely focus on your mistake.		
You regularly use phrases like mistakes happen and you cannot win them all.		
You are often afraid of trying new things because you believe you would not be good at them.		
You see mistakes as a good thing.		
I think I must put 100 percent into everything I do or I will fail.		
Average is not good enough for me.		
I get overwhelmed because I have too much to do.		
I have so many shoulds in my life that I rarely enjoy myself.		
I am a martyr.		
I am afraid if someone sees I was less than perfect, they would reject me or disapprove.		
I miss opportunities for intimacy in a relationship because I will not take a risk unless I can control the outcome.		
I react negatively to suggestions related to me or my work because I take it as criticism of me as a person.		
If someone is unhappy with what I produce, they are unhappy with me.		
I often feel burned out.		

The Solutions

Examine each quiz carefully and take the results seriously. Ask your friends or family about the results. Take the tests periodically to see if anything has changed. Allow your responses to help you begin the process of negating your feelings of perfectionism. Remember, a little perfectionism is not bad, it is only when it takes control of your life can you feel destructive effects.

The Resources

The following Web sites offer more information about whether you are a perfectionist:

Think Quest, *www.library.thinkquest.org*

Blogthings, *www.blogthings.com/areyouaperfectionistquiz*

Discovery Health, *www.discoveryhealth.queendom/com/questions/perfectionism_abridged*

Briomag, *www.briomag.com/briomagazine/quizzes*

iVillage. *www.quiz.ivillage.com/cgi-bin/goodhousekeeping/tests/perfectionist*

All the Tests, *www.allthetests.com*

Forget About Diets, *www.forgetaboutdiets.com/loss/perfectionismcancreateloss*

The following books offer more information on whether you are a perfectionist such as:

When Perfect Isn't Good Enough: Strategies for Coping with Perfectionism (New Harbinger Publications, 1998)

Perfectionism: What's Bad About Being Too Good (Free Spirit Publishing, 1999)

Overcoming Perfectionism: The Key to a Balanced Recovery (HCI, 1990)

Perfectionism: Theory, Research and Treatment (American Psychological Association, 2002)

Freeing Our Families from Perfectionism (Free Spirit Publishing, 2001)

Perfecting Ourselves to Death: The Pursuit of Excellence and The Perils of Perfectionism (InterVarsity Press, 2005)

Never Good Enough: Freeing Yourself from the Chains of Perfectionism (Free Press, 1999)

24

Stress and Limited Resources

We all need the right resources in our lives to help fight against stress. It is ironic that in a world full of rapidly changing technologies designed to make our work and personal lives easier, that finding the resources to keep up with our lives can be so challenging. When our needs collide with this lack of resources, we can be assured that stress will follow.

The Challenge

Resources is a buzz word for a variety of elements you need in your life. At your workplace you will need the people on the job to help you succeed as well as the most basic of technical resources including computer systems and software, fax machines, cell phone technology, tracking devices and updated manufacturing equipment. In our personal lives, resources might include personal items for cooking and managing our homes as well as people and services available to us including our families, professionals and service personnel. These resources are not always available to us as we need them and we can feel stuck in trying to acquire the proper resources or upgrade what we have. This can lead to frustration, not doing the job properly and stress. We can acquire new resources or better use the resources available to us. The challenge is to understand what resources we need or have, what we can reasonably expect to receive, how to ask for additional resources and how to use them properly to justify their acquisition. Maintaining the proper amount of resources will mean staying up-to-date on what is available and some creativity, but it is vital in getting the job done and avoiding the frustration of feeling this close to failure.

The Facts

Recognizing a lack of resources can affect many people in the process of doing a project. This can start from the top down through the project manager to the workers who are being asked to complete the project with limited resources. The stress from making the process work without necessary resources can also filter down and have an adverse effect on everyone involved. This stress can manifest itself in a feeling of frustration over being asked to do the seemingly impossible and possibly to performing the work at a less than satisfactory level.

Limited resources can include a variety of elements such as:

- Not enough staff to perform the project;
- outdated or lack of necessary equipment from basic office equipment to manufacturing systems;
- lack of proper training to understand and perform the task properly and
- not enough time to reasonably do the project and maintain other elements in the workplace.

If you are being told to do a project without the proper resources, you are actually being told to sacrifice quality. For example if you need five engineers but only have two, the quality of the work will drop. One way to bring this to management's attention when they are asking you to do a project without the necessary resources is to talk about quality. Do not just ask for more resources, ask what level of quality is required. This argument is much more likely to give you the additional resources you need.

The Solutions

The best time to identify resources is when the project is in the earliest planning stage. This might include the time when the RFP is being prepared and can focus everyone's attention on the basic question: Can we do this with the resources we currently have? If the answer is no, and the response is properly evaluated it can lead a business to pass on a certain project or look at ways to improve resources prior to commencing work.

Sometimes adding to resources can be a temporary measure and involve outsourcing various aspects of the project or hiring temporary help to complete the work needed. The downside to this is a loss of control over the work process and having to find qualified temporary or contract employees and bringing them up to speed on what the company expects. It can include extra levels of supervision that can take time from people who need to be working on the project. When the process works it can give you some go-to resources to add as needed for future projects.

Equipment that is necessary for this project, but perhaps not for the long-term needs of the company, can possibly be leased for a certain amount of time. Your staff will still need to be trained on the new equipment and there may be maintenance issues involved, but a good supplier should be able to supply the necessary training and maintenance back-up.

One approach to dealing with limited resources is to rethink the schedule to focus on quality and delivery. This means quality will not drop when resources are low if each schedule milestone is framed around the available resources. For example, if there are only resources for three weeks of quality work, then that is what should be scheduled for and delivered. These short milestones will trade low quality for high and give more frequent deliveries on the project. The downside is it may take longer for the entire project to be completed, but delivering high quality in increments could be worth that trade off.

The people who hold the budget strings in any business have heard the same arguments about needing more resources beyond their ability to count. Everyone is always asking for more and sooner or later they are going to turn a deaf ear to the request, no matter how justified it is. One way to get around that deafness is to come to them with ideas on how to make the project work and not simply holding out your hands for more money that may or may not be readily available. You can do this by:

- Understand that great ideas do not necessarily have to cost great amounts of money.
- Find ideas that make good economic sense in the short and long term.
- Start to believe that the tighter the resource box you are operating in, the more creative can be the solutions. Accept the challenge.
- Find ideas that might save money in the long run, rather than just spend it in the short run.
- Stay positive and challenge yourself and your work group.
- Review the big ideas in business and see that many of them did not require great outlays of money.
- If you can sell a good idea, it will often attract the resources you need.
- It is true that necessity is often the mother of invention and when things look difficult, the best ideas will emerge.
- Revise your idea if it does not fly and persevere in presenting it to management. Many times it takes repeated efforts to sell a new idea.

One way to work with limited resources is to network or work with collaborators or partners. By networking effectively you may discover ways to maximize resources or new sources of personnel and equipment you were not previously aware of from innovative suppliers to firms that can help provide you with temporary staff. A good arrangement with collaborators and partners can have them supply a portion of the work needed, using their resources, without having to add substantially to yours. The downside to working with collaborators or partners is giving up a certain amount of control over the work itself, but, if you find the right people and create workable agreements that include verifiable deliverables and ways out of the agreement. This can work very well for you and help you get the work done with limited resources.

The Resources

The following Web sites offer more information about stress and limited resources:

Scott Berkun, *www.scottberkun.com/forums/pmclinic*

Small Business Association, *www.sba.gov*

Rossiter & Company, *www.rossiterandco.com*

Fasten Network, *www.fastennetwork.com*

Wikihow, *www.wikihow.com/Work-With-Limited-Resources-on-a-Project*

United States Chamber of Commerce, *www.uscoc.com*

Project Perfect, *www.projectperfect.com.au*

The following books offer more information on stress and limited resources such as:

Work and the Workplace: A Resource for Innovative Policy and Practice (Columbia University Press, 2006)

Managing Human Resources: Productivity, Quality of Work Life, Profits (McGraw-Hill, Irwin, 2002)

Making Collaboration Work: Lessons from Innovation in Natural Resource Management (Island Press, 2000)

It's Ok to Ask 'Em to Work: And Other Essential Maxims for Smart Managers (AMACOM/American Management Association, 1999)

ROI At Work (ASTD Press, 2005)

The Art of Project Management (O'Reilly Media, Inc., 2005)

The One-Page Project Manager: Communicate and Manage Any Project With a Single Sheet of Paper (Wiley, 2006)

Part Six:

Dealing with Personal Stress

25

Stress and the Family

Stress can go beyond just yourself. Stress can effect the dynamics of the entire family including your spouse and children, in some cases even your parents and other relatives. The stress you are feeling can easily affect your interaction with your family in a negative way that can cause stress among your family members. You can bring your stress home with you from work or have it enter the family scene from other aspects of your personal life and where your head is at in the particular moment. Stress can also be caused by the family in having to deal with issues that are part of your family life.

The Challenge

Family stress can cut both ways. Your stress can easily affect how you deal with your family and how they will deal with you. It can cause deep unhappiness and confusion among the people you love the most. It can take you into a downward spiral of ill effects that can come back and haunt you in many ways. Also, your family can contribute to your stress in ways that we do not readily recognize. We all know we have to deal with the issues and demands of the family, but sometimes these issues can be overwhelming and cause us tremendous stress. The issues may include dealing with an ill parent, going through domestic disputes with our partner that could even lead to divorce, what our children and teenagers are doing and what behavior patterns are troubling you. In some ways, it can be more difficult to deal with family stress because the stressors are people we love and cannot separate from. We can leave a stressful job situation and move on. This is almost impossible and undesirable when we look at ways to deal with our family. We can feel stuck in a stressful family situation, and this feeling can also add to our stress. Luckily, family stress can be positively dealt with. The challenge is to recognize the effects of our stress on our family or the presence of stressful factors in our family life, coming to terms with the stress, maintaining positive lines of communication and seeking help in dealing with family stress. We have to function in some type of family unit and there will always be stress in this most intimate of settings. The key is to work through the stress and enhance the loving feelings that make our families one of the most important parts of our support system.

The Facts

A common definition of family stress is a real or imagined imbalance between the demands on the family and the family's ability to meet those demands. The seriousness of the family stressors can be determined by how the family perceives the nature of the stress. A sudden event that can be seen as damaging may be perceived as a crisis and this has to be dealt with immediately.

There are a variety of events in our family that can cause our stress. Some may be triggered by our behavior, others are outside of our control including:

- Dealing with a catastrophic injury or illness to a close family member, especially to our parents who may need to make changes in their lives and hard decisions in their health care;
- financial disputes with members of our family because of loans or other issues;
- tension with a spouse that has either been ongoing for some time or based on a specific incident, such as an extra-marital affair, which could lead to divorce;
- blending two new families as part of a new marriage;
- behavior patterns by children that involve illegal or destructive activities;
- moving to a new home or a new location and
- even planning what should be a pleasant activity, such as a vacation.

It is easy to inflict our own stress on our family. We may feel stressed by work pressures, and, instead of communicating these stresses and our feelings about them, we retreat into a shell or act out with anger. This can cause confusion and hurt and ultimately stress out our families.

There are specially trained therapists for the family. These professionals can help the entire family deal with stress aspects in their lives and look for positive ways to handle the stress. A family therapist might start by meeting with just you or you and your spouse and then move on to deal with other members of your family, first in private and then later as a group. This can be a lengthy and challenging process, but, when led by the right person, it can provide an excellent way to recognize and deal with stress in our family lives or deal with a crisis situation.

The Solutions

Honest communication with our family can present unique challenges. We have structured our family environment based on certain factors that may not easily lend themselves to communication. We may be used to having the final say in all of our family activities and as this changes when our children grow older, we have trouble communicating our frustration over our changing roles. The family may have trouble expressing their feelings over the changing aspects of their lives and how this fits into the family. It is difficult, but if we can find some time every few days to sit down, avoid distractions and honestly discuss how the family is functioning, we can help deal with the stress. This means turning off the television, ignoring phone calls and creating an atmosphere that is non-judgmental. Once these parameters are met, communication can be enhanced.

Quite often our views of our immediate family, spouse and children, are colored by how we were raised as children. If our parents were strict disciplinarians we might emulate that behavior or go against it by being more permissive to not raise our children the way we were. The most troubling degree of this is if our parents were mentally and physically abusive and these very destructive patterns of behavior have passed down to us. If we can understand how our upbringing influences how we deal with our own family, we can free ourselves from unproductive patterns of behavior and move into a more positive family relationship.

Dealing with family stress often involves coping skills. These are developed over time and take real work. Coping is accomplished with resources from both inside and outside the family. This is how the family can remove the stressor, live with hardships or develop new resources in a response to a crisis. Families who do a good job of managing stress:

- Do things as a family and not withdraw from each other during times of stress;
- build esteem in each other and themselves by showing appreciation and letting other family members know they understand;
- develop social support within the community by meeting new friends, joining clubs and using community facilities and
- develop and use a range of tension-reducing devices such as exercise, relaxation, keeping a positive outlook and being involved in activities.

Just as it can in other aspects of our lives, getting organized and maintaining a clean family environment can help immeasurably in reducing family stress. Quite often having a trash-filled house or car, a dining table that is packed with items that have nothing to do with eating or not properly taking care of trash in the home can cause stress that cannot easily be identified. Taking the time to clean out the house and do necessary chores can make you feel better as well a providing a positive activity for your family. You might also look at better organizing your schedule and reducing the number of activities your children are involved in to concentrate on other aspects of the family.

We usually have to attend various types of family gatherings from birthday parties to weddings and everything in between. These social occasions often provide opportunities to rehash old hurts rather than enjoy our large family. We may find ourselves not attending important family events because of events that have transpired between us and our family members. Family gatherings are not a good time to cause ourselves more stress. Some simple ways to avoid this are:

- Try to resolve the conflict away from the gathering. Ask the person involved in the conflict if he or she would like to try to resolve it in some different and private venue.

- Forgive and forget what has happened in the past. Letting a disagreement fester into a feud will not help you feel any better. If you cannot resolve the conflict, try to let it go.
- Remove the person from your life if what the other person did was abusive and there is no reason to expect the behavior to change in the future. You can severely limit the your dealings with this person, and while this is a solution of last resort, it is sometimes necessary for your own emotional health.

The Resources

The following Web sites offer more information about stress and the family:

Clemson Extension, *www.cdc.gov/nasd/docs*

American Family Physician, *www.aafp.org*

Stress About, *www.stress.about.com*

Article City, *www.articlecity.com/articles/family*

Pioneer Thinking, *www.pioneerthinking.com/ara-familystress*

Michigan State University Extension, *www.msu.edu*

The Consultation Center, *www.theconsultationcenter.org*

The following books offer more information on stress and the family such as:

Family Stress Management (Sage Publications, Inc., 2001)

Stress Between Work and Family (Springer, 1990)

Family Stressors: Interventions for Stress and Trauma (Routledge, 2004)

Handbook of Stress, Trauma, and the Family (Taylor and Francis, 2004)

Stress, Coping, and Health in Families: Sense of Coherence and Resiliency (Sage Publications, 1998)

Families and Change: Coping With Stressful Events and Transitions (Sage Publications, 2005)

Family Stress: Classic and Contemporary Readings (Sage Publications, 2002)

26
Stress, Relationships and Intimacy

Relationship difficulties present their own type of stress. Often, we consider stress caused by relationships and intimacy to be with a significant other or a spouse. But, relationships can also include how we deal with our friends, immediate family and children. Intimacy does not have to be considered necessarily physical intimacy involving sexual issues, but can simply mean a feeling of relating to someone beyond the usual and relying on him or her to confide in and keep our secrets. If we feel stymied in our relationships and intimacy with others, it can lead to real stress in our lives.

The Challenge

Most of us seek some type of significant relationship in our lives. This usually means having someone with us in a romantic relationship, but there are other relationships that can be important to us. Usually what defines a successful relationship is the ease with which we can be with someone else and the trust we bring to the relationship. This involves feelings of intimacy that include the ability to be physically intimate, but also the feeling that a person has our back, that we can freely express our emotions to them and be able to have them help us in a non-judgmental way. Relationships and intimacy are key aspects to our mental and even physical health. Developing them and dealing with them can take effort and be stressful, but not having anyone in our lives we can trust can lead to even worse stress, that can manifest itself in poor physical health. The challenge is to find someone we can develop a relationship based on intimacy, working on the relationship and not taking someone for granted, note]ing when changes can occur in a relationship and how we have to deal with those changes, and when it may be time to end a relationship because it is causing us more harm than good. A relationship can be immensely rewarding when we approach it informed and open.

The Facts

We seek some relationships, others are simply part of our lives. For most of us relationships include:

- A significant other such as a girlfriend, boyfriend, live-in partner or spouse;

- a non-romantic relationship with a person of either sex;
- a warm and ongoing friendship and
- relationships with immediate family such as parents, children or siblings.

Much of our relationship problems actually come from within us and not from the other person. They can be generated from hidden conversations and action patterns. The problem is we do not notice or acknowledge the role we play, but are tempted to blame the other person for our problem in the relationship.

There are several behavior patterns we manifest that can lead to problems with our relationships and cause us stress:

- Being very critical and judgmental of those we are in relationship with;
- blaming the other person in the relationship without taking time to look at ourselves.
- forgetting the differences in others that initially attracted us to them and using these differences now to hurt the relationship;
- invalidating other people's opinions and points of view believing they are always wrong and we are always right; and
- failing to acknowledge the problems and taking action to move ahead with the relationship.

One of the most important elements for maintaining a successful relationship is communication. Most of us do not know what separates productive from non-productive communication and how communication is based on both verbal and non-verbal signals. Good communication is not just sharing feelings or thoughts, but to communicate in a way that is meaningful to someone else.

Marriage relationships are unique and can cause significant stress in our lives. Some of the major factors of marital stress include:

- Believing our spouse is not affectionate, or not as affectionate as he or she used to be;
- a spouse with an unforgiving attitude;
- how finances are handled or mishandled;
- lack of communication;
- not finding quality time to spend together;
- extramarital relationships;
- dealing with extended families and step children and
- dealing with relatives and in-laws.

We cannot generate an intimate relationship if we do not have access to our own feelings and ideas. Another person cannot insert intimacy into our lives if we are out of touch with ourselves. Our intimate experiences involve emotional, cognitive, social, physical, sexual and spiritual aspects of our lives. True intimacy is one of the ultimate expressions of the human experience and is why we strive so hard to find it.

The Solutions

Similar to dealing with other stressful parts of our lives, we can take a systematic approach to dealing with stress caused by perceived problems with a relationship or level of intimacy. This approach includes:

- Define your problem specifically. Do not just say my partner does not love me anymore but identify what makes you think so.
- Relate to each of your problems by acknowledging you are responsible in some way for the problem.
- Identify specific conversations and action patterns that may be causing problems in your relationship.
- Take actions to neutralize the stress by challenging stress-producing conversations, examining and disrupting knee-jerk behavior and creating relationship enhancing contexts.
- Remind yourself that often your hidden patterns are built into your physical presence and not just in your mind.
- Repeat the previous steps if your problems persist or seek professional therapy

Committing to someone else means accepting certain promises regarding our behavior in the relationship. This goes beyond the process of taking a formal vow such as in a marriage ceremony, but recognizing what is involved in successful personal relationships:

- Promoting the health, well-being, personal growth and success of your relationship partner;
- communicating openly and honestly;
- telling your relationship partner if something important is bothering you;
- dealing with problems or conflicts in way that allows you and your partner to feel satisfied and not frustrated;
- keeping your promises or atoning for any slips you might make and
- doing whatever it takes to preserve the relationship if it is important to you, regardless of how this fits into your comfort level.

Dealing with someone else in a relationship often involves negotiation so we can mesh our needs with the other persons. Negotiations can be very casual but usually depend on some specific guidelines:

- Each person in the relationship should be free to request what they want or need.
- Each person should feel free to decline a request they cannot honor properly.
- Conflicts or differences of opinions should be resolved so the relationship partners feel they have won.
- Each participant should commit to what works for the relationship.

Beyond feelings of a troubled relationship, there are some physical elements that can be noted to determine if a relationship may be a stressor:

You have nothing in the house that comes in pairs.

There are no photos on display that just show you and your partner.

Your bed is unmade and your bedding is worn out or dull.

- Your bedroom lock does not work and there is no sense of privacy in the bedroom.
- Your rooms are harshly lighted and you never use candlelight.
- One of you has taken over more space than the other.

Reaching intimacy with someone else depends on our own feelings and why we want to feel this intimacy, but there are elements that can help build intimacy:

- Knowing yourself;
- practicing good communication;
- using reciprocal feelings of intimacy;
- keeping your intimate feelings alive and
- trusting the other person as you would trust yourself.

The Resources

The following Web sites offer more information about stress, relationships and intimacy:

Stress Cure, *www.stresscure.com*

Life Positive, *www.lifepositive.com/Mind/psychology/stress/social-anxiety*

Bell Online, *www.bellonline.com*

Self-Help Vocabulary, *www.self-help.vocaboly.com/archives/881/how-stress-affects-relationships*

Emotional Wellness, *www.emotionalwellness.com/intimacy*

Self-Help Magazine, *www.selfhelpmagazine.com*

Natural Health Web, *www.naturalhealthweb.com*

The following books offer more information on stress, relationships and intimacy such as:

Naked Intimacy: How to Increase True Openness in Your Relationship (McGraw-Hill, 2002)

The New Intimacy (HCI, 1997)

Saying What's Real: 7 Keys to Authentic Communication and Relationship Success (HJ Kramer/New World Library, 2005)

The Courage to Trust: A Guide To Building Deep and Lasting Relationships (New Harbinger Publications, 2005)

Sex, Love, and the Dangers of Intimacy: A Guide to Passionate Relationships When the Honeymoon is Over (Thorsons, 2002)

He's Scared, She's Scared: Understanding the Hidden Fears That Sabotage Your Relationships (Dell, 1995)

Lasting Love: The 5 Secrets of Growing a Vital, Conscious Relationship (Rodale Books, 2004)

27

Stress and the Single Life

For the most part we are social creatures who depend, to some extent, on maintaining a positive mental attitude by surrounding ourselves with a support group of friends and family. This often leads to relationships that may or may not include living together or getting married. It involves having a partner in our life who can help us enjoy the world around us and face the stressors of modern life. Dealing with this partner can have tremendous rewards as well as significant dangers, but most experts believe we function better with someone close to us. This is not always possible, whether because of our own attitudes towards relationships, opportunities or other factors we do not have control over. Living single can be stressful and we have to recognize how this stress is caused by being on our own.

The Challenge

Woody Allen once made an analogy to having a relationship by telling the old joke where a woman goes into a psychiatrist's office and asks for help because her husband thinks he is a chicken. The psychiatrist asks why she did not bring the husband with her to be cured, and she said she would have but they need the eggs. Allen uses this to point out that relationships with other people can be messy and painful, but, ultimately we need the eggs. Many experts in human behavior believe it is very important to have somebody sharing our lives, but some of us may choose to live the single life for any number of reasons. Living single can bring stress into our lives, or make it harder to deal with the stress we encounter on a daily basis. This does not mean we have to maintain a close relationship to have a happy life, but we need to know how to live single without adding to our stress. The challenge in this is to understand why we choose the single life, what benefits we derive from it, how having a close partner can help or add to our stress and what options we have to no longer be single. We must choose carefully when we want to live with someone else and then be prepared to work hard to maintain a successful relationship. The benefits can be significant to lowering our level of stress, but we have to look at the pitfalls as well.

The Facts

There are many reasons why people may choose to live single, some based on their own feelings, others based on outside circumstances:

- Dissatisfaction with previous relationships;
- a need to find out what living alone will be like;
- satisfaction with other relationships that do not involve a close relationship with one person;
- unwillingness to go through the effort of finding a life partner and
- a personal propensity for wanting to be live by oneself and not have to report to any other human being.

An added factor to the stresses of living alone and the challenge of finding a partner is to be a single parent. Not only do we have to deal with the challenges of raising a child on our own including all the stressors that is involved in the activity, we have to balance the time and emotional demands with finding someone to have in our life. And, this someone has to be willing to be in a relationship with more than just you and recognize the demands a child will have on the relationship.

Unfortunately popular culture and easy therapy make it sound easy and attractive to live single. You are shown images of friends socializing, roaming the town and playing sports. What is left out are the hassles of maintaining a household, paying bills, shopping for essentials and cooking alone. This feel-good attitude can give us false expectations of what it is like to live single and add to our stress if we believe we are not living in the same way. One element that is frequently omitted but can be very important is the lack of emotional support we receive when we live single. There is no one there at the end of the day to discuss what we are dealing with and help us share the load. To cope with the single life, you must understand the realities of it and how you can deal with it in reality and not fantasy.

The Solutions

A virtual cottage industry has developed over the years in trying to find partners for people. Some of these methods move from practical to absurd and have been used for comedic purposes. Other commercial attempts to link people are more serious. Often, though, we can find methods to finding partners that do not involve organized dating events, placing personal ads or using Websites to find people:

- Taking up outside activities such as sports or cultural related that puts you into contact with other people who share your interests;
- joining clubs and other groups that meet on a regular basis;
- helping out with charitable causes that involve performing activities with others;
- being introduced to someone by a mutual friend that may include a blind date and

- meeting people at the workplace, although work relationships can present a variety of problems and some companies are adamant about barring outside relationships between employees especially if they involve supervisors and people under them.

If you are living single and see this situation not changing in the near future, or having no real desire to pursue a relationship, there are several ways to reduce your stress:

- Meditate daily and envision whether you want a relationship and who that might be with.
- Surround yourself with caring friends or family. Sometimes a good support system can just provide you with a way to blow off steam.
- Set realistic expectations for your dating life, your children's place in that life, your personal finances and the needs of your job. Avoid trying to be perfect or finding the perfect person for you. That person does not exist.
- Get a handle on your daily responsibilities by breaking down big jobs into smaller, and more doable projects. This will help you organize your life which can also reduce stress.
- Delegate your household responsibilities by hiring help or asking friends or family to help with larger projects. In some cases, you can seek help in cooking or child care just to give yourself a break.
- Put your finances in order.
- Exercise, eat properly and get plenty of sleep.
- Find activities you enjoy that get you out of the house.
- Learn how to say no to outside requests you simply do not have time to do.
- Look for the good things in your life and expect these things to continue and grow as you move through your life.
- Create a daily routine that helps you focus your life and maintain a proper balance when dealing with your children.
- Discipline your children fairly and enlist their help in maintaining a good life balance. If your children are old enough, they should know what type of situation you are dealing with and be willing to help. Be consistent in your discipline from one event to another and between children.
- Maintain a polite and workable situation with your ex-partner if children are involved. It is easy to let the strong emotions of a break-up or divorce color your judgments against the partner, and these emotions can get in the way of finding peace and moving on with life. In some cases, you might want to visit a therapist to discuss your anger and how you can improve your relationship with your ex-partner.
- Celebrate things you have accomplished on your own, especially if they are elements of your life that were taken care of by ex-partners.
- Do not just jump at any chance to meet somebody, even if you are being fixed-up by a trusted friend. Ask a lot of questions, and, if the fit does not feel right, take a pass on it.
- Let yourself have some time when you do nothing. Not every minute of your life has to be filled with fun activities. The more you schedule, the less fun they may be.

The Resources

The following Web sites offer more information about stress and living single:

Christian Dating, *www.christian-dating-service-plus.com*

Lifetime for Women, *www.lifetime.com*

Stress and the Single Mom, *www.stressandthesinglemom.com*

Living Single Again, *www.livingsingle.com*

Unmarried, *www.unmarried.org/single*

Salon, *www.salon.com*

Ask Men, *www.askmen.com*

The following books offer more information on dealing with stress and living single such as:

The Art of Living Single (Avon, 1990)

Positive Discipline for Single Parents: Nurturing, Cooperation, Respect and Joy in Your Single-Parent Family (Prima Lifestyles, 1999)

50 Wonderful Ways to Be a Single-Parent Family (New Harbinger Publications, 2002)

Single and Loving It: Living Life to the Fullest (Harrison House, 2003)

Living Every Single Moment: Embrace Your Purpose Now (New Hope Publishers, 2004)

Living Alone and Loving It: A Guide to Relishing the Solo Life (Fireside, 2002)

Living Alone Creatively: How 12 People Do It (iUniverse, Inc., 2006)

28

Stress and Children

We are sometimes so wrapped in our own stress that we can ignore or deemphasize the stress felt by our children. We may believe that children, especially younger children, could not be feeling any real stress, or, if we could handle the stress of our childhood, then there is no reason our children cannot do the same. By the time we realize our children are displaying the mental and physical manifestations of severe stress, it may be too late to head the problems off early. We are not being selfish or unaware parents, but, rather are just using past precedents in a way that are not helpful to the current situations of our children.

The Challenge

Stress factors for pre-teen children, those usually under the age of high school students, have changed and grown in much the same way that they have for adults. These stressors may cover a variety of factors from dealing with a family situation, handling the demands of friends who can be unconsciously cruel, the pressures of an increasingly difficult school load and the needs of outside activities that can be overbooked to the point where a child does not have time for simple play or relaxation. Added to this stress are the changes in hormones and other body systems that go along with growing and the sometimes absurd images and expectations children are presented with from modern entertainment and advertising. Child stress can lead to the same type of debilitating conditions that adult stress has and have profound effects on the overall health of the family. The challenge is to understand the reality and nature of children's stress, where the stress is coming from, what the stress is doing to the child, finding ways to reduce the stress through home and daily activities, and, if necessary, finding professionals who can help reduce the stress through therapy. Seeing stress in your children may mean stepping back and taking an honest assessment of behavior patterns, but for the health of your children and your family, this awareness is vital.

The Facts

Children can be open to even more stress than adults over disasters that affect their lives. The disasters can result in separation anxiety and other factors that make it difficult to accept what may be just a temporary situation.

A child's reaction to stress can vary with the child's stage of development, coping ability, the length of time the stressor continues, the intensity of the stressor and the amount of support the child receives from family, friends and community. Some of the most significant reactions of children to stress include:

- Lack of self-control;
- thumb sucking in public;
- regression in toilet training;
- bed wetting;
- changes in eating habits;
- difficulty in speech and sleep;
- uncontrollable crying;
- regression to infant behaviors;
- whining;
- aggression;
- loss of concentration;
- feeling of disillusionment;
- lack of self-esteem with rebellious behavior and
- tantrums.

Part of the problem in dealing with childhood stress is having your child express their feelings to you. Children seldom have the ability to articulate their feelings of anxiety. These feelings do not really make sense to them. They may be able to express physical symptoms such as an upset stomach, headaches or aches of muscles and joints, but these can be misinterpreted to be simply from a physical cause and not based on a mental condition. If your child is not responding in a timely manner to physical treatment, your physician may attempt an interview with him or her regarding her feelings and activities and then recommend a therapist who specializes in pediatric therapy or working with families.

All of us went through some type of stress in our childhood and this experience can be both a good and bad thing. We can help our children understand the transient nature of stress and talk to them regarding what aspects of their lives may be stressing them based on our own experiences with school or family. However, if we thought we just gutted out any problems with stress, we may be tempted to expect our children to do the same and not quickly seek the help they need. We must recognize our children are different from us and different from their close relatives and are going to respond to stress in many different ways.

There are several common forms and causes of childhood stress that can affect any child no matter what his or her background is:

- A feeling of not fitting in with friends;
- a sense that of not doing well at school and not knowing how to improve;
- response to a home situation such as parental strife or a divorce;
- a backlash from getting pushed into activities the child does not enjoy;

- overloading a child's schedule with activities he or she may have requested but are not aware of the ramifications of having too much on their plate and
- peer pressure where friends are picking on the child and setting up cliques that do not include him or her.

A child dealing with a specific trauma goes through a progression of feelings:

- Terror including body problems and crying;
- rage or anger which releases adrenaline into the body;
- denial that can include withdrawal from normal life;
- unresolved grief that can move into depression or major character changes and
- shame and guilt because the child blames him or herself for the trauma

The Solutions

More so than in the past, stress in our child's life may be based on romantic or sexual feelings and issues of abusing alcohol or other drugs. There are positive ways to steer your child from the negative aspects of these issues.

We want our children to have a well-rounded life beyond school and may be tempted to overload their schedule with outside activities such as cultural, sports or service-related. Our children may want to participate in a large number of outside activities but do not understand how too much could be a bad thing. These activities that we may have to say no to or schedule creatively include:

- Extra school work that involves activities such as being part of a council or club;
- recreational activities such as playing in a band or acting in a school play;
- sports activities that are either intramural or competitive with other schools;
- participation in organized groups such as the Boy Scouts or church groups and
- a large amount of social contact for parties or other events.

One of the areas a child can be stressed is in the classroom. Maintaining a positive contact with your child's teacher and attending parent-teacher conferences can help you determine if your child's teacher is contributing to stress. Is the teacher paying fair attention to your child? Is the room arranged to maintain a positive impact? Is the day planned well and are routines consistent?

You can help your child deal with destructive stress in several ways:

- Show how your child can cope with stress in a healthy way.
- Be proactive and plan plenty of time for play and for informing children of any possible stressful changes in their lives.
- Help your children think through the consequences of their actions. Ask open-ended questions about what the solutions to their problems could be.
- Help your children separate reality from fantasy.
- Find time to talk about stressful events and everyday activities.
- Use stories and books to show how stress can be dealt with. Avoid the over stimulation of television.

- Get your child involved in producing some type of art.
- Try to get your children to act out coping skills by creative play.
- Allow, within limits, to give your children some type of control over their lives and to voice their opinion about what is going on in the family.

The Resources

The following Web sites offer more information about stress and children:

North Carolina State University, *www.ces.ncsu.edu*

About Our Kids, *www.aboutourkids.org*

Prepare Respond Recover, *www.prepareresponderecover.com/childrensneeds/*

Iowa State University Extension, *www.extension.iastate.edu*

At Health, *www.athealth.com/Consumer/disorders/childstress*

American Academy of Child and Adolescent Psychiatry, *www.aacap.org*

American Psychologist, *www.americanpsychologist.com*

The following books offer more information on dealing with stress and children such as:

Indigo Dreams: Relaxation and Stress Management Bedtime Stories for Children, Improve Sleep, Manage Stress and Anxiety (Lori Life, 2006)

The Handbook for Helping Kids With Anxiety and Stress (Youthlight, Inc., 2003)

Post-Traumatic Stress Disorder in Children (American Psychiatric Association, 1985)

Reducing Stress in Young Children's Lives (National Association for the Education of Young Children, 1987)

Controlling Stress in Children (C.C. Thomas, 1985)

Helping Children Cope With Stress (Jossey-Bass, Inc. Pub, 1997)

Children's Stress and Coping: A Family Perspective (The Guilford Press, 1993)

29

Stress and Teens

Growing into and through adolescence can open a teenager to very real stress. Nowadays this stress goes beyond the usual aspects of self-image, desire for freedom and dealing with school. Modern teenagers are facing stress factors that include many things that either did not exist or were rare including intense peer pressure and acceptance, dating, sexual conduct, drugs and academic challenges that can be very daunting to a success minded teenager. Teens have to deal with these stresses and find ways to cope with them. Sometimes they need help but cannot always articulate these needs. Growing up in modern society is not for the squeamish.

The Challenge

It is never easy, nor has it ever been, to deal with the angst and attitudes of having a teenager in the home. Unless you are one of the rare parents who have perfectly adjusted teenagers who live in a perfect world, dealing with teens and their stresses can be challenging at best and frustrating at worst. Modern teenagers are not only going through the physical process of adolescence and the changes in their bodies that can translate into behavior issues, they are often dealing with the psychological aspects of having to deal with peer pressure and cliques in their social environment and school and the pervasive feelings that they are the only ones who have ever gone through this process and the adults in their lives cannot possibly understand what they are dealing with. Unfortunately, given the challenges facing modern teenagers, this can be true. Teens are now facing issues most parents did not have to including sexual issues, the presence of drugs and alcohol that can be readily available and increased pressures to show academic success to advance into what is perceived as a good college or university. Most of these pressures will ultimately turn out to be able to be dealt with and a teenager will discover that life is workable. But, sometimes the stress involved in the variety of areas of a teenager's life can lead to debilitating physical and mental conditions and behavior that can be destructive. The challenge is to recognize that teenagers are experiencing real stress in their lives, trying to relate those stressors to what we experienced growing up, finding ways to communicate our ability to understand and help with these stressors and, if necessary, finding professional help to ease this stress. Having a teenager in the house can be frustrating, but rewarding, and you must keep in mind that, in most cases, your teenager will survive these years as you did.

The Facts

Often we add to the stress in our teen's life by providing things we think they need. This is especially true of outside activities such as sports or cultural activities. Many teens are literally overbooked with these activities and have little time to relax, read, watch television or do something that does not provide stimulation. The teen usually wants to do these things for any number of reasons and it is up to the parent to understand when these activities have become too much and need to be reduced. If your teen cannot drive yet, these activities can be stressful to you as well as you make time in your day to transport them to and from these activities.

Like adults, most teens experience harmful amounts of stress when they perceive a situation has become difficult, dangerous or painful. They do not have the resources yet to cope with these stresses and this can actually add to the stress being experienced. Some common sources of stress for teenagers include:

- School demands and frustration in trying to meet them;
- negative thoughts and feelings about themselves that frequently revolve around self-image and impossible-to-meet standards shown in popular culture;
- changes in their bodies, especially a strong generation of growth hormones;
- problems in dealing with friends and peers at school where relationships can become destructive;
- living in what is perceived as an unsafe environment or neighborhood;
- the marital difficulties, separation or divorce of parents or challenges of a new blended family;
- family problems with other relatives, sometimes revolving around dealing with a family member with a chronic and serious illness;
- the death of a loved one;
- choosing from a variety of education choices;
- living at home while wanting to be on their own;
- finding a job and having money to do what they want
- taking on too many non-academic activities and having too high expectations in succeeding or excelling at every activity and
- dealing with the pressures of family financial difficulties.

If these stressors are not properly dealt with they can lead to anxiety, withdrawal, aggression, physical illness or poor coping skills that may involve turning to reckless behavior, drugs or alcohol.

The Solutions

One of the first indicators there may be something wrong with your teen is the feedback you receive from their school counselor. Through modern culture and perceptions, the image of a school counselor has taken a beating over the last few years, but, the truth is these are trained and motivated individuals who want to help your teen cope with high school, plan for the future and deal with issues in their lives.

They recognize they are not actual therapists, but can be very helpful in giving you an early warning that something is wrong with your teen and getting help from therapists who specialize in teen counseling or family therapy. If the school counselor contacts you with a concern, you should take it seriously and investigate what the problem may be and what can be done.

Teens that develop a relaxation response which includes decreased heart and breathing rate and a sense of well being will feel less helpless and have more choices in responding to stress in a healthy way. Parents who recognize their teens are experiencing a high level of stress can help in these ways:

- Monitor your teen's health, behavior, thoughts and feelings to see if they are being affected by stress.
- Watch for your teens overloading on school work and outside activities and listen carefully to their concerns.
- Learn stress management skills for yourself and use these as a model for your teenagers to use.
- Support your teenager in sports and positive social activities as long as these do not become too much to handle adequately.

Teenagers can be encouraged to take on coping mechanisms that will help ease stress including:

- Exercising and eating regularly;
- avoiding excess caffeine intake which can increase anxiety and feelings of agitation;
- avoiding illegal drugs, alcohol or tobacco;
- learning relaxation techniques such as breathing and progressive muscle relaxation;
- developing positive assertive skills;
- rehearsing and practicing situations which can be stressful;
- learning practical coping skills such as time management and breaking large jobs into doable tasks;
- decreasing harmful self talk by replacing negative thoughts with neutral or positive thoughts;
- learning to feel good about doing a competent job rather than demanding perfection;
- taking a break from stressful situations by listening to music, talking to a friend or even spending time with a pet and
- building a reliable network of friends who can help cope in a positive way.

A parent should wok to understand what works best for a teen to cope with stress then work to enhance these skills with the teen, sometimes through simply talking through how to deal with a stressful situation. On the other hand, if a parent knows a teen is stuck with a particular teacher or peer who is causing stress, he or she can help the teen put that relationship in perspective and lessen the stress.

The Resources

The following Web sites offer more information about stress and teens:

American Academy of Child and Adolescent Psychiatry, *www.aacap.org*

Advanced, *www.library.advanced.org/13561/english/teen_stress*

Health Center, *www.thehealthcenter.info/teen-stress/causes-of-stress*

Children First, *www.childrenfirst.nhs.uk*

Kids Health, *www.kidshealth.org*

Family Education, *www.life.familyeducation.com*

Teen Matters, *www.teen-matters.com*

The following books offer more information on stress and teens such as:

Dealing with the Stuff That Makes Life Tough: The 10 Things That Stress Teen Girls Out and How to Cope with Them (McGraw-Hill, 2003)

Too Stressed To Think? A Teen Guide To Staying Sane When Life Makes You Crazy (Free Spirit Publishing, 2005)

Fighting Invisible Tigers: A Stress Management Guide for Teens (Free Spirit Publishing, 1995)

Hot Stones and Funny Bones: Teens Helping Teens Cope with Stress and Anger (HCI Teens, 2002)

The Complete Idiot's Guide to Dealing with Stress for Teens (Alpha, 2001)

The Handbook for Helping Kids With Anxiety and Stress (Youthlight, Inc., 2003)

30
Stress and Seniors

We never pass an age boundary when stress cannot attack us. From childhood on we are open to stressors in our lives that merely change over time. This is also true as we age into our senior years. Stress on senior citizens can represent a unique challenge as they try to cope with the changes in their health and lifestyles. The stress may also be from the interactions they are having with their families. No matter what, senior stress is an issue that we will all have to deal with.

The Challenge

Even if we have reached comfortable retirement, we can be open to particular stress factors that affect senior citizens. These stressors can come from within as we face the unstoppable prospect of aging and realizing we may only have a certain time left. They can come from deteriorating health due to aging. They can come from catastrophic situations where we must deal with conditions such as Alzheimer's Disease. Sometimes the stress can come from a change in lifestyle where we have to abandon our old homes and look at different ways to live including the daunting prospect of living in a nursing home. It can come from a feeling that we have lost control of our lives and are no longer in contact with our families. In short, senior stress is very real and must be dealt with proactively by the senior and the family. The challenge is to understand the nature of senior stress, identify the particular stressors, come up with ways to cope with the stress and find ways to maintain a positive outlook on life and self-image. Senior stress can be dealt with, but it must be treated seriously and not just regarded as a phase someone is going through.

The Facts

Reactions to stress in seniors can sometimes be confused with the symptoms of other conditions they are having. These include indigestion, aches and pains and sleep disorders. While it is possible these symptoms can be brought on by physical problems that have nothing to do with stress, the stress can amplify them or be masked by concerns.

Stress is the wear and tear on the body caused by constant adjustment to our living environment. Any element of change in our lives can cause stress and there are many changes going on in a senior's life. Stress causes our body to tense up and increase heartbeat and breathing rate. Most people need to have some relief from stressors, but as people age, the ability to reach relaxation after a stressful event becomes more difficult. Age may cause the systems in the nervous system that respond to stress to simply wear out.

We can feel psychological stress at any age. However, seniors have sources of stress that are unique to the process of aging:

- Seniors may feel fear over losing control of their lives and environment. They may no longer be able to live by themselves. Moving to a long-term retirement center or care facility means shrinking the environment and losing some possessions and control. Even more traumatic is the move into a nursing home. This is one of the top stressors in senior lives and means losing much control over their environment and activities. Leaving the familiar life and moving to an unsure environment would be stressful at any age, but even more so for the senior who realizes their life has changed probably forever. This stress can easily lead to depression which only makes the situation more difficult.
- Seniors may experience stress due to financial factors. The money saved over a lifetime and the reliance on a pension may no longer be enough to pay the bills, especially when the cost of living in a retirement center is added on. People living on a fixed income are much more susceptible to the effects of inflation and medical costs.
- The loss of friends and family can cause stress. This is especially true with the loss of a spouse.
- Seniors can feel loss through lowered physical strength and coordination.
- An inability to remember things, whether it is related to a physical condition or not, can be a major stressor for seniors.
- Sometimes a senior will be called upon to be a regular babysitter for active and young grandchildren. While it is nice to be needed, this can cause stress in a senior's life.
- As we age we are more susceptible to chronic or potentially life-threatening illnesses. Much of this comes from the natural aging process. We may find ourselves in poor health when we have lived most of our lives in good health. This type of stress can also occur when we are facing a dire physical condition existing in a spouse or loved one.

The Solutions

It is often difficult for a parent who is entering the senior years to admit to stress. This can be wrongfully seen as a sign of weakness and something that need not be shared with children who can help care for them. As we grow older, we are reluctant to admit our weaknesses including our lack of ability to handle new stressors. The one thing to accept as we age is to be honest about our feelings and ask for help when we need it, including help doing chores and getting around. As a close relative to a senior, you should never discount the feelings of stress and just chalk it up to growing old and needy.

People respond to stress in many different ways including crying, withdrawal and depression. You should let the elderly person have as much independence as possible. But, if stress is seen to interfere with a senior's eating, health or normal daily activities, you should work to seek out professional help for them that includes some type of therapy.

Even for seniors, changes in the workplace can be stressful. The retirement age in the United States in most companies is 70, but many people, for economic or social reasons, work into their 70's. Seniors must be able to adjust to using new technologies and to compete with younger people in the workplace. The stress of having to do so may make a senior retire before he or she is ready.

Sometimes, animals can provide companionship and stress relief for the elderly. Current research has shown that having a pet can reduce blood pressure and other stress symptoms in a senior. Many nursing homes and live-in care facilities allow pets to regularly visit the residents to boost their spirits and help alleviate stress.

No matter the age, meditation, deep breathing and exercise can provide relief from stress. Meditation does not require any great physical strength. Exercise when properly planned can be very helpful. This may include some form of mild aerobics, swimming in a low-impact environment, formal stretching or playing a game, such as golf. Even a low-impact form of yoga can be very helpful in relieving senior stress.

More than at any age, seniors must eat regularly, eat right and avoid tobacco, caffeine and alcohol. They must be aware of any side effects to medications they are taking that can cause anxiety and discuss those side effects with their pharmacist or physician.

Dealing with stress can be more challenging for a senior, but there are several basic things that can be done and be effective such as:

- Eating right and getting proper nutrition by avoiding fast-food and junk;
- avoiding smoking, drinking or prescription drug abuse;
- exercising regularly;
- maintaining an active social life by getting together with friends or families and taking part in the activities available by senior services or centers;
- volunteering to help others, now that the senior has more time to do this;
- maintaining positive thoughts about the quality of present life and how they have experienced their lives to date;
- developing a new hobby and setting time aside to do it on a regular basis;
- keeping health and fitness as important goals and
- learning to relax by finding a quiet place to meditate for 10-20 minutes every day; also a senior can relax by taking a walk, reading a good book and listening to favorite music.

The Resources

The following Web sites offer more information about stress and seniors:

American Association of Retired Persons, *www.aarp.org*

The Mayo Clinic, *www.mayoclinic.com*

Healthopedia, *www.healthopedia.com/stress-and-seniors*

MotherNature, *www.mothernature.com*

Discovery Health, *www.health.discovery.com*

Healthy Ontario, *www.healthyontario.com*

Colorado State University Extension, *www.ext.colostate.edu*

The following books offer more information on senior stress such as:

Strength Training for Seniors: An Instructor Guide for Developing Safe and Effective Programs (Human Kinetics Publishers, 1999)

Senior Moments (Byrd & Byrd, LLC, 2005)

Savvy Senior: The Ultimate Guide to Health, Family, And Finances for Senior Citizens (Hyperion, 2004)

Early Bird Special!!! And 174 Other Signs that You Have Become a Senior Citizen (1st Books Library, 2004)

Body & Being: How we age (cc design & publishing, 2007)

Comprehensive Stress Management (McGraw-Hill, 2003)

Tao of No Stress: Three Simple Paths (Healing Arts Press, 2002)

31
Stress and the Caregiver

Throughout our lives we are asked to be caregivers for someone suffering from an illness or injury. In most cases, this caregiving is temporary and does not require a great deal of physical or mental effort. We may feel some temporary stress over the caregiving demands, but this stress will quickly dissipate once we are no longer called on to help with care. However, in some cases the caregiving must go on for a long time or seemingly have no end and require extraordinary action on our part. This is when caregiving can be the most stressful to the caregiver.

The Challenge

A child with a broken bone or the sniffles will probably get better fairly quickly. A spouse or friend with a temporary condition may require some degree of help, but will probably be able to take care of themselves and even resent intrusion in their lives. We may help here as caregivers, but the real work for the caregiver is when we are trying to help someone with a condition that requires intense attention and the use of our time. Often, this type of caregiving is done for elderly parents or occasionally a spouse with a debilitating condition. We are consciously happy to help, especially when it is for someone who has helped us in the past. However, unconsciously we may start to develop feelings of resentment or being torn between the needs of our lives and the needs of the person receiving care. This mixture of satisfaction and frustration can lead to tremendous stress which can affect the quality of care we are giving. We need to understand the very real stress of the caregiver and how to overcome it. The challenge is to be honest with ourselves regarding the demands being placed on us, seeing how this stress is affecting our lives and finding solutions to caregiving issues that may free us up to some extent. We can never reasonably shrug off the illnesses or injuries to those we love, but we must get a handle on the stress and try to get rid of it. Then we can provide the care needed and feel happy that we are available to help.

The Facts

The most simple definition of a caregiver is they are the people who take care of other adults, most often parents or spouses who are ill or disabled. Caregivers can plan on helping with several daily tasks:

- Grocery shopping;
- house cleaning;
- cooking;
- shopping for essentials;
- paying bills and handling finances;
- making sure medicine is being taken;
- toilet use;
- bathing;
- dressing and
- ensuring the person is eating properly.

As the population ages, especially among baby boomers entering their later years, the need for caregiving is certainly going to expand. This means more and more younger relatives are going to have to help with their parents or older relatives. If you are young enough that you have not had to deal with the concerns of being a caregiver, you must expect to have to do this sometime in the future.

One of the key elements to keep in mind with the caregiver relationship is the psychological aspect of the needed care. Assuming that in most cases, the person needing care will be a parent, the caregiver and the person needing care must deal with a troubling reversal of roles. Up until the situation arrived for caregiving, the parent was used to living alone and before that being responsible for the care of their children. Now, the situation is exactly reversed and they must depend on the abilities and judgments of their children. This can easily lead to conflict and resentment, which must be dealt with by allowing the person needing care the ability to still make some decisions as much as possible.

Caring for another person takes a lot of time and effort, plus it means juggling caregiving responsibilities with other necessary activities. Many caregivers report they are less able to take care of their own health in terms of exercise and nutrition. Caregivers often end up feeling angry, anxious, isolated and sad. This is especially true of people providing care for someone with Alzheimer's Disease or some other form of dementia. Women caregivers are more prone to stress than males and those who care for spouses are more likely to feel stress than those who provide care for parents. You may be suffering from caregiver stress if you are feeling these symptoms:

- Sleeping problems;
- change in eating habits resulting in gaining or losing weight;
- feeling tired all of the time;
- loss of interest in activities you used to enjoy;
- easy irritation, anger or sadness and
- physical problems such as frequent headaches or stomach aches.

The Solutions

Pre-planning for caregiving needs can be essential, even before the need occurs.

This is similar to pre-planning for a funeral. The pre-planning will help you mesh your abilities with the possible requirements of someone who will need care and will include several items you should all agree on:

- Where will the person needing care live?
- Will the person needing care need to sell personal items to downsize their lifestyle and sell an existing home he or she can no longer care for?
- What will be the living arrangements for the spouse of the person needing care?
- How will the care needed be paid for and what other financial elements should be settled?
- What are the expectations for you in providing care and what services can be hired, such as a visiting nurse or professional caregiver?

In a caregiving situation, it may be ultimately necessary to move the person needing care to an extended care facility or nursing home. Studies have shown that these types of moves and the loss of independence they represent can be one of the greatest stressors for the person needing care. It can also be a major stressor for the caregiver who can feel guilt over making a move that had to be done. It is essential to find a comfortable facility with a good reputation, take the time to thoroughly inspect the facility, make sure the staff is properly caring for your loved one and, perhaps most importantly, make the commitment to visit often and stay with the person for a substantial time.

There are a variety of ways you can help relieve your stress as a caregiver including:

- Find out about community caregiving resources. You can find reliable help through organizations such as the National Family Caregiver's Association, *www. nfcacares.org* or the National Family Caregiver's Support Group, *www.aoa.gov/ caregivers*.
- Ask for help from other people and accept it when offered.
- Maintain your social life and stay in touch with friends and family.
- Establish a daily routine, prioritize and make lists.
- Turn to faith-based groups for help.
- Join a support group for caregivers in your situation such as the Alzheimer's Association, *www.alz.org*.
- Visit your physician for a checkup and discuss any symptoms of depression or sickness you are feeling.
- Try to get enough sleep and rest.
- Maintain a healthy diet rich in fruits, vegetables and whole grains and low in saturated fat.
- Take it one day at a time.
- Meditate and relax.
- Accept the mixed feelings you have.

If you need help in caregiving you can ask your local Area Agency on Aging through *www.aoa.org.* or *www.eldercare.gov*. Depending on your needs they can help you with:

- Transportation for you or the person needing care;
- meals for the person needing care in their home;
- adult day care and home care;
- cleaning and yard work services;
- home modification for the disabled;
- referrals to senior centers;
- hospice care;
- support groups and
- legal and financial counseling.

The Resources

The following Web sites offer more information about stress and the caregiver:

Women's Health, *www.4women.gov/FAQ/caregiver*

Caregiver Stress, *www.caregiverstress.com*

Healthopedia, *www.healthopedia.com/stress-and-seniors*

Family Doctor, *www.familydoctor.org*

Senior Magazine, *www.seniormag.com/caregiverresources*

Senior Living About, *www.seniorliving.about.com/od/healthnutrition/a/caregiverstress_2*

4Therapy, *www.4therapy.com/consumer/conditions*

The following books offer more information on stress and the caregiver such as:

The Fearless Caregiver: How to Get the Best Care for Your Loved One and Still Have a Life of Your Own (Capital Books, 2003)

Taking Time for Me: How Caregivers Can Effectively Deal With Stress (Prometheus Books, 1992)

Stress Reduction for Caregivers (Routledge, 1999)

A Guided Journal for Caregivers (Healing Arts Communications, 2004)

Quick Tips for Caregivers (Healing Arts Communications, 2000)

The Emotional Survival Guide for Caregivers: Looking After Yourself and Your Family While Helping and Aging Parent (The Guilford Press, 2006)

A Caregiver's Survival Guide: How to Stay Healthy When Your Loved One Is Sick (InterVarsity Press, 2000)

Part Seven:

Tips for Reducing Overall Stress

32

Managing Your Time

Much of the stress in our lives can come from the feeling that there is never enough time in the day to accomplish what we need or want to do, whether this is at work, in our family or in other social situations. We feel crushed under a wave of expectations that quickly replace tasks we accomplish with a whole set of new ones. We have to add these tasks into what is already expected of us and the stress of wondering how to do all of this can lead to debilitating conditions and an inability to get anything done. We have learned some time management skills throughout our lives, but now we have to hone those skills to better meet the demands that are placed on us by our current lives.

The Challenge

How often have you sat back in wonder at all the demands on your time and consider how it could be possible to do all of them and still have a life? We see an endless stream of expectations and have to figure out what to do and when to get it done. Sometimes this eating at our time can cause tremendous stress that can manifest itself emotionally and physically in destructive responses to the stress of feeling we do not have the time necessary to meet the demands asked of us. In practical terms. This sense of time not working for us can lead to some practical problems such as not getting a task done because of procrastination, doing a less than adequate job on a project just to get it over with and forgetting to do things because they have slipped out of our consciousness. Time management is a term that is frequently used to help solve this problem, but many of us do not really understand how to manage our time and handle other time issues in ways that can either relieve our stress or, at least, minimize it. We need to rethink how we manage time and what the effects of proper time management can be. The challenge is to understand when our management of time is not working properly, finding ways to better manage our time, learning how to schedule projects and seeing the benefits involved in making the effort to manage our time more effectively. Time can be our friend if we use it properly and this proper use can vastly minimize the stress of modern life.

The Facts

Our time can be spread out over a variety of areas that need our attention. This can vary depending on your own situation but in general includes:

- Work and related activities;
- education including formal school and continuing education;
- family responsibilities including home improvements and planning for vacations;
- social activities with friends and
- volunteer or charity-related activities.

One of the effects of poor time management is the tendency to procrastinate on a project because we cannot see how to address it. Procrastination is a destructive practice because it stops us from getting the job done and then adds to our stress by being aware there are things we are not accomplishing. Everyone tends to procrastinate in some areas of their lives, but when the practice becomes chronic, it can represent a major stressor.

One of the areas we may procrastinate or waste time is coming to a decision. We may agonize over whether we are making the right decision. A good rule is to never take more time to come to a decision than it is worth. There will always be some risk over what cannot be foreseen happening in the future. Realize this and you will be more likely to come to a decision.

If you have the time and ability, conduct a time study to see how well you manage your time and where you can improve. You might decide to up your time to top priority projects to one-third of your day and this can guide your study. If possible, ask your boss or trusted co-worker to look at your time study and make suggestions on how you are doing.

The concept of time management is really a myth. There are only 24 hours in a day, and you cannot change that. What you can do is better manage your work or life to fit into a 24-hour day.

Many people are proud of their ability to multi-task, doing several different jobs at once. But, unless you are a professional chef, multitasking is a bad practice and does not adequately allow us to concentrate on what we are doing and what is important. Mindfulness is a good alternative to multitasking.

The Solutions

Time management has become a major buzzword for business people. Companies may pay lip service to time management, but be unwilling to help employees better manage their time, or look at their own business practices to see how they might have a negative effect on good time management skills. Sometimes companies will send employees to time management seminars or bring in experts to help employees manage time, but, if they are not willing to follow up on these lessons, the time involved in going through this training is wasted.

You can better manage your time not only through attitudes and psychological techniques but also by using practical tools available to help you manage your time. These tools vary in complexity and effectiveness, and how we use them depends on our comfort level, but the most common time management tools available to us are:

- Online resources and planning sheets;
- elaborate calendars such as Dayplanners that can help employees map out their time;
- a simple daily schedule;
- reminder programs we can have on our computer or fed to our cell phones and
- simple to-do boards where we can list what needs to be done and in what type of time frame.

Here are some simple suggestions to better manage your time:

- Put your goals in writing and then set priorities.
- Focus on your objective and do not get lost in the activities.
- Set one important objective per day and work to achieve it.
- Rid yourself of at least one time waster in your life every month.
- Create a daily to-do list and prioritize the activities. Cross them off your list as you do them.
- Try to accomplish the most important or daunting things in your day first.
- Set time limits for every task you undertake.
- Do things right the first time to avoid wasting time in doing them again.
- Find an hour of uninterrupted time every day for your most important tasks.
- Finish what you start and do not jump from one thing to another.
- Take some time for yourself to reflect on what happened and plan ahead.

Create a 10-minute list. These are items that should only take about 10 minutes or less to accomplish but keep getting shoved aside. Do these minor tasks during breaks in the day and you will be surprised at how much you are accomplishing.

When you feel a project is overwhelming and you cannot figure out how to schedule for it, consider taking the large project and breaking it up into smaller, more doable tasks. Each task accomplished should lead to the next and ultimately meet the demands of the project. This can help you manage your time and get things done.

Getting organized is a terrific way to manage your time. You will probably be amazed at how much time you waste every day in trying to find a needed file or other item for your work or personal life. By having a cluttered workspace, you invite wasting time. Take the time every week to go through your in-box, including your email in-box, and file or toss anything you do not need. Take the items from your desk and create files or put them in stacks that make sense. This ability to put your hands on something when you need it will help you save time.

When looking at the time we spend away from our job, one concept is to focus on what you need to do versus what you want to do. You need to separate your activities into these categories and find a balance that works for you. You will probably feel better by planning something you want to do every day and not to get bogged down by the things you believe you need to do.

The Resources

The following Web sites offer more information about managing your time better:

Find Articles, *www.findarticles.com*

Self Help Solutions, *www.selfhelpsolutions.homestead.com/time1*

Stress About, *www.stress.about.com/od/managetimeorganize/f/time_management*

Get More Done, *www.getmoredone.com/tips1*

Mayo Clinic, *www.mayoclinic.com/health/time-management*

Management Help, *www.managementhelp.org*

Business Town, *www.businesstown.com/time/time-secrets*

The following books offer more information on managing your time better such as:

The 25 Best Time Management Tools & Techniques: How to Get More Done Without Driving Yourself Crazy (Peak Performance Press, 2005)

Time Management: Increase Your Personal Productivity And Effectiveness (Harvard Business School Press, 2005)

Time Management from the Inside Out: The Foolproof System for Taking Control of Your Schedule (Owl Books, 2004)

Time Management (McGraw-Hill, 2003)

The Time Trap: The Classic Book on Time Management (MJF Books, 2002)

10 Natural Laws of Successful Time and Life Management (Business Plus, 1995)

Time Management: Proven Techniques for Making the Most of Your Valuable Time (Adams Media Corporation, 1998)

Just Say No

Most of us want to be helpful. We want to be of assistance to our family and our friends. We want to show the people we work for and with that we are willing to put out the extra effort to get the job done. We want to be involved in a charity cause that will genuinely do some good. We accept all these duties and challenges and then wonder why we feel stressed. We have loaded ourselves with burdens that we could avoid by using one simple word: no. This does not have to come with attitude and you may feel compelled to explain why you cannot be available or provide the type of assistance being asked. But, if you learn how to say no you will be better able to apportion your time and be of service to others without loading yourself up with unwanted stress.

The Challenge

From an early age, most of us have been taught to get along with people by agreeing to duties that we may or may not have time to do. We have been told that good people say yes to requests for help, similar to the lesson taught us by the good Samaritan. This thinking can lead us to take on extra work duties or obligations that we cannot say no to and then resent later on when the other stressors in our lives feel overwhelming. We wonder why we did not say no to the request in the first place and believe we are now stuck with a chore we did not really want to do and are under equipped mentally and physically to perform. At the very least this will result in a destructive feeling of resentment to the person who asked us to help. At the very worst, this can lead to doing a less than acceptable job on the request because we now feel believe we cannot handle the request properly. Learning how to say no, for most of us, is an acquired talent that requires us to place the refusal in the proper context and to do it in such a way that it will not cause hard feelings from those who made the request. The challenge is to recognize when we place ourselves in position of stress by accepting duties beyond our current ability to handle them, what is involved in saying no, why we feel uncomfortable in saying no and how to do so in a positive way that will preserve our relationships and maintain our sanity.

The Facts

Not being able to say no and then later regretting it is a form of passive aggression. We go about performing the unwanted task in such a way that the person we are helping is well aware of our resentment and may be tempted to take back the chore. This lack of communication is much more destructive than just saying no.

Not saying no puts us in the place of being a people pleaser and gives us more importance in other people's lives. We become the go-to people who can be relied upon to help no matter what. While this can make us feel good, it can ultimately lead to feelings of inadequacy that no matter what we take on, people will never like us enough to make ourselves feel good.

Although this can change depending on the situation and the type of person you are, there are three basic ways to say no:

- The unassertive no is accompanied by weak excuses and rationalizations. If you feel a lack of confidence when you say no you may feel you need to support your answer with lots of reasons to convince the requester that you really mean it. This can lead, in some cases, to you inventing an excuse to support your no answer. This can backfire if your lie is exposed and you will end up sounding ineffective because you had the need to invent an excuse to support your answer.
- The aggressive no is done with an air of contempt. Instead of a simple response you have to add on statements that only make the requester feel bad. This can even lead to making an attack on the person making the request. This is all unnecessary and can lead to very bad feelings.
- The assertive no is probably your best option. It is simple and direct and, if it requires some type of explanation, should make that short and simple. If you cannot help someone because you have another commitment, simply inform them and let it go.

You can feel more comfortable saying no if you practice saying no to at least one thing every day. This should be a reasonable response and not capricious. When you have said no and you feel justified in it, reward yourself and give yourself credit for practicing this important two-letter word every day.

According to psychologist Sharon Newman, women are more often than men taught to be nurturing and caring. This makes it harder, often, for women to say no to requests. Newman found, in general, that men are better in brushing people off.

Sometimes we are trapped having to say yes because saying no is unavoidable. There are some techniques to say yes to something you may later have to refuse:

- Explain you can accept the request this time, but ask the person how you can help them plan better for the next time.
- Agree, but remind them that they own you one.
- Tell them yes, but take control of the situation by saying you will come back to them with a schedule.
- Place a condition on your acceptance, such as the amount of time you can spend helping them and stick with it.

The Solutions

Saying no in a positive way often depends on analyzing who is doing the asking and our history with that person. Some people use us and others to perform tasks they could do themselves. They, in a sense, become co-dependent on us, a feeling that some of us like. If you believe the person making the request of you is using you to do something they could do themselves, there is nothing wrong with asking why they need help and refusing it if we feel that is an appropriate response. In some cases, our ability to say no will be severely limited by the person who is doing the asking. We are far less likely to say no to an infirm relative or friend or to our boss, but these situations have to be analyzed individually.

Even though it is the most productive way of refusing a request, the assertive no is still not easy for many of us and might require a strategy to make it more usable. This strategy can include:

- Ask for time to think over your answer. While you are thinking over your response, remind yourself that the decision is yours alone.
- Use nonverbal assertiveness to reinforce your no answer. Use a firm and direct voice. Look into the person's eyes when you say no and shake your head along with your verbal response.
- Keep in mind that no is an acceptable response. If you believe no is the preferred answer to the request, remember it is honest and authentic to say no.
- If you end up agreeing to something you wanted to refuse, you will feel resentful throughout the time you do whatever you agreed to. This wastes energy and will cause you discomfort. It is unnecessary if you just say no when you need to.
- If you have to say no to someone you would help under different circumstances, use an emphatic response to ease the rejection. If someone asks you to watch their children and you cannot, tell them no, express your sympathy with their situation, tell them why you cannot do it and that you would under other circumstances.
- Start your response sentence with the word "no." It is easier to maintain your commitment to refuse a request if it is the first word you use.

Before you have to say no to a friend in a delicate situation, you can actually practice saying no to others that will make you feel more comfortable with the word. These situations include:

- The clerk who wants your phone number or Social Security Number;
- the person behind the returns desk at a store;
- the telemarketer who disturbs your dinner;
- the perfume demonstrator at the store;
- your friends' pets when they bother you or jump on you and
- the secretary who takes your call and then asks if you mind if he or she puts you on hold.

One of the most likely places you will be asked to say yes when you should probably say no is at the job. When a superior throws another urgent task at you there are ways you can refuse the task without looking like a slacker or a non-team player:

- Remind the supervisor that you are working on other projects that have already been identified as top priorities.
- Ask your supervisor for help in ranking how this new project should fall on your list of existing priorities.
- Explain that you may be able to do everything including the new task that has been asked of you, but the work will not be up to the usual high standards you have demonstrated and are expected of you.

The Resources

The following Web sites offer more information about just saying no:

Get More Done, *www.getmoredone.com*

Temple University, *www.temple.edu/counseling*

Crystal Links, *www.crystallinks.com*

Iowa State University Extension, *www.extension.iastate.edu*

Self Growth, *www.selfgrowth.com*

Life Script, *www.lifescript.com*

Online Organizing, *www.onlineorganizing.com*

The following books offer more information on just saying no such as:

The Power of a Positive No: How to Say No and Still Get to Yes (Bantam, 2007)

How to Say No Without Feeling Guilty: And Say Yes to More Time, and What Matters Most to You (Broadway, 2001)

Saying No: A User's Manual (The Virtual Press, 2003)

Too Busy: Saying No Without Guilt (InterVarsity Press, 2002)

"The Answer is No:" Saying It and Sticking to It (Perspective Publishing, 1994)

When I Say No, I Feel Guilty (Bantam, 1985)

The Art of Saying No (World Leisure Marketing, Ltd., 1994)

34

Taking Care of Yourself

Too often we take care of everyone else and leave nothing for ourselves. To reduce your stress, you must learn how to take care of your own needs. This does not mean developing selfishness but helping yourself by taking care of what is important to you. The benefits to this attention to yourself can filter down to others and your relationships at work and in your personal life. We have to ultimately live by ourselves in many ways, and the ability to take care of our needs is vital to a healthy life.

The Challenge

It can often feel as if everyone and everything is trying to take a piece of ourselves away. We face seemingless endless challenges and demands from work and from our social lives. We have to report on time, meet expectations, perform our jobs in an exceptional manner, provide material possessions for our families, listen and try to understand their needs and finally deal with the demands of charitable activities. These demands can leave little time to meet our own needs. Sometimes the belief that we have to meet these needs makes us feel as if we are being selfish and concentrating on ourselves when others also need us. But, we do not recognize that not taking care of ourselves means developing deep-seated stressors that can cause problems with other aspects of our lives. We have to take the time and effort to meet our needs so we can better be a productive part of others' lives. The challenge is to recognize when we are not taking care of ourselves, placing this need to meet our own needs in context of other things that are required of us, identifying what those needs are and meeting them in a way that can be beneficial to us and to others. You have to meet your needs and be yourself to really succeed and enjoy your life, and you can do this without hurting others. The end result is a happier and more content you who can work through the other situations in your life.

The Facts

Taking care of yourself can seem like selfishness. We are taught to help others first and to worry about our family and friends before we worry about ourselves. This type of selflessness is worthwhile, but does little to help you avoid stress. The key is to balance your needs with others and to take the time necessary to meet your needs without sacrificing what others need. Most therapists will tell you that you cannot help others until you learn how to help yourself.

Communication is a key element in taking care of yourself. You must learn how to express to your co-workers or your family that you need to have some time to do something for yourself, even if that is as simple as a relaxation exercise such as deep breathing or progressive muscle relaxation. Let the person know you will not be available for a certain amount of time, unless it is an emergency, and take the time you said you would. Thank your co-workers or family afterwards and explain that this meeting of your needs was helpful and you appreciate their cooperation and understanding in meeting it.

Taking care of yourself often means finding balance in your life. A balanced life, balanced between obligations and things we like to do, usually means:

- Working in a job that is challenging and gives you a sense of achievement rather than frustration;
- finding a method of play which is relaxing and joyful;
- finding love that is not necessarily romantic or sexual, but a love of one person for the friendship and support he or she offers and
- having spirituality that connects you to something larger than yourself.

You probably have heard of the term a vicious circle which means you are repeating negative activities with the same results and then adding on to them. You can replace the vicious circle with a benevolent spiral that moves you upward when you find pleasant activities, enjoyable things to consider and satisfying things to accomplish. You can feel trapped in a vicious circle, but if you make the effort to break free of it, the effort can bear fruit.

The Solutions

You may feel the need to take care of yourself after witnessing or being part of a traumatic event, such as an accident or criminal activity. You may feel disruptions in your emotions, cognitive abilities, physical condition and behavior. Talk to people about what happened to you and do not keep your feelings bottled up. If necessary, and if you are feeling destructive thoughts, you may want to visit a professional therapist.

There are specific ways to take care of yourself and your needs depending on what is going on in your life. There are some general ways you can take care of yourself including:

- Learn how to air your feelings. Keeping them bottled up is very destructive. Just beware of hurting others. Share your downs and disappointments with a trusted friend or family member. Expressed feelings can be changed feelings.
- Do not compare yourself with others by admiring what they have while ignoring what you have. Envy breeds self-disgust. Do not put anyone higher than you.

- Form a small, reliable group of people you can turn to for emotional support. You should all agree to be there for each other. Make rules to offer advice only when it is asked for, listen without interrupting for comment and take turns talking and listening.
- Take the time to play. Play is not a negative or frivolous activity, it is any activity you do because it feels good. You deserve to take time to play, it is important.
- Remember to laugh. You should be willing to especially laugh at yourself. Look for the obvious humor around you and let your hair down by doing something silly and totally unexpected every so often.
- Protect your right to be human and do not let others put you on a pedestal. Being on a pedestal means people expect you to be perfect and will feel angry when you inevitably are not and are seen to let them down.
- Learn how to say no. Saying no can be a difficult process, but once you become comfortable with saying no to unreasonable expectations, requests or demands you will find that you actually have more compassion. Then when you say yes to somebody's request, you will feel better about yourself and the people who are asking you for help.
- Look at a job or career change if you are miserable in your current work situation. You must first determine if the job itself is not working or if certain people at your job, including your boss, are causing your distress. Find the things you enjoy about your job and pay more attention to them. All jobs have unpleasant aspects and you should not fixate on the negative.
- Stretch your body. Find a way to work up a sweat by exercising or playing a sport. Go for a walk with the dog. Ride your bike. Make an effort to park farther from the door at work or when you go shopping. Walk up or down stairs instead of taking the elevator. You do not need to belong to a health club to gain some needed activity in your life. Also eating properly and avoiding junk and caffeine can help you feel better.
- Practice being a positive and encouraging person and not somebody who just sees the negative. When you give others a word of encouragement, you will feel better and build up the best part of yourself.
- Look at enhancing your spiritual life. Slow your pace down. Sit quietly and listen to your inner voice. Meditate on the things that bring peace, beauty and serenity to your life. You can do this through a traditional religion or from a more alternative form of spiritual growth.
- Remember to have me time in your day, or schedule a day or week off to unwind.
- Try to use relaxation techniques to get a good night's sleep on a consistent basis. Avoid oversleeping because of depression.
- Do not sweat the small stuff and, as the saying goes, it is all small stuff. Most things tend to work out for the best and worrying about them will not help.

The Resources

The following Web sites offer more information about taking care of yourself:

Self Help Magazine, *www.selfhelpmagazine.com*

California Division of Human Resources, *www.hr.ucdavis.edu/ASAP/Articles/TakeCare*

Palo Alto Medical Foundation, *www.pamf.org/teen/parents/emotions/lifeskills*

Mountain Valley Center, *www.mountainvalleycenter.com*

My Sistahs, *www.mysistahs.org/features/care*

University of Iowa Counseling Service, *www.uiowa.edu/~ucs/trauma*

Society of Clinical Care Medicine, *www.sccm.org/SCCM/MyICUCare/Support+Brochures/Taking_Care*

The following books offer more information on taking care of yourself such as:

Taking Care of Yourself: Strategies for Eating Well, Staying Fit and Living in Balance (Sounds True, 2002)

Taking Good Care of Yourself: For Kids Going Through Separation and Divorce (Children of Separation and Divorce Center, 1994)

The Caregiver's Survival Handbook: How to Care for Your Aging Parent Without Losing Yourself (Perigee Trade, 2004)

The New Mom's Companion: Care for Yourself While You Care for Your Newborn (Sourcebooks, 2003)

Good Samaritan Faith: A Strategy for Meeting Needs in Your Community (Regal Books, 1984)

Before Love Dies: Getting Your Needs Met in Relationships (Legacy Publishers International, 2005)

The Lies We Tell Ourselves: Overcome Lies and Experience The Emotional Health, Intimate Relationships, And Spiritual Fulfillment You've Been Seeking (Thomas Nelson, 1999)

34

Asking for Help

Many of us pride ourselves on our ability to take care of things ourselves. We have been taught since childhood to be self-reliant and, when the chips are down, trust no one but ourselves. We can be reluctant to look outside ourselves because we do not trust anybody else to be of real use and because we have too much pride in our own ability to handle any situation. But, there are many times when we have to swallow our pride and do something we might find difficult: asking for help.

The Challenge

Asking for help, for many people, can be seen as a sign of weakness. And, when overused, it can be a crutch to use when there are things we could and should be able to do for ourselves. But, most of us have times in our lives when we need to ask for help. This can be regarding a work situation, life situation or our own emotional health. The help we ask for may be from colleagues or friends, or from professionals. The information and help we receive may not be as useful as we hoped and will have to be analyzed as to whether the help can be incorporated into our situation. But, we will never reach that decision if we are unwilling to give in from time to time and ask for help. Most people are flattered to be asked for help or advice and we should not assume we are being a burden on them, just as we should not assume asking for help means we cannot handle our lives. The challenge is to understand the need to occasionally ask for help, identify the issues in our lives we may need help with, finding people we can reasonably ask for help and have faith in their ability and then using that help in our lives. You are not an island and you will need help sometimes in your life. It can be less painful than you think when you let go and simply ask for help.

The Facts

Asking for help is a skill that has to be learned. If not properly used it can be counterproductive and not make you feel any better about asking. Often, you have to make sure you make the request so you receive the help you really need and not what the other person perceives you need. This means you have to think about what you are asking for and the best way to frame the request. If it appears you are not hearing what you need to hear, politely restate your question and better focus the request for help so you get what you need.

One of the areas that can be the most difficult is asking for help dealing with our lives from a professional mental health therapist. If your stress is affecting you physically or causing depression, it may be time to turn to a professional. It can be hard to ask for help from a stranger, it may make you feel vulnerable or ashamed you cannot handle the problem on your own. Remember that needing help and admitting the need is not a sign of moral weakness. We have a responsibility to ourselves and our loved ones to seek professional help if we believe we need it. You may be reluctant to receive therapy because you wonder what people will think of you. It is really not their business to know, and the ones you share this information with should be able to understand the importance of therapy and what it can do for you. Even though our culture sometimes tells us to be rugged individualists, there are times we have to ask for help. Keep in mind you would not hesitate to consult a lawyer to help with legal matters or an accountant to help with your taxes. Seeing a professional therapist is really not different.

Keeping mum is not the best idea if you feel you need help. There are facts to back up the need to ask for help and the negative consequences in not doing so. According to a recent study by OfficeTeam, a leading staffing service specializing in highly skilled professionals:

- 37 percent of survey respondents said not asking for help is the biggest networking mistake by professionals.
- 25 percent cited not keeping in touch with contacts as the biggest mistake.
- 22 percent listed not thanking people for their help as the biggest mistake.
- 13 percent said burning their bridges with past employers as the biggest mistake they made in networking and asking for help.

The Solutions

There are a variety of sources you can ask for help depending on what you need and how you feel about the person you are requesting the help from. These sources include:

- Your supervisor or boss concerning your workload or questions on specific projects;
- a work colleague who can either give you advice or help you shoulder some of the work on a project you have become bogged down with;
- a friend regarding a situation in your personal life with anything from a lift to an appointment if your transportation is disabled to a loan of money;
- a family member such as a spouse, parent or sibling who may be able to help with a situation involving your personal life and
- a professional such as your physician or a therapist if you feel you are having trouble handling things around you under your own power.

Do your mental homework before asking for help and develop a go-to list of help givers based on this homework. These steps include:

- Listing your needs on a piece of paper and how those needs might change over time.
- Decide which needs you can and want to meet yourself and mark them off the list.
- Decide which needs have to be met by others.
- List the people who can help you meet those needs and match them to the need. Also include the skills, abilities, expertise and availability of those people who can help you.
- Decide which needs must be met by a professional health care provider.

One of the environments you are most likely to ask for help is at work. This will frequently mean asking your supervisor or boss for help. A good boss should be willing to help and will do what he or she can to meet your needs. But, to make the process work as well as possible, here are some simple rules for asking for help at work:

- Do everything you can first to work through the problem. Work out whatever you can with your working peers before asking for help upwards in the organization.
- Ask for help in private and away from other workers if at all possible. Be discreet and choose your forum carefully.
- Work out a time in advance to make your request so you know you will have the attention you need. Do not just spring a request for help on somebody.
- If you think you need help, ask as soon as you have made the determination. It is tempting to wait while you try to solve the problem yourself, but this can just make it worse. Do not wait to make a panic request.
- Deliver the main request early and do not beat around the bush to get to it.
- Know what you might need for help and give the other person options to choose from. You can always finish your request by asking if the person has any other ideas.
- Define the problem and tell somebody the solution you have in mind. Ask for specific help and be clear while being open to other alternatives.
- Make your request interesting and proactive rather than negative or whiny.
- Be prepared to accept the help you are offered and report later how this help worked out for you. Stay positive in your assessment and thank the person for the help.

The Resources

The following Web sites offer more information about asking for help:

Point Lookout, *www.chacocanyon.com/pointlookout*

St. Vincent Health, *www.stvincent.org/ourselves/mentalhealth/locations/indy/consumers/asking*

It's My Life, *www.pbskids.org/itsmylife/emotions/depression/article6*

Find Articles, *www.findarticles.com*

To-Done, *www.to-done.com/2005/07/knowing-when-to-call-for-help*

Caring to the End, *www.caringtothend.ca*

Arbias, *www.arbias.org.au/client-information/asking-others-to-help-you*

The following books offer more information on asking for help such as:

Mayday!: Asking for Help in Times of Need (Brett-Koehler Publishers, 2007)

How Can I Help? Stories and Reflection on Service (Knopf, 1985)

Help is Not a Four-Letter Word (McGraw-Hill, 2006)

I Am Not Sick, I Don't Need Help (Vida Press, 2007)

You Don't Have to Learn Everything the Hard Way: What I Wish Someone Had Told Me (Kadima Press, 2004)

Strategic Help Seeking: Implications for Learning and Teaching (Lawrence Eribaum, 1998)

When Someone Asks for Help: A Practical Guide for Counseling (InterVarsity Press, 1982)

36

Changing Yourself and Your Response to Stress

What is inside of us and how we use those attitudes to respond to stressful situations can often make the stress worse. We have to learn how we can change our inner feelings and our knee-jerk responses to stress to rise above the stressors. Changing anything in your life can be difficult, but this process is essential in adapting to modern life and the stress it presents. Changing can mean the difference between adequately dealing with stress or surrendering to it.

The Challenge

Very few of us believe we are perfect. And, that is because we are not. We all carry a lot of baggage with us that helps us to determine our response to the stress around us. This baggage may be acquired as early as childhood and be very difficult to change. But, changing yourself, while remaining true to your nature, can be invaluable in dealing with a rapidly changing world. At the same time this change in yourself can affect how you respond to stress. You may start replacing anger and frustration with acceptance and constructive thoughts. You may change your attitudes regarding the stressors you receive at work, from your family or from you social life. The challenge is to understand the importance of changing yourself and your responses, how to go about doing so in a way that does not cause you more stress and determining how these changes are better able to help you handle the challenges you face. You should never be afraid to examine yourself and change when necessary. The only constant in life is change, and you need to embrace the process and make it work wonders for you.

The Facts

Before you can change yourself and your response to stress you have to know your patterns of behavior. This takes honest introspection, sometimes with the help of a therapist and should include these questions:

- Do I go with the flow or get upset?
- Do I cling to my anger and let it ruin my day?
- Do I take my work problems home with me?
- Do I take my personal life to work with me?
- Do I feel generally discontented with my life?
- Am I suffering from physical ailments or lack of sleep?

To cope with our lives and our stress we often turn to substance abuse, most noticeably alcohol. While there is nothing wrong with having a drink with dinner or going out for a beer with our friends, when we find that stress or the perceived feelings of stress trigger overuse of alcohol, we need to take a serious look at our life habits and how we should be responding to them.

There are many definitions of stress, but one of the most common is that stress, both cognitively and physically, occurs when we experience an imbalance between situational expectations and the perceived resources available. We get stressed out due to the relationship between demands placed on ourselves and the time, energy and resources we have to successfully meet or overcome the demands.

The Solutions

It is often our perceptions of the demands placed on us that trigger one of two common cycles:

- The I-can cycle occurs when we look at the situation and judge that it is acceptable, non-threatening and, as much as possible, under our control.
- If your appraisal leads to I-cannot, this triggers an entirely different cycle. We view the situation presented to us as negative and focus on the negative qualities of the task rather than the real possibility for succeeding. This triggers the physiological response to negativity and can lead to health issues.

Our appraisals can be very subjective and can take place automatically without critical thought. This appraisal can trigger the domino effect of our response. These negative feelings can cause us great stress. Here are some ideas to head off these negative feelings and change your responses to them:

- Think about how your subjective appraisals of situations immediately affects your thoughts and physical condition.
- View the stress as challenging rather than debilitating.
- Keep in mind how much physical pain such as aching muscles, digestive disorders or headaches are related to your negative thoughts. Try working on your stress appraisal and response before you have to resort to pain medications or other medicines.
- You cannot live a stress-free life, but you can change the way you think about the demands you place on yourself and work on fostering an optimistic attitude. This positive outlook can help you feel more energized and creative resulting in success.
- Plan your downtime and fun the same way you would approach work or social expectations. Do not make this time an afterthought. Finding time to get away from things and have fun can be terrific ways to prevent stress and help you maintain a positive outlook.

To change yourself and your responses to stress, consider the four A's: avoid, alter, accept or adapt.

You can avoid a lot of needless stress by:

- Taking control of your surroundings. Find a different way to get to work including mass transit. Save some time at lunch by taking a bag lunch and eating at your desk.
- Avoiding people who bother you. If someone at work gets on your nerves avoid sitting next to him or her at meetings and avoid their cubicle.
- Saying no. It is important to know when and how to say no to work you cannot reasonably perform.
- Turning off your access to the news including newspapers, radio or television if you feel the condition of the world around you is depressing or stressing you.
- Prioritize your to-do list and get rid of the lower rung items you do not have time to do.

Take inventory during times of stress and then find ways to alter your situation so things can work better in the future:

- Be honest and respectful with other people by asking them to change their behavior and be willing to do the same.
- Communicate how you feel openly by using I statements.
- Do not be afraid to take risks. Inaction can cause more tension than making a mistake.
- Practice good time management techniques.
- Be proactive in setting limits to what you can do in advance and then stick with them.

Sometimes you just have to accept the things that life deals you but you can cope still by:

- Talking with someone you trust in your office or your social life.
- Forgiving someone who has made you angry. Let the negative go and you will feel better.
- Remembering to smile throughout the day and do not just sit at your desk scowling at your computer.
- Practicing positive self-talk and do not beat yourself up. Avoid I-am-terrible-at-this thoughts and replace them with I-am-having-temporary-trouble-with-this.
- Learn from your mistakes. We often learn more about the things we may have done wrong and not repeat the action.
- See stress as an opportunity to motivate you and get you going on a project, as long as it is used in moderation.

If you perceive you cannot cope with a stressful situation, it may be time to adapt your standards or expectations, and can be the most helpful ways to fight stress. These adaptations include:

- Adjusting your standards and redefining cleanliness, success and perfection.
- Practicing thought-stopping where you stop gloomy thoughts immediately. Let the stressful situation go and do not dwell on it.

- Try looking at your situation from a new reference point. Replace frustration with a feeling of opportunity.
- Writing down the things in your life that bring you joy, then review that list when you are feeling stressed.
- Using your humor and imagination to take the sting out of a stressful day. There is always something you can laugh at.
- Concentrating on the big picture. Think if the stressful situation will matter to you in a year. The answer is usually no and can help you feel better about the stressor.

The Resources

The following Web sites offer more information about changing yourself and response to stress:

Columbus Business First, *www.columbus.bizjournals.com*

Mayo Clinic, *www.mayoclinic.com/health/stress-relief*

Michigan State University, *www.healthed.msu.edu/fact/stress_response*

ADHD, *www.add_adhd-help-center.com/stress/response*

Arthritis California, *www.arthritis.ca*

Stress About, *www.stress.about.com*

Medical Moment, *www.medicalmoment.org*

The following books offer more information on changing yourself and responses to stress such as:

A Clinical Guide to the Treatment of the Human Stress Response (Springer, 2002)

Beyond the Relaxation Response (Berkley, 1985)

Stress Response Syndromes: Personality Styles and Interventions (Jason Aronson, 2001)

Exercise and Stress Response: The Role of Stress Proteins (Informa Healthcare, 2002)

Posttraumatic Stress Disorder: Acute and Long-Term Responses to Trauma and Disaster (American Psychiatric Publishing, 1997)

Treatment of Stress Response Syndromes (American Psychiatric Publishing, 2002)

Stress in Life and at Work (Sage Publications, 2001)

37

Changing the Situation

When we experience stress we tend to internalize it. We wonder what we can do to adjust our attitudes and our expectations to better cope with the stress or manage our response to it. We look at how we can get different attitudes from co-workers, family or friends to help us deal with stress. But, sometimes the nature of the stress is more endemic than just what is inside us and governs our reaction. Sometimes chronic stress is based on the situations we are facing in our lives. If this is the case, and we are facing stress we cannot change within our own behavior, we have to look at ways to change the situation to cause us less stress.

The Challenge

What is causing your stress? Could it be your own attitudes, your upbringing or the support you are not receiving from people around you? Or could it be the situation you find yourself in that is causing the stress no matter what you change within yourself? This situation may be something you have to deal with at work, problems in your personal life or the changes in your dealings with loved ones. While it may seem more difficult, sometimes you have to work to change your situation by taking active steps rather than just trying to deal with the situation. The challenge is to recognize when your stress is based on situations rather than your internal feelings, deciding what can be done to change the situation, making the needed changes and evaluating how the change in situation is affecting you. Changing your situation can affect many people and many aspects of your life, and while the change can be challenging, it may be the only reasonable option you have for easing your stress. Remember, changing a situation is not a cure-all and should be undertaken only when other options are exhausted.

The Facts

Working to change a life situation can be frustrating and lead to additional stress. It can involve many different elements that need to be addressed, not the least of which is other people's reaction to the changes you are trying to make. You must anticipate this resistance and be prepared to come to terms with it and not give up your efforts.

One of the most stressful situations we will ever face is divorce, especially if there are children involved. While the divorce may ultimately result in feelings of relief from relationship stress, in the short run the situation can be very stressful for three main reasons:

- Reorganizing and taking more responsibility for daily tasks that used to be shared;
- the feeling of losing significant relationships and some important possessions and
- needing to work to establish a new and fresh identity as an individual rather than one part of a married couple.

One of the ways to relieve stress is to write regularly in a journal or diary. You can also do this to evaluate your situation, identify your stressors and list them out one at a time. You might be surprised at how many of these stressors are related to your situation.

The Solutions

Changing a work situation can be especially difficult depending on your position. You will have to deal with your boss and your fellow co-workers, but there are ways to work to change an unacceptable work situation that often leads you to work extra hours and place demands on you that cannot be met:

- Talk to your boss honestly about what is troubling you and offer solutions to make your situation better.
- Meet with your workgroup and immediate co-workers, and, without blaming anybody, express your frustrations and what you might want to do to relieve them.
- Request an intervention by bringing in an outside consultant or coach who can help redirect your efforts and help change the work situation.
- Be prepared to exercise the nuclear option and leave your current job, even if you have nothing special lined up yet. Your health is the most important thing.

You can survive and adapt from a divorce, but you must be prepared to do some work to make the change in this stressful situation work as well as possible. This work will include:

- Accepting the divorce and striving to make peace with your ex-spouse. You must realize that nastiness only begets nastiness in return. Try to forgive the former spouse for any wrongs you think were done to hurt your situation. Examine honestly your own role in the relationship including: remembering the reason for choosing your mate and learning what you would want differently now; accepting your individual contributions to the break up and exploring how your past may have played a role in marital situation struggles.
- You must balance being a single person versus being a single parent. You owe it to yourself to eventually enter into another relationship and must recognize how that will work with your extended family.
- Reorienting your goals to concentrate on the future instead of thinking of ways to punish someone for what happened in the past. If you are adjusting well, you are ready to move on.

Once you have identified your stressors in your situation you can easily classify them to make them more manageable and place them in the context of your life. These classifications include:

- Predictable situations are those which can be foreseen and avoided such as being late or not managing your time well.
- Escapable situations are those that are unavoidable, but which you can remove yourself from by limiting involvement with people with negative attitudes.
- Tolerable situations are those that cannot be changed or avoided but have to be endured. Once we realize the situation will not be changed, it may be easier to deal with it.
- Inspirational relationships may serve as motivators for creative action to deal with stress. Creative thinking is a good way to live your life and can be major stress reducer.

As the pressure from dealing with a stressful situation rises within you, there are ways you can ease the pressure and lessen the stress:

- Identify the cause of your stress and do not just react. Take a moment to figure out exactly what bothered you.
- Choose your response, even if you cannot change the stressor. How large is the stressor, or is it from a combination of factors in your situation? How much control do you have over the situation? Is the stressor in the past, present or future? You cannot change the past, but you can make changes in the present and expect they will affect your future.
- Face your stressor head on and take action as quickly as possible. Sitting around feeling paralyzed by a stressful situation will not be helpful. Take your response one step at a time and expect it may take several steps to change a situation. Trust your responses and move forward with them. Set realistic goals and realize if you are not resolving your stress you may not have set your goals properly or set them too high.
- See a physician or therapist if you feel your stress is harming your life.
- Expect to make mistakes. We all do and we usually learn from them
- Reduce any dependence you might have on alcohol and drugs and replace that with relaxation techniques or physical exercise.
- Maintain your self-confidence and self-esteem. Know you can change your situation if your really want to.
- Do not overextend yourself in your work or personal situations. Commit to changing the situation and you can reduce your stress more easily than if you only pay lip service to making the changes.
- Work to get along with people as long as you do not believe you are sacrificing your own self-respect to do so. You do not always have to like someone to deal with them effectively in your work or life situations.

The Resources

The following Web sites offer more information about changing the situation:

Iowa State University Extension, *www.extension.iastate.edu*

Crisis Center, *www.crisiscenter.com/dstress*

Stress Hardy, *www.stresshardy.com*

Fasten Network, *www.fastennetwork.com*

Wikihow, *www.wikihow.com/Be-Calm-In-a-Stressful-Situation*

Mayo Clinic, *www.mayoclinic.com/health/stress-management*

Indiana University Southeast, *www.ius.edu/ASC/PersonalCounseling/SurviveStress*

The following books offer more information on changing the situation such as:

Changing for Good: A Revolutionary Six-Stage Program for Overcoming Bad Habits and Moving Forward (Collins, 1995)

Understanding and Changing Your Management Style (Jossey-Bass, 1999)

Evolve Your Brain: The Science of Changing Your Mind (HCI, 2007)

Kindness: Changing People's Lives for the Better (Messorah Publications, Limited, 2000)

Brainstyles: Change Your Life Without Changing Who You Are (Simon and Schuster, 1997)

Stress: Living and Working in a Changing World (Whole Person Associates, 1998)

Changing Directions Without Losing Your Way: Managing the Six Stages of Change at Work and in Life (Tarcher, 2001)

Part Eight:

Tips for Relieving Overall Stress

38

Exercising

One of the top New Year's Resolutions is to exercise more. We correctly see exercise as a way to improve our appearance, build up our strength and endurance and lose weight. We may not realize that daily or regular exercise can also be vital in reducing stress. Many very busy people find ways to include exercise in their day because it makes them feel better. Exercise can also help alleviate the physical problems of feeling stress by relieving aches and pains and improving our digestion. There are a dozen reasons for exercising, reducing stress is easy to ignore but can be treated very effectively with a wise regimen of exercise.

The Challenge

People who decide to begin or enhance an exercise program will find a variety of reasons to do so, but sometimes forget to include stress reducing as part of the program. Stress can be reduced through a variety of exercise, even the counter-intuitive practice of competitive sports. Nowadays, we have a variety of methods to exercise available to us. What we choose to use will depend on our needs, our current physical condition and the goal of the exercise. We may not recognize the positive aspects of using exercise to reduce stress, but find this result is happening to us. You can choose from formal and traditional methods of exercise that use gyms, equipment and weights. You can opt for classes in aerobics and movement. You can ride a bicycle, either stationary or out in the open. You can jog or run. You can institute a regimen of walking. You can find relaxation exercises that can be done at work or at home without having to go through the effort of finding a special place and changing clothes. You may explore holistic methods that involve yoga or meditation. The important thing is to find a method of exercise and commit to it. The challenge is to understand what exercise can do to relieve stress, knowing what effect exercise will have on your body and mind, what limitations and other aspects of your health that will affect your choice of exercise, finding someone who can help you through the process and evaluate and change the exercise if needed. When used properly, exercising can make you feel wonderful and give you the energy you need to deal with the every day stress of life and the extraordinary stress we are all sometimes subject to.

The Facts

It was not that long ago that people did not need to engage in organized exercise. The challenges of everyday life through hunting, farming and dealing with the challenges of the times would usually provide enough exercise for almost anyone. As we developed through the 20th and 21st centuries, we have developed a more sedentary lifestyle that does not get us moving as much as we should. We now need to recognize this fact and find ways to add exercise to our lives.

Vigorous exercise does more than build up muscles, bones or cardiovascular capacity. It can release endorphins into our bloodstream. These naturally-occurring chemicals are like natural opiates and can stimulate a feeling of contentment and pleasure in us that is similar, but preferable, to what we might get from ingesting a substance such as alcohol or a narcotic. The endorphin high does not last that long, but no matter its duration, it can help us relax and ease the stresses in our lives in a positive way that also enhances other important health factors.

Swimming or water sports can provide an excellent form of exercise that can be enjoyed by almost any age group and can allow us to get away from our daily lives for a certain amount of time. Most people associate swimming exercises as the tedium of doing laps in a pool, but they can also include sports like water polo or aerobics that are held in a pool and provide extra resistance to the effort being put out. Water aerobics are particularly beneficial to seniors.

If you can get your heartbeat and breathing elevated for just 15 minutes each day, or at least three days a week, you can enjoy the benefits of aerobic exercise. If you believe an elevated heart rate could be dangerous for you, you can wear an armband or other similar monitor of your heart rate. You should never start any form of new exercise without consulting your physician, especially if you have a condition that could cause you problems.

The rise in popularity of holistic medicine has interested many people in using holistic techniques to exercise. Any form of activity that involves increasing heart rate, breathing or stretching are beneficial in relieving stress and holistic exercises may be worthwhile in pursuing. These include:

- Breathing and progressive muscle relaxation that includes formal breathing techniques and progressive muscle relaxation that uses a pattern to relax the body muscles.
- Mediation techniques that include stress coping meditation, mind focus and deep relaxation audio.
- Yoga in a variety of forms that need to be carefully evaluated for their benefits and risks.
- Tai chi, a formal regimen of movement that provides exercise and focuses the mind.
- Massage therapy practiced by a trained and certified professional.

The Solutions

You do not have to be an adult in the prime of your life to exercise. Children as young as babies can be exercised through flexing. The same is true for seniors who can also do simple stretching exercises to increase mobility and enhance cardiovascular health. Smaller children can do calisthenics. Older adults can engage in yoga, low impact aerobics and weight lifting to help alleviate stress, build up muscle tone and strengthen bones. The key is to fit the type of exercise with the age group and to not expect very young or older people to be able to do the same type of exercises as other adults or teenagers.

Organized sports can also be an excellent form of exercise. The muscles and coordination to play sports such as softball, basketball, tennis, volleyball or combat sports such as karate and tae kwon do can be very well developed during the training and actual play. Even playing a relatively low impact sport such as golf can provide excellent mobility exercise and even more if the player actually walks the course and does not rely on a motorized cart. One just has to be careful that they are in proper shape to play a certain sport and recognize that almost any sport can include the possibility of injuries that could limit, temporarily, future exercise.

Many people believe they have to spend a lot of money on a health club to get exercise, and, while these facilities usually have excellent equipment and classes taught by experts, there are other, less expensive ways to find exercise venues:

- Public parks that may or may not include field houses;
- a YMCA or YWCA facility that typically are less expensive than health clubs;
- bike paths or walking paths;
- the home with exercise equipment from stretching bands to weight lifting machines and
- the workplace where you can do simple stretching or lifting exercises at your desk or work station.

Stretching has become one of the most popular forms of exercise, especially for senior citizens. Stretching must be approached in a systematic manner or it can be counterproductive or even injurious. Before starting any stretching be sure to warm up with five minutes of walking, dancing or riding a stationary bank. There are two major forms of the same type of exercise. Static stretching exercises are the most common form where the stretch is held for 10-20 seconds. They can be relaxing and improve flexibility. Dynamic stretching exercises puts the body in motion and stretches are not held. They are frequently used to warm up for aerobics. Basic stretches include:

- Neck stretches, where most people carry their stress;
- shoulder, back and arm stretches;
- sides and waist stretches;
- abdomen and shoulder stretches;
- shoulder rolls;
- pelvic tilts;

- pelvic twists;
- knee to chest lower back stretches;
- knees to chest gluteal stretch;
- leg stretches;
- inner thigh stretches;
- inner thigh/groin stretches;
- hamstring stretches;
- calves stretch and
- front of thigh stretches.

The Resources

The following Web sites offer more information about exercise and stress relief:

Stress Relief Exercises, *www,stress-relief-exercises.com*

Tufts University, *www.nutrition.tufts.edu/consumer/balance*

Help Guide, *www.helpguide.org/mental/stress_relief_meditation_yoga_relaxation*

How to Be Fit, *www.howtobefit.com/exercise-to-relax*

Ezine Articles, *www.ezinearticles.com/?Tips-For-Relieving-Stress-By-Exercise&id*

Emax Health, *www.emaxhealth.com*

Spine Health, *www.spine.health.com/topics/conserv/backexercise*

The following books offer more information on exercise and stress relief such as:

The Power of Yoga: Health, Exercise, Stress Relief & Relaxation, Mind & Spirit (Basic Health Publications, 2004)

Instant Meditation for Stress Relief: Breathing Techniques and Mental Exercises for an Immediate Sense of Calm and Well-Being (Lorenz Books, 1998)

Instant Stretches for Stress Relief: Instant energy and relaxation with easy-to-follow yoga stretching techniques (Barnes & Noble Books, 2001)

Turn Stress into Bliss: The Proven 8-Week Program for Health, Relaxation, Stress Relief (Fair Winds Press, 2005)

The 15-minute Executive Stress-relief Program (Perigree Trade, 1992)

Aerobic Walking The Weight Loss Exercise: A Complete Program to Reduce Weight, Stress and Hypertension (Wiley, 1995)

Exercise for Good Health (Living Well, Staying Healthy) (Child's World, 2003)

39

Writing

Writing it down can be a terrific way to deal with the stress in your life. Writing can be hard work, but, when it involves our more intimate feelings and acknowledgement of our problems, it can be very cathartic. Often, this writing is not meant to be seen by anybody but ourselves, but you can share your writings or your feelings with a trusted friend or therapist. The process of writing it and then reviewing it periodically can help you not only focus on what is troubling you, but how you went about dealing with it.

The Challenge

Writing can seem like dauntingly hard work, but it does not have to be. Writing at its core is a way to express ourselves in ways that we may not be able to articulate verbally. It involves looking into ourselves and discovering what is bothering us and being able to write it down. The writing is usually in the form of a journal or daily diary that may be meant to be only seen by us. Doing the writing does not mean we have to be skilled writers, but merely willing to take up the pen or sit at the keyboard and express ourselves. It can turn into a great pastime and regular writing can help relieve our stress by allowing us to look at what is inside. The challenge is to understand what we wish to write about, finding a medium that works for us, setting up a schedule, getting the words on paper without worrying about them being perfect, reviewing what we have written and learning from the experience. A few minutes of writing every day can mean the relief of hours of stress and may lead us to discover talents we never knew we had.

The Facts

Many therapists encourage the keeping and sharing of journals. This is called journaling. The concept is to write down, on a daily basis, the things that have happened to us and how we feel about them. The journal could be kept in a formal style or exist as notes that perhaps only we understand. The journal would be shared with the therapist, if appropriate, or referred to as part of a therapy session. Some days may seem less eventful than others, but the chances are there is something that has happened that can be worth including in a journal.

There are specific benefits to writing about your day and your feelings in a journal including:

- Reducing symptoms of arthritis, asthma and other health concerns;
- fortifying the immune system which can help prevent a number of illnesses and
- improving cognitive functioning.

Another form of stress-relief writing is through Scrapbooking. This combines the use of photos, inspirational sayings and writing your comments or goals about what they represent to you. Some people create a wish scrapbook at the end of the year, but these types of exercises can be done throughout the year.

Keeping a journal is similar to one of the major steps in a 12-step program where participants, usually those trying to fight an addiction, are encouraged to list their strengths, weaknesses and areas they want to improve on. As the start of a journal, you may want to include such items to begin the process of self-examination and revise them as your life changes and your awareness of who you are begins to change.

Journal writing for teenagers can be a vital way to let off steam. You should encourage your children to write down their feelings and problems on a daily basis. Emphasize you believe this is important and are doing the same thing. Also, assure them that anything they write down is private and you will not pry into it, unless your teen wants to share the writing with you or a therapist under a family therapy process.

Some people take their writing public by creating a personal blog that talks about aspects of their lives. It is usually a good idea to keep your actual identity a secret regarding this blog and use only a dedicated email address for people to respond. You may get flamed or nothing but junk answers, but your blog may make you feel better and help somebody else deal with similar problems.

One of the most beneficial aspects of writing about your stress is to improve your sleeping habits. Many times we have trouble falling asleep at night because we are endlessly replaying the events of the day and how we feel about them. Simply by writing about your concerns, possibly close to when you are going to bed, can help you relax and sleep better.

The Solutions

You can certainly take classes to be a better writer, but often it is important to ignore what we think is our lack of ability and proceeding with the writing. Most of us have had some type of experience writing, whether it is for school or work. And, while staring at a blank page can feel scary, once you let your mind go and the words flow, it is not as hard as we thought it would be. The key is to not self-judge your ability as a writer but to simply sit down and do it.

Do not strive for perfection in your writing. Just get the words down on paper. Many people tend to freeze up thinking their journal writing has to be perfect in grammar and without misspelling. But, that would only matter if you are turning it in as a class project or job report. If it is just for your own use, you can use sentence fragments, not worry about subject-verb agreement and spell it so it looks right. If you do feel a need for perfection, get a draft done as soon as possible and go back to edit what you have wrote. It will never be perfect, nor should it have to be.

Writing is a process that is different for everyone. We all have ways that seem right when it comes to putting down our ideas, but, if you are starting fresh with writing after not having done it for yourself for some time, here are some ideas to help the process:

- Find a quiet place and consistent time to write and stay with your schedule, even if you do not feel like writing on that particular day.
- Try to limit your writing to the events of that day.
- If you are writing about a stressful situation, explain your thoughts and feelings about the perceived stress.
- Write openly and honestly and do not worry about meeting some standard of formal style.
- Be sure to not just concentrate on the negative, but also include positive elements of your day and positive thoughts about what is going on with you.

Journal writing to relieve stress is sometimes called expressive writing. This type of writing concentrates on your private feelings, and, as a general rule should not be shown to anybody, including those close to you. This will allow you the freedom to be as honest or open as you want without worrying about offending someone else's feelings. Your writing is for your benefit and not usually for other consumption.

Consider only reviewing your journal on a weekly basis. This gives you a chance to think some more about what happened and better process what is in your journal. Reviewing it on a daily basis may end up adding to your stress.

Create a special environment for your writing. If you are writing at a desk, buy a small bulletin board and keep it at eye level. Put photos, cartoons or inspirational sayings on the bulletin board for you to refer to as you write. If you write just in a chair, keep a writer's pillow handy. It should be a different color and size than the rest of your furniture cushions. When you write, get it out and use it as an arm rest. It may sound silly, but it can help.

The Resources

The following Web sites offer more information about writing to relieve stress:

Parenting, *www.parenting.org*

Associated Content, *www.associatedcontent.com/article/211096/write_to_relieve_ stress*

Ezine Articles, *www.ezinearticles.com/?Stress-Management--How-Writing-Can-Relieve-Stress*

Essortment, *www.essortment.com/lifestyle/journalwriting_snad*

Relishing Life, *www.relishinglife.com/71/turn-to-writing-for-stress-relief/*

42 Explore, *www.42explore.com/journl*

Journal For You, *www.journalforyou.com*

The following books offer more information on writing to relieve stress such as:

Journal to the Self: Twenty-Two Paths to Personal Growth – Open the Door to Self-Understanding by Reading, Writing and Creating a Journal of Your Life (Grand Central Publishing, 1990)

Journal Jumpstarts: Quick Topics and Tips for Journal Writing (Cottonwood Press, Inc., 1996)

Life's Companion: Journal Writing as a Spiritual Practice (Bantam, 1990)

Writing to Heal: A Guided Journal for Recovering from Trauma and Emotional Upheaval (New Harbinger Publications, 2004)

Journal Keeping: Writing for Spiritual Growth (InterVarsity Press, 2002)

Writing Down the Days: 365 Creative Journaling Ideas for Young People (Free Spirit Publishing, 2000)

Daily Warm-Ups: Journal Writing (Walch Publishing, 2004)

40

Letting Feelings Out

We have been taught from our earliest years to not cause a scene and maintain control. This means we frequently bottle up negative feelings until they get too much and cause us both mental and physical problems. These negative feelings can make us feel like exploding sometimes and we do not always know how to handle them. Finding ways to let our feelings out can be very beneficial in maintaining a mental balance and dealing with stress in a positive way. It can mean unlearning certain types of behavior and coping mechanisms and discovering that, when done correctly and in a way that is not meant to hurt people, it can be accomplished and can be helpful to let go of these feelings.

The Challenge

If we do not let our feelings out from time to time we can feel like we are going to explode. This means that we will sacrifice positive ways to let feelings out and take on negative methods that may include yelling and basically holding a tantrum. These types of behavior can cause more harm than good and seldom lead to ways to relieve stress. We have been conditioned to believe that it is a sign of weakness to seek ways to let our feelings out, that strong people should be able to maintain an equilibrium and shove stressful feelings down and go on with their lives. All this self-control accomplishes is a feeling that we are losing control of our feelings and our lives. We cast around trying to find ways to let the feelings out, and, if we do not have good ideas or a plan of action, we can feel growing frustration that can lead to debilitating effects and add to our stress. There are many ways and resources we can use to positively let our feelings out and you can use these to help in your process. The challenge is to know when we are holding on to too many negative feelings, how those feelings are affecting our lives and finding positive ways to let them out than can make us feel better without burdening others. Once we come to terms with the importance and benefits of letting our feelings out, we can move on to a place of better health, reduce our stress and move on with our lives. All we have to do is make the effort and find out how letting negative feelings out can be of great benefit and not that hard to do.

The Facts

Although we will concentrate on negative feelings in our lives, feelings of frustration, anger and despair, sometimes even positive or neutral feelings can pile up inside our heads. We have to separate them from the negative feelings and learn how to place them in their proper context. We can share them and look for ways to enhance the benefits of these positive feelings. Finding a way to use our positive feelings can be just as important as finding ways of dealing with negative feelings.

Letting feelings out is a skill we all should work on developing, but it can be especially useful for singles. People with a strong support group of relationships such as a boyfriend, girlfriend, wife or husband may find it relatively easier to let out feelings because we trust these people with our feelings. Living single can make this process a little more challenging.

Negative feelings usually go through a process that can be headed off at any time before they become truly destructive. We go from acknowledging that something negative has happened to us at work or in our daily lives, we replay the experience and how we should have dealt with it, this progresses to mild irritation at what happened to us grows to full-blown aggravation, finally to frustration and anger. Soon we find we are thinking constantly about what has happened until we are losing sleep, suffering headaches or getting chronic indigestion.

There are no bad feelings, just the way we deal with them. Keep these ideas in mind as you deal with negative feelings and do not beat yourself up over having them:

- Try to acknowledge your strong emotions.
- Describe your feelings rather than displaying them.
- Remember you are entitled to feel any way you like as long as you are not hurting someone else.
- Acknowledge the help of someone we express our negative feelings to and tell them how much you value their presence and help.
- Do not be afraid to admit uncertainties in how you feel. You can do more harm than good in pretending you know what is going on with you, when you really do not.
- You do not always need words to help you let out negatives. Sometimes simple human contact, such as holding someone's hand and sitting silently, can work as well as talking it out.
- You are not the only one with regrets in your life. Everyone has them and those close to you should be willing to listen to yours.
- Cry if you feel like it. It is not a sign of weakness, but a sign of sensitivity. Good friends may feel gratified you feel comfortable enough with them to cry, if that is how you feel.

The Solutions

There are several people we can turn to let out our feelings including:

- Family members who are willing to take the time to listen to us and not judge us for being honest;
- friends who we know will be sympathetic to us and help us deal with the feelings in our lives based on their own experiences and honest knowledge of us and
- professionals such as therapists, psychologists or psychiatrists.

If we are dealing with negative feelings associated with certain types of behavior we can turn to support groups to help us work with people who share the same types of issues and can help us deal with them. A good example of this are anger management groups where people who believe they are expressing inappropriate levels and types of anger work together to lessen these impulses and find ways to express anger that are less destructive.

For the most part our lives are pretty good. Most things that happen to us and generate feelings are positive, but they can get shoved aside in the wake of thinking about negative feelings. Part of letting feelings out is placing them in a context and realizing that much of what happens around us, especially on the job, has nothing to do with us. It is easy to accept the negatives and hold them close, but letting them out is essential in maintaining a balance in our lives.

How you deal with letting go of negative feelings will depend a lot on what the situation is and what else is going on in your life, but, in general there are several useful ways to let go of negative feelings:

- Recognize the seriousness of uncontrolled emotions. Unchecked negative feelings can wear on your body and nervous system until you feel sick. All of your agonizing over negatives rarely solves the problem.
- We often feel we should stew over our hurts and negative feelings for as long as we want. But, it can be easier to deal with negatives by putting a time limit on how long we feel them. Tell yourself you are only going to deal with the negatives for a certain amount of time and every minute spent on the negatives take away from the positives. Do not cheat on this time limit, when the subject comes up again, tell yourself you have more productive ways to spend your time.
- Engage your mind with something else. Take a walk, do a household chore, socialize with friends or do a hobby. Do something that takes some degree of concentration to take you away from your negatives.
- Turn the situation over to a higher power. This may be God or some type of spirituality, but this concept that is a major component of 12-step programs, can be vital in taking away bad feelings.
- Do not give up on letting negatives out and expect they will not disappear immediately. This is a skill that takes time to learn and if it does not initially succeed in the long run, try again. Work for a little progress each time you let your feelings out.

Writing it out can help you let go of negative feelings without burdening others. Let your thoughts stream without filtering, schedule enough time during the day to write, find a place where you can concentrate and feel safe, use music if it is not distracting, relax through breathing, keep it simple and show how you feel, do not tell about it.

The Resources

The following Web sites offer more information about letting feelings out:

Inspiration for Singles, *www.inspiration-for-singles.com/catch-yourself*

Health and Age, *www.healthandage.com*

Caring to the End, *www.caringtotheend.com*

At Health, *www.athealth.com/consumer/disorders/expressfeelings*

Growing Aware, *www.growingaware.com.au*

Kids Health, *www.kidshealth.org/kid/feeling/thought/talk_feelings*

Coping, *www.coping.org*

The following books offer more information on letting feelings out such as:

The Power of Letting Go: 10 Simple Steps to Reclaiming Your Life (Multnomah, 2006)

Thinking Out Loud (Tate Publishing, 2007)

Living With Loss And Grief: Letting Go, Moving On (Overcoming Common Problems (Sheldon Press, 2006)

How to Take the Grrrr Out of Anger (Three Rivers Press, 1996)

Stamp Collecting for Dummies (Free Spirit Publishing, 2002)

Leading Out Loud: Inspiring Change Through Authentic Communications (Jossey-Bass, 2003)

Cutting More Ties That Bind: Letting Go of Fear, Anger, Guilt, and Jealousy So We Can Educate Our Children and Change Ourselves (Weiser Books, 1994)

41

Finding A Hobby

Modern life often beats us down to where we want to spend our time off simply sitting in front of the television or sleeping. We ignore one of the best ways to deal with stress: finding a hobby. Hobbies can take many forms and involve different types of money and commitment, but when used properly they can pull us away from the stress of every day life and allow us to enjoy activities that have nothing to do with earning a living or handling family life. Many of us do not know how to go about finding a hobby we can pursue, but with a little effort, we can find things we enjoy and use them to the advantage of our mental health.

The Challenge

When was the last time you engaged in a hobby? Within the last few days, few months or you cannot remember when? Hobbies in an electronic age of television, DVR's, the Internet and videogames may seem quaint, but they developed over hundreds of years as an important element of our lives. Their very frivolousness was just what many of us needed to help pull us away from our regular lives and plunge us into a different world. They are relaxing and challenging and can provide a sense of accomplishment that we sometimes do not so easily find in our work lives or personal lives. Sometimes hobbies are something we pursue on our own, sometimes they are part of a more organized club or association, sometimes they are both. Whatever their form, a pleasant hobby can be instrumental in maintaining a balance between work and relaxation. The challenge is to realize when we could use a hobby in our life, finding an activity that we genuinely enjoy and can perform to a feeling of accomplishment, deciding whether we want this activity to include others and being prepared to change the activity if we find that it is not providing the relief from stress we were hoping for. There are a tremendous variety and resources for hobbies and even the very act of searching for an activity can help us deal with stress. All you have to do is want to find a satisfying hobby and allow yourself the time to adequately pursue it and give it a chance to work wonders in your life.

The Facts

Hobbies have been around for a very long time and their definition is in the eye of the beholder. Basically, a hobby is any leisure activity that diverts you from your daily life and occupies empty moments. Some people may look at very high-ticket pursuits, such as aviation or yachting as a hobby, hobbies that most people cannot afford. Others may look at collecting as a type of hobby, collecting from coins to toys to expensive items such as antiques, wine or art. Some view craft type work as a type of hobby, which may include sewing, carpentry or building furniture. The one thing they all have in common is they provide an escape from everyday worries and life through an activity that really does not impact the needs of our daily lives. As such, hobbies can provide terrific releases from stress, as long as the hobby remains a past time and does not turn into an obsession.

Most hobbies are designed to be enjoyed by yourself, but a hobby can also provide a way to socialize. These methods include:

- Organized clubs that meet to discuss aspects of the hobby;
- groups that get together to perform the hobby as part of an exhibition or competition;
- classes, offered through community centers or community college continuing education classes and
- social events that celebrate the hobby and get people together who share the same interest, including conventions and informal gatherings.

Many scientific studies have shown that doing art or craft hobbies can help keep your brain active. Learning and enjoying a new skill can actually grow your brain by changing the size and structure of the brain neurons. A study in the New England Journal of Medicine shows that doing a mentally challenging hobby helps minimize memory loss in older adults. A physical hobby can help with ailments such as arthritis, although you may have to be a bit more creative in how you do a hobby if you are now suffering pain. Think of a hobby as exercise for your mind and sometimes your body.

The Solutions

There are an almost endless variety of sources to find information on every type of hobby. These can range from books to magazines to Websites with helpful hints. Indeed, many hobby-related Websites feature message boards or blogs where hobbyists can share ideas and observations. Using the Internet has also made it much easier to acquire supplies for a hobby, which used to have to be purchased at a hobby shop or by mail order catalogs. Shopping Websites such as eBay provide excellent ways for collectors to find and purchase items as well as ways for people to make money selling items they are not interested in but might be worth substantial money to a dedicated collector.

While there are almost countless activities that can count as a hobby, you might be tempted to explore activities that most people do not necessarily think of taking up as a hobby:

- Gardening is a wonderful stress reliever. It gets you out of the house and into the sunshine and fresh air. It gives you an opportunity to work with living things and the earth. The end result can provide beauty for your home or food for your table.
- Photography can be a great hobby, whether you are simply looking to improve your basic skills or create real art. It can be done with traditional 35mm film and a dark room or with a digital camera and a computer. As you work with a camera you start to see the world in a different way and it can seem like a more beautiful place for your daily life.
- Scrapbooking takes your collectibles and memorabilia and combines a form of journalism with artistry to create a unique entity for displaying your cherished memories. Scrapbooking allows you to take a break from stress and create lasting art that others can enjoy.
- Maintaining a saltwater aquarium provides the same diversions as a regular aquarium with the unique challenges and beauty of keeping healthy saltwater fish. Many aquarium enthusiasts are much more into saltwater than freshwater aquariums.
- Puzzles, whether they are crosswords, sudoku, or jigsaw puzzles let you focus on something besides your stress and allow you to work your brain power.
- Like photography, drawing allows you to get into your artistic side and can help process your emotional life. Drawing might include sketching, water color, charcoal or painting with oil or acrylics. You can choose still lifes, landscaping and other subjects. You can take classes that can help you meet other enthusiasts.
- Needlework including needlepoint, knitting or crocheting has been going through a major resurgence in recent years with a variety of stores, books, magazines and Websites available for enthusiasts. You can do needlework while you talk to other people or watch television. And, contrary to some popular belief, needlework is being enjoyed by more and more men and not just women.
- Playing a musical instrument is a wonderful way to challenge yourself and create art. You may want to start with piano lessons using a relatively inexpensive electronic keyboard. By using headphones, you can avoid bothering your family or neighbors. Learning the piano can teach you the basics of music and allow you to move to other instruments. You can take lessons or use Websites or CDs to learn the basics.
- People dealing with severe stress are often encouraged to use journaling to write down their feelings and what is stressing them out. This journaling can lead to an attraction to other forms of writing from autobiography, family or fiction. You can share your writing with others or keep it to yourself to enjoy.

The Resources

The following Web sites offer more information about finding and enjoying a hobby:

Stress About, *www.stress.about.com/fuandgames/tp/hobby*

Natural Family, *www.naturalfamilyonline.com*

Ezine Articles, *www.ezinearticles.com/?Stress-6-Top-Ten-Stress-Relieving-Hobbies*

Indian Child, *www.indianchild.com/Hobby*

Malone Counseling, *www.canville.net/malone/getahobby*

Deal With Stress, *www.dealwithstress.com/Hobbies-As-Stress-Relief*

Family, *www.family.com*

The following books offer more information on finding and enjoying a hobby such as:

Choosing Your Retirement Hobby (Dodd, Mead, 1976)

Basic Model Railroading: Getting Started in the Hobby (Kalmbach Publishing Co., 1998)

How to Sell Toys and Hobbies on eBay (Entrepreneur Press, 2006)

Crafting for Dollars: Turn Your Hobby into Serious Cash (Three Rivers Press, 1996)

Stamp Collecting for Dummies (For Dummies, 2001)

Reef Secrets: Starting Right, Selecting Fishes & Invertebrates, Advanced Biotope Techniques (TFH Publications, 2003)

Get a Hobby: 101 All-Consuming Diversions for Any Lifestyle (Collins, 2007)

42

Volunteering

Most of us have very busy lives. Between work and family or social demands we find our days are full to bursting. We may believe we can do no more, but ignore the possibility of volunteering in our community. Sometimes a relatively short amount of time devoted to volunteering can work a lot of positive in our lives. Volunteering can make us feel we are spending some of our time and energy to improve the world around us, and this can be a very positive way to fight off stress. Volunteering should not be seen as a burden but as an opportunity to do others some good while we help ourselves.

The Challenge

We may believe we are not really doing anything positive in our lives, even though we are very busy. We are performing our jobs, maintaining a family life and paying the bills, but something is missing. Quite often this missing piece of our lives is giving back to the community through volunteering. Many people react in disbelief when the concept of volunteering is presented to them. They do not see how they can find the time to effectively volunteer by ignoring the relative ease of the process. If we take a hard look at our schedules and how we spend our time, we may be amazed at the time available to do some type of volunteering. The process can be fun and provide us with very positive feelings of accomplishment. Volunteering can take on many forms and involve a variety of time commitments. We can work with individuals, act as a mentor, help in church activities, promote a political candidate or cause, help in our church or simply work with a fund-raising event. The challenge is to recognize the importance of volunteering, finding the resources available to effectively volunteer, making a commitment to the process and sticking with it and changing our activities if the form of volunteering we initially choose is not working to our satisfaction. Volunteering is not a luxury, for most of us it is a form of duty to our communities and to ourselves. The opportunities are many and the time needed does not have to be daunting. All we need to do is make the effort and reap the very real rewards in helping others without the need for financial reward.

The Facts

A good working definition of a volunteer is someone who serves in a community or for the benefit of the environment because they choose to do so. Many people volunteer through a non-profit organization called formal volunteering, other people serve less formally as an individual or part of a group. They are harder to identify. A volunteer does not get paid or receive other compensation. Within the formal and informal volunteers there are several categories such as:

- An international volunteer works outside the community or country, usually related to a developing country.
- An online volunteer contributes time and effort through online work such as translating documents, proofreading material, preparing proposals, research, creating Web pages, moderating online discussion groups and managing other online volunteers.
- A sports volunteer helps with youth sports activities by coaching teams, refereeing games or organizing the league.
- A museum volunteer can help with selling tickets, working in the museum shop or handing out information. Some are specially trained to lead tours or answer questions and are called docents.
- A youth volunteer is a younger person, typically between 12-21 years of age, who do voluntary work in the community to add to their resume for college or work consideration.
- A Peer Health Education volunteer helps with medical programs by leading support groups and providing information as needed to medical patients with special needs.

Under the less-than-desirable conditions, volunteering can feel like work. It should not. Volunteering, if done properly, can mean putting in some time and having to do things you commit to similar to work, but the rewards are entirely different. While you hopefully will have some spiritual rewards in doing a job properly and in following a satisfactory career path, the main reason most of us work is to earn a living. In volunteering there is no monetary reward and the benefits of doing it more hard to quantify. It can be much more rewarding than work and make you feel like you are doing some real good.

In some ways, volunteering can be more political than work or social life. The truth is people sometimes volunteer for the ego boost involved in doing so and can treat their volunteering activities as jealously as they do their work. They create hierarchies for themselves and can keep other volunteers shut out of the process. There may be some mind games involved in volunteering and you need to understand the politics involved in the organization or cause you are volunteering for to get the most out of the experience and not have it become a negative part of your life.

Volunteering can not only make you feel better and relieve stress, it can also add to your work skills. You can improve your communications and interpersonal skills and also improve your communication. It can also increase your ability to find a job. According to a Canadian study, 28 percent of unemployed volunteers said that volunteering had helped them obtain a job and 62 percent of unemployed volunteers believed to would help them find a job in the future.

The Solutions

Many people get into volunteering to put something on their resume or feed their egos. There is nothing wrong with this if the volunteering is worthwhile, but sometimes this can lead to problems. Your volunteering should revolve around two things: doing good for others and doing good for yourself by taking on activities that make you feel good and help you deal with the stress of the rest of your life. If you invest too much of your ego and other psychic demands into volunteering, you can defeat its purposes.

Volunteering can not only do good, it can introduce us to other people. Finding new friends or even romantic relationships can be challenging. Usually, finding them at work can present problems in that the work situation can change and relationships can suffer or disappear. Finding new acquaintenances through volunteering means you will spend time with people who share your interests and are far more likely to be around in the long run. It is similar to meeting people through a hobby, but volunteering is usually more formal and goal-oriented.

You need to recognize your motivations when you decide to volunteer. It will help you find a good fit for your activities and keep you focused. Those motivations include:

- Altruism or volunteering purely for the benefit of others, although some believe there is always some aspect of personal gain to volunteering;
- improving the quality of life in the community through organizations or individual contacts;
- giving back to the community the things we enjoy about it and the benefits of our own good fortune;
- a sense of duty means we believe volunteering is necessary for our good feelings;
- religious convictions lead people to volunteer because it serves the teaching of their church;
- networking means you can meet people through volunteering who may be able to help you in other areas of your life and
- social aspects that help you meet new friends and form relationships.

When you decide to volunteer for an organization you may be asked some questions to make sure you are a good fit for the goals and work of the organization including:

- Why do you want to volunteer for the organization?
- What do you already know, or think you know, about the organization?
- How many hours a week can you volunteer?
- What are your interests?
- What do you do for a living?

- What special skills do you have?
- Do you have transportation?

By the same token, you should ask some simple questions when you decide to volunteer for an organization such as:

- What will be expected of me as a volunteer?
- What kind of training will I receive?
- How many other volunteers are there?
- How much time do you expect me to commit?
- What type of people do you already have as volunteers?

The Resources

The following Web sites offer more information about volunteering:

Center on Philanthropy, *www.philanthropy.org*

Volunteer Canada, *www.volunteer.ca*

Essortment, *www.ncnc.essortment.com/benefitsofvol_rwig*

Time Bank, *www.timebank.orog.uk/aboutgiving/benefits_vol*

National and Community Service, *www.nationalservice.gov/about/role_impact*

Points of Light Foundation, *www.pointsoflight.org*

Volunteer Match, *www.volunteermatch.org*

The following books offer more information on volunteering such as:

Make a Difference: America's Guide to Volunteering and Community Service (Jossey-Bass, 2003)

Giving from Your Heart: A Guide to Volunteering (iUniverse, Inc., 2005)

Volunteering: The Selfish Benefits: Achieve Deep-Down Satisfaction and Create That Desire in Others (Committee Communications, 2001)

How to Live Your Dream of Volunteering Overseas (Penguin, 2001)

The Busy Family's Guide to Volunteering: Do Good, Have Fun, Make a Difference As a Family (Robins Lane Press, 2003)

Volunteering to Help the Environment (Children's Press, 2000)

Volunteering: The Ultimate Teen Guide (The Scarecrow Press, 2007)

43

Relaxing Your Body

Many of us might express our concerns over stress to friends or family and are told to just relax. This seems to be a cure-all for feeling stressed. But, when it comes to finding ways to relax we are often at a loss. We do not know how to relax the tension that we feel except through methods that may cause us much harm as any benefit, such as turning to alcohol, oversleeping or using illegal drugs. We need to learn how to relax our bodies and how this process can help us deal with the stress of everyday life. That way, the next time we are told to relax, which is always good advice, we will know what that means to us and how to go about doing it.

The Challenge

Relaxing our bodies is a skill we must learn. You cannot rely on simply sitting still for a few minutes and hope this is really going to help you relax. You must learn and practice techniques that can actually bring you the benefits of relaxation: reducing stress hormones, easing tension and providing perspective on how we feel and what we are doing in our lives. Relaxing our bodies can be done almost anywhere at any time, whether you are at home, in your vehicle, at work or in other stressful situations. As we become more experienced in relaxation for the body techniques, we will see their positive results and be prompted to maintain the regimen of relaxing our bodies. Our physical being easily manifests the debilitating aspects of stress and relaxing can help our body cope with those effects. The challenge is to recognize what the benefits of relaxing the body are, what techniques are most effective to us and evaluating their effectiveness in case we want to change the techniques. We are not bound to any relaxation regimen and can pick and choose what works best for us. Whatever we choose, the key is to maintain some type of regimen and use relaxation for the positive benefits it can provide. Just relax and deal with stress in a positive way. Just know how to do so.

The Facts

Medications are often turned to or prescribed as ways to relax our bodies. These medications prescribed to us by our physician or a psychiatrist might include anti-depressants or tranquilizers such as valium. These can be effective in helping us relax, but the danger with medications is developing a reliance on them and adjusting their dosage. There also might be side effects, such as drowsiness, that we have to deal with. If at all possible, it is preferable to find other methods rather than medication to relax our bodies, keeping the possibility of medication in a supervised environment as something to turn to if other techniques do not do the job needed.

Do not equate sleeping with relaxing your body. While sleep is certainly important to our overall health and can help us feel refreshed, sleeping too much will actually increase our stress. Chronically oversleeping is often a symptom of depression and will not really make us feel better rested. It is the quality of the sleep we are getting, and not the quantity that can help us fight against the stressors in our lives.

There are a variety of formal techniques you can learn and practice in a class environment, or through DVDs or Websites including:

- Pilates which uses specially designed equipment or mat instruction and can build strength without bulk, lengthens and stretches muscles and creates posture awareness;
- Yoga, a series of poses and postures done while focusing your breathing and relaxing your mind, promoting deep relaxation, body awareness, strength and flexibility;
- Qi gong uses deep meditation visualization, breathing and slow, easy movements to restore a life-giving balance and help you feel relaxed yet energetic with enhanced breathing, flexibility and strength and
- Alexander Technique in which you perform basic tasks such as standing up and walking while a teacher gives you cues and adjustments to help you move more easily, helping free your muscles from tension and restoring balance and good posture.

The Solutions

Often we can take classes or seminars in relaxing our body. This will help us learn relaxation techniques, but we still need to practice them on their own. Some of the venues or programs we may use to help us relax our bodies include:

- Exercise classes that help us release our stress while strengthening our bodies;
- yoga classes in a variety of formats that allow us to learn stretching techniques that can relax our bodies and
- short-term seminars that can be attended to learn some basic relaxing techniques.

One of the most used and most effective of techniques to relax our bodies is using progressive muscle relaxation. This can be done in a variety of areas from home to work, but you have to set up the proper environment for relaxing your body. This means finding a relatively quiet place where you can be undisturbed for about 15 minutes. Use a comfortable chair where you can sit up straight with your feet on the floor. Sit comfortably and pay close attention to how you feel as you begin and progress through the exercises. Note any stiffness or tightness and if you are experiencing any aches or pains. When you know how you feel before you begin relaxing, you will know how you feel when your body is relaxed.

Your arms can easily tense up when you are stressed. Relax them by:

- Slowly inhale and exhale while you have your eyes closed.
- Bend your right hand back at the wrist and briefly hold the tension. Relax your hand and then do the same thing with your left hand.
- Tighten both hands into fists and hold the tension. Feel that tension spread up your arms towards the elbows. Then relax.
- Bend both arms at the elbows and raise your hands towards your shoulders. Tighten up the biceps muscles, hold and relax.
- If you avoid moving your arms around, they will become more relaxed.

Your face can experience and express feelings of stress. Even without knowing it, our facial muscles can tense up and be a cause of headaches. You can relax your facial muscles by:

- Raise your eyebrows up as far as you can and hold them. Then relax. This helps relax the muscles in your forehead.
- Squeeze your eyelids tight together. Hold the tension, then relax.
- Bite down and clamp your teeth together. Be aware of the tension around your jaw. Relax the jaw muscles. Be careful not to grind your teeth.
- Bend your head forward as if you are trying to touch your chin to your chest. Feel the tension you feel at the back of your neck and relax. This will relax your neck and also your face.

Turn your attention to your upper body. It is a frequent monitor of the stress level in your overall body. Relax your upper body muscles by:

- Raise your shoulders as high as you can, let them drop all at once and relax.
- Do two things at once for your chest. Take a deep breath and hold it while trying to touch your shoulder blades together by pulling your arms back. Hold them and relax.
- Pull in your stomach as if you are trying to touch your backbone with your stomach, then relax.
- Arch your back out and away from the chair and you will feel the tension along the spine. Then relax.

Finally, turn your attention to your legs and feet. You can help them relax by:

- Place your feet flat on the floor. Press down on them and feel the tension spread up the back of your legs. Then relax.
- Relax your thighs by starting with your right leg and raising it up in front of you. Note the tension building, then relax. Do the same thing with your left leg.
- Bend your toes up as if pointing towards the ceiling and feel the tension around your feet and ankles. Repeat the exercise, then relax.

Deep breathing can be used in the same way as progressive muscle relaxation and be done just about anywhere. Deep breathing can also relax your mind as well as your body. One way to do deep breathing is:

- Lie on your back with a pillow under your head. Bend your knees, using a pillow under them if necessary, and your stomach will relax.
- Place one hand on your stomach just below your rib cage.
- Slowly breathe in through your nose. If this is working, your stomach will feel like it is rising.
- Exhale slowly through your mouth and completely empty your lungs. You will feel your stomach fall.
- Repeat this breathing several times until you feel your body calm and relax. Try practicing this method daily.

The Resources

The following Web sites offer more information about relaxing the body:

Lessons 4 Living, *www.lessones4living.com/how*

University of Georgia, *www.uhs.uga.edu/stress/relax*

iVillage, *www.ivillage.co.uk/dietandfitness*

Mindtools, *www.mindtools.com/stress/RelaxationTechniques/PhysicalTechniques*

University of Maryland, *www.umm.edu/sleep/relax_tech*

WATE-TV, *www.wate.com*

1000 Advices, *www.1000advices.com/guru/happiness_relaxation_4ways_mc*

The following books offer more information on relaxing the body such as:

Instant Calm: Over 100 Easy-to-Use Techniques for Relaxing Mind and Body (Plume, 1995)

How to Free Yourself from Nervous Tension: An Exact, Scientific Method for Relaxing Your Body and Mind (Regnery, 1955)

Body Mind Mastery: Creating Success in Sport and Life (New World Library, 1999)

Yoga Body, Buddha Mind (Riverhead Trade, 2004)

Thinking Body, Dancing Mind: Taosports for Extraordinary Performance in Athletics, Business and Life (Bantam, 1994)

Stress Relief & Relaxation Techniques (McGraw-Hill, 2000)

Relaxation Techniques (Pustak Mahal, India, 2004)

44

Relaxing Your Mind

The debilitating effects of stress attack both our bodies and minds. It can make our bodies feel tense and ill, and it can cause our minds to work against our productivity. Mind stress often means obsessing over the causes of stress and feeling that no matter what we do, we cannot rise above the stressors in our lives. Luckily, like methods of relaxing the body, there are ways to relax your minds so that stress has a lesser effect. These techniques are usually formal and more than simply taking a minute for yourself.

The Challenge

You may feel you have worked hard and mastered techniques for relaxing your body whether this is formal such as yoga or less formal methods. But, have you learned any techniques to relax your mind? In many ways, relaxing the mind is far more difficult than relaxing your body. Your mind is a complex mechanism that processes the world around you in many ways, some of which can cause stress in your life. Relaxing the mind means pulling away from the world around you in a productive way and finding ways to cope with the everyday stress of your life. The challenge is to understand the effects of stress on your mind, how this stress can be relieved through relaxation techniques, what types of techniques are best for you and evaluating how they are working. Think of your mind as a tense muscle similar to what you would find in your body and you will be helped in finding effective ways to relax it. This relaxation is not necessarily physical, but mental and relies on techniques that work on our feelings and perceptions rather than the physical makeup of the mind and the chemicals it releases. Relax your mind and your body may follow along and your stress will alleviate in a relatively short time.

The Facts

By its very nature, relaxing your mind gets inside of your head for a while and then figuring out how to remove yourself from a stressful situation. You must first acknowledge what is going on in your head and then be willing to take the steps to productively deal with it. Once you do that, you have a chance to relax your mind.

Relaxing your mind is actually a conscious activity and not just the act of sleeping or staring mindlessly into space. You have to be prepared to make an effort to relax your mind and do the work necessary. You should find that the work involved is not odious, but, rather, enjoyable and a good way to conquer the stress in your life. Look around for the technique that works best for you and stick with it. Practice it once or twice a day and do not expect immediate results. It can take repeated use over a number of weeks before you notice any effect.

A good therapist or counselor can help you develop ways to relax your mind. He or she will work with you to discover the causes of your stress and what will work for you. Avoid quick-fix cures or techniques that seem faddish, they probably are. Explore the tried and true methods and look for the beneficial effects you are seeking.

It is never too early or late to work on relaxing your mind. Children or teenagers who are experiencing stress-related problems can easily do mind relaxation exercises and may be more open to developing skills that adults might view as frivolous. Seniors who are suffering stress can benefit greatly from mind relaxation and the exercises save them the physical impact of body relaxation techniques.

If you feel things are starting to get out of hand and your mind cannot keep up with the stress, finish what you are doing and take a break. If someone is making you stressed, excuse yourself and get a little exercise and fresh air before returning to the situation. Other mind relaxing techniques include listening to soothing music, even making a tape or burning a CD you can play in your car or over a portable music player. Avoid, if possible, stimulants such as caffeinated coffee, tea, carbonated drinks and chocolate. Modulate your voice when you talk out loud to someone else or to yourself in private.

The Solutions

Meditation is one of the oldest and most relied on forms of relaxing your mind. While many people understand the concept of meditation, or use prayer as a form of meditation, they may have never explored how to do it properly. You can take a class or use other resources to get the most from meditation, but the technique basically comes down to:

- Sit or lie in a relaxing position, using a mat if necessary, and wear loose and comfortable clothing.
- Close your eyes and concentrate on a calming thought, object or even word. This is sometimes referred to as a mantra.
- Do not worry if other thoughts pop into your mind while you are trying to concentrate. This is perfectly normal. Just try not to dwell on them and remain focused on your image or sound.
- If you are having trouble meditating, try repeating the thought or image out loud or barely under your breath. You may want to play soothing music in the background.
- Recognize as you gradually become more and more relaxed and remember what you did to achieve that.

Visualization is a great way to reduce stress and also works out your imagination. You can do visualization in almost any environment as long as the process does not threaten your physical safety. Basic visualization includes:

- Sit or lie down in a comfortable position.
- Imagine a pleasant and peaceful scene such as a sunset, forest or the beach. Picture yourself in this scene.
- Focus your attention on this scene for a set amount of time, any time you are comfortable with, then gradually return your attention to the present.

Drawing and coloring may seem like children's activities, but they can be very helpful in meditating and relaxing your mind. One of the best ways to use drawing or coloring is to employ a mandala. The mandala is a Sanskrit word that denotes a circle or polygon in real life and can symbolize community and connection. Mandalas are intricate designs and you can focus on coloring them while you are meditating. Focus on the process and how it feels to do something as simple as color. Not only is it relaxing and calming, but when you are finished you have a pleasant work of art to add to your home or office. You can obtain mandalas in books or print them from Websites.

If you are having trouble settling your mind and going to sleep at night, you might investigate the Quiet Ears technique of mind relaxation. It is easy to do and quite effective involving:

- Lie on your back with your eyes closed.
- Place your hands behind your head and make sure they are relaxed and in a comfortable position.
- From your hand position, place your thumbs in your ears so that you close the ear canal. Be careful not to insert your thumbs too far into the ear.
- Listen to a high-pitched rushing sound. This is normal.
- Listen to the rushing sound for 10-15 minutes.
- Place your arms at your sides, relax them and then go to sleep. Repeat as needed.

Getting organized and developing time management skills can help you relax your mind and deal with the stress of your work life. Make a to-do list and break down your tasks in order of priority. As you complete each task, mark it off your list and review the list at the end of the day. You should be pleased at seeing how much you have accomplished.

The Resources

The following Web sites offer more information about relaxing the mind:

American Association of Retired Persons, *www.aarp.org/health/staying_health/stress*

University of Georgia, *www.uhs.uga.edu/stress/relax*

Mayo Clinic, *www.mayoclinic.com/health/meditation*

Whole Fitness, *www.wholefitness.com/relaxing*

University of Maryland, *www.umm.edu/sleep/relax_tech*

Stress Vacation, *www.stress-vacation.com/relaxation*

Mindtools, *www.mindtools.com/stress/RelaxationTechniques/RelaxationResponse*

The following books offer more information on relaxing the mind such as:

How to Meditate: An Illustrated Guide to Calming the Mind and Relaxing the Body (Ulysses Press, Seastone, 2000)

Turning the Mind into an Ally (Riverhead Hardcover, 2003)

Ageless Body, Timeless Mind: The Quantum Alternative to Growing Old (Harmony, 1994)

Body Mind Balancing: Using Your Mind to Heal Your Body (St. Martin's Griffin, 2005)

Healing with the Mind's Eye: How to Use Guided Imagery and Visions to Heal, Body, Mind and Spirit (Wiley, 2003)

The Attention Revolution: Unlocking the Power of the Focused Mind (Wisdom Publications, 2006)

The High-Performance Mind (Tarcher, 1997)

Part Nine:

Stress Reduction/Relief Worksheets

45

Stress Level Chart

We will feel some form of stress throughout our lives and must work out ways to deal with it. But, we cannot handle stress as well if we do not understand how much stress we are feeling and what the nature of it is. Keeping a chart of our stressors helps us understand our changing levels of stress and what we might do about them. Understanding our level of stress is the starting point to a healthier, more well-adjusted life.

The Challenge

You would never approach a difficult task in your life or undergo a physical assessment by a physician without using or looking at a chart of your symptoms or the elements in your task. The same is certainly true when dealing with stress, in fact it may be even more important since the stressors in our lives can be harder to identify and more subjective. You can use the charts below to see how they relate to your stress and what you are experiencing. This is an essential element of dealing with stress and should take the time needed to complete and understand it. You can customize the charts for your own needs and adapt them as your life changes. They should be a fluid element in your quest for self-awareness. The challenge is to understand the need for stress charts, identifying honestly what is bothering you or might bother you and then forming a plan to deal with it. Chart your way to better health and handle your stress by taking a few minutes to complete these charts.

Stressful Life Events

Fill out the list below and answer yes to any action that has applied to you in the last two years. This will give you some indication of what stressors have recently been bothering you. Be honest and factor in as many behaviors as possible.

SIGNIFICANT LIFE EVENT	YES	NO
Minor violations of the law		
Stressful holidays		
Changes in number of family get-togethers		
Change in eating habits		
Change in sleeping patterns		
Taking on a small mortgage or loan		
Change in social activities		
Change in recreation patterns		
Change in work hours or conditions		
Change in residence		
Change in schools		
Trouble with the boss		
Revision of personal habits		
Change in living conditions		
Spouse begins or stops work		
Children begin or end school		
Change in responsibility at work		
Son or daughter leaving home		
Trouble with in-laws		
Foreclosure of mortgage or loan		
Taking on a large mortgage		
Change in number of arguments with spouse		
Change to a different line of work		
Death of close friend or relative		
Change in financial state		
Sexual difficulties		
Gain of new family member		
Business readjustment		
Pregnancy		
Change in health of family members		
Material reconciliation		
Retirement		
Fired or laid off at work		
Marriage		
Personal injury or illness		

SIGNIFICANT LIFE EVENT	YES	NO
Jail term		
Marital separation		
Divorce		
Death of spouse		
CHANGES IN BODY FUNCTIONS AND PHYSICAL HEALTH		
(Have you or someone else noticed these		
signs of stress?)		
Backache		
Muscle tension		
Nervous stomach		
Breathing problems		
Frequent urination		
Fatigue		
Dizziness		
CHANGES IN EMOTIONS AND FEELINGS		
(Have you or someone else noticed these signs of stress?)		
Irritability		
Sadness		
Worry		
Tension		
Anger		
CHANGES IN BEHAVIOR		
(Have you or someone else noticed these signs of stress?)		
Sleep problems		
Eating too much or too little		
Wanting sex more or less than before		
More use of alcohol		
Use of illegal drugs		
CHANGES IN HOW YOU THINK		
(Have you or someone else noticed these signs of stress?)		
Trouble remembering things		
Difficulties concentrating		

How to Measure Your Stress

Once you have identified a stressor, you need to evaluate its severity. The simple quiz here gives you an opportunity to rate the major stressors in your life and identify what might need the most work the soonest. A score of under 40 points indicates your level of stress is tolerable; 41-60 points indicates your stress is not too bad but needs improvement; more than 61 points indicates your level of stress is too high and you need to work on the individual items that rate high. Re-evaluate your stress after a month and see what has changed.

STRESSOR	No Stress 0	Little Stress 1	Some Stress 2	Good Deal of Stress 3	Great Deal of Stress 4
Personal injury or disease					
Injury or disease of family members					
Burden of work					
Burden of personal life					
Conflict with spouse					
Conflict with family members					
Economic problems with household expenses					
Increase in unresolved problems					
Lack of information on child education					
Tedious personal life					
Lack of sufficient time for own interests					
Drop in income					
Feeling that work is in a crisis					
Lack of communication on job					
Alienation from job and co-workers					
Lack of help in life					

STRESSOR	No Stress 0	Little Stress 1	Some Stress 2	Good Deal of Stress 3	Great Deal of Stress 4
Increase in debt					
Loss of regular income					
Loss of back up income					

Checking Stress Levels

Below is another simple quiz to measure your stress level based on specific stressors. Fill it out by circling the proper answer on how you have felt in the last six months and look at the results carefully.

STRESS QUESTION			
How are your energy levels?	Low	Moderate	High
Do you have trouble falling asleep or staying asleep?	Sometimes	Frequently	Rarely
How would you rate your level of confidence?	Low	Moderate	High
How often do you suffer minor ailments?	Frequently	Occasionally	Rarely
How often do you feel irritable?	Rarely	All the time	Sometimes
How do you cope with change?	Defensively	Look for the advantages	Find a way through
Do you have feelings of fear or panic?	Often	Rarely	Sometimes
Do you feel worried?	Rarely	Sometimes	Often
How well do you cope with conflict?	Seek win-win solutions	Roll with the punches	Avoid it at all costs
Do you feel emotional or cry easily?	Rarely	Sometimes	Frequently
Do you get neck, shoulder or back pain?	Frequently	Sometimes	Rarely or never
Do you feel apathetic, as if nothing matters?	Frequently	Rarely or never	Sometimes

Stress Frequency Chart

You can track the monthly frequency of your stress with the chart here on how many times a month you feel this way. Add up the score when you are finished filling it out. A score of 0-20 means your stress level is low, although it is never too early to develop good stress management skills; a total between 20-40 means you have moderate stress and should begin to implement stress management to avoid physical problems; a score of 40-60 means you are stressed out and should take strong action to deal with it, including seeing a therapist.

STRESS SIGN	0	1	2	3
Felt tense, nervous, anxious or upset				
Felt sad, depressed or hopeless				
Felt low energy, exhausted, tired, unable to get things done				
Could not turn off thoughts long enough at night or on weekends to feel relaxed and refreshed the next day				
Unable to sit still				
Felt losing control of feelings				
Preoccupied with a serious personal problem				
Been in unpleasant situations and hopeless to do anything about them				
Felt tired in the morning with low energy to get through day				
Had problems concentrating or remembering things				
Could be doing a great deal more to take care of yourself and stay healthy				
Have little control of events in life				
Cannot seem to accomplish desired effect				
Frustrated by bad breaks and people not measuring up				
Very high standards for own activities				
Life is empty and has no meaning				
When something difficult is coming, think about all the ways it can go poorly				
Run into problems that cannot be solved				
Not able to give to the people who are close				
Not felt close to or accepted by family and friends				

The Solutions

Any or all of these quizzes can give you a good idea of your stress level. Remembering that we all experience some level of stress, pay attention when the results seem high. Discuss these stressors with you family, friends or a therapist and then dig into what you can do to alleviate the stress.

The Resources

The following Web sites offer more information about stress levels:

Med India, *www.medindia.net/patients/calculators/life_sressor*

World Room, *www.worldroom.com/pages/womensworld/stress*

Eurofound, *www.eurofound.europa.eu*

Agnet, *www.agnet.org*

Bupa Co., *www.bupa.co.uk/health_information/asp/quizzes/stress/stress*

Kids Data, *www.kidsdata.org*

The following books offer more information on stress levels such as:

Getting Things Done: The Art of Stress-Free Productivity (Penguin, 2002)

101 Creative Strategies for Helping Children with High Stress Levels (YouthLight, Inc., 2005)

10 Simple Solutions to Stress: How to Tame Tension and Start Enjoying Your Life (New Harbinger Publications, 2007)

The Stress Management Handbook (McGraw-Hill, 1999)

Stress and Health: Biological and Psychological Interactions (Sage Publications, Inc., 2004)

Stress Busting Through Personal Empowerment (Routledge, 2004)

Good Stress, Bad Stress: An Indispensable Guide to Identifying and Managing Your Stress (Marlowe and Company, 2002)

46

Sleep Level Chart

Sleep is a critical element of our lives, one that is often interrupted for people who are suffering from stress. According to the National Sleep Foundation, most people need an average of eight hours of sleep per night for optimum function. However, most American adults are averaging only about seven hours of sleep or night and many of them are getting around three hours per night. If you are sleeping too much or too little, you may be suffering a sleep disorder based on stress. The sleep problem can add to your stress as you try to find ways to get a good night's sleep. By charting your sleep, potential sleep disorders and some methods to enhance sleep, you can get the rest your mind and body require.

The Challenge

To understand your sleep levels, you must understand the nature of sleep. It is far more than just laying down and relaxing and the quality of the sleep is sometimes more important than the quantity you are receiving. Your night's sleep can be divided into two crucial phases:

- Non-rapid eye movement sleep, NREM, takes up about 80 percent of your sleep time. It begins with general relaxation culminating in the deepest sleep levels when protein synthesis, growth hormones, the immune function and the mind's overall health are given a boost. This most rejuvenating sleep takes up about 50 percent of the adult's sleep time.
- Rapid eye movement, REM, takes up about 25 percent of your sleep time and is the most important period for mental revitalization. Dreams that occur during REM are a sorting of free-floating ideas that may be troubling you. Prolonged REM deprivation has been linked to excessive anxious or emotional behavior.

The National Sleep Foundation estimates nearly $100 billion are lost annually in business due to mistakes made by workers because of lack of proper sleep. This lack of sleep can also lead to on-the-job accidents. Sleep loss can add to driver fatigue and is a major cause of automobile accidents.

Our daily, stress-filled lifestyles contribute to a lack of proper sleep, making it harder to fall asleep or taking time away from a good night's sleep to meet other demands.

Late-night shift workers and the elderly are also more prone to sleep disorders because of physical issues or a feeling of not being tired. The challenge to understand and deal with your sleep levels is to adequately chart your sleep, recognize if you are suffering from a sleep disorder, avoiding behavior that can interfere with sleep and, if necessary, visit your physician for a complete sleep study. Getting a good night's sleep is a key to maintaining a more stress-free and healthy life.

Sleep Patterns Chart

Your physician will probably ask you to chart your sleep patterns before coming in for a thorough evaluation. It will only take you a few minutes of the day to honestly record your sleep levels. For the times shown on this chart place a D for the time you went down and a U for the times you have woke up for any significant length, usually 20 or more minutes, during the night. You can also shade in the time you have been asleep.

DAY/TIME	8 PM	9 PM	10 PM	11 PM	12 PM	1 AM	2 AM	3 AM	4 AM	5 AM	6 AM	7 AM
SUNDAY												
MONDAY												
TUESDAY												
WEDNESDAY												
THURSDAY												
FRIDAY												
SATURDAY												

Causes and Types of Sleep Disorders

Sleep problems can affect everyone from children to teens to adults to the elderly. They may be a non-specific problem that plagues our sleep or represent measurable primary or secondary disorders. Use this chart to indicate what type of sleep level problem you believe you are having and use it to consult with your physician over your sleep levels and patterns.

COMMON SLEEP DISORDER	YES	NO
Desire to go to bed earlier than usual		
Difficulty falling asleep		
Frequent waking during the night and lighter sleep		
Waking up earlier than usual and not feeling refreshed		
Feeling tired in the daytime		
Needing frequent naps during the day		
More fragmented sleep with rapid sleep cycles		
Decrease in deep sleep		

COMMON SLEEP DISORDER	YES	NO
Poor sleep hygiene with irregular sleep hours, use of alcohol before bedtime and napping		
Pain or medical illness that keeps you from sleeping well including need to urinate, arthritis, asthma, diabetes, osteoporosis, heartburn, menopause and Alzheimer's Disease.		
Side effects from medications		
Lack of exercise, a too sedentary lifestyle		
Psychological stress		

PRIMARY CLINICAL SLEEP DISORDERS	YES	NO
Insomnia		
Sleep apnea		
Narcolepsy		
Jet lag		
Shift work		
Sleepwalking		
Sleep Terrors		
Restless legs		
Periodic limb movement		

SECONDARY CLINICAL SLEEP DISORDERS	YES	NO
Adjustment insomnia		
Advanced sleep phase		
Bedwetting		
Behavioral insomnia of childhood		
Bruxism, teeth grinding		
Central sleep apnea		
Circadian rhythm sleep disorder		
Confusional arousals		
Congenital central alveolar hypoventilation syndrome		
Delayed sleep phase		
Dissociative disorders		
Eating disorders		
Environmental sleep disorders		
Excessive fragmentary myoclonus		

SECONDARY CLINICAL SLEEP DISORDERS	YES	NO
Groaning		
Hallucinations		
Hypersomnia		
Hypoventilation/hypoxemia		
Idiopathic hypersomonia		
Idiopathic insomnia		
Insomnia due to drugs, medical conditions, mental disorders or unspecified causes		
Insufficient sleep syndrome		
Irregular sleep-wake rhythm		
Leg cramps		
Long slumber		
Movement disorders		
Nightmares		
Paradoxical insomnia		
Parasomnia		
Psychophysiological insomnia		
Recurrent hypersomnia		
REM sleep behavior disorder		
Rhythmic movement		
Short sleeping		
Sleep paralysis		
Sleep starts		
Sleep talking		
Snoring		

Treating Sleep Level Disorders

You do not have to experience sleep disorders and rely on therapy and drugs. There are many lifestyle changes or homeopathic approaches to improving sleep that have been shown to be effective. You should chart the ones you have tried and what they have done to help.

SLEEP DISORDER TREATMENT	TRIED	UNTRIED	RESULTS
Avoid caffeine, nicotine or alcohol before going to sleep.			
Avoid exercise at least four hours before bedtime			
Leave worrying outside the bed			
Keep other activities out of the bedroom such as family activities, television and work			
Avoid forcing yourself to sleep by going to another room to watch television or read until feeling sleepy			
Maintain a comfortable bedroom temperature			
Reduce noise levels			
Avoid stimulation before sleeping			
Take your time getting ready for bed			
Maintain good nutrition			
Keep a regular sleep schedule			
Expose yourself to sunshine during the day			
Separate yourself from a snoring partner			
Go to bed earlier			
Monitor medications for sleep-hindering side effects			
Reduce stress levels			
Limit use of sleep aids or sleeping pills			
Minimize liquid intake before bedtime			
Combine sex and sleep			
Record worries or concerns in a journal before sleeping			
Check off items on a to-do list, think of tomorrow's schedule and let go			
Listen to calming music or a sound machine			
Read a relaxing book			
Get a massage from your partner			
Talk about what is troubling you			

The Solutions

Use these charts to start to understand your sleep levels and what you can do to improve them. The quality of your sleep depends on awareness and action and you can have neither until you examine your sleep. If you are one of the lucky ones of us who never experience sleep problems, you can still use these charts to see what you are doing well. Discuss the results with your partner and listen to any concerns he or she may have regarding your problems sleeping or excessive snoring. They can lead to other health problems and should be taken seriously. Then try to relax and get a consistent good night's sleep. You may be amazed at how much better you feel about your life if you are sleeping properly.

The Resources

The following Web sites offer more information about sleep levels:

National Sleep Foundation, *www.sleepfoundation.org*

Bryn Mawr, *www.serendip.brynmawr.edu*

Sleep Medicine Center, *www.sleepmedicinecenter.upmc.com*

Sleep Education, *www.sleepeducation.com/Disorders*

Help Guide, *www.helpguide.org/life/sleep_aging*

Baby Center, *www.babycenter.com*

The following books offer more information on sleep levels such as:

Sleep Disorders for Dummies (For Dummies, 2004)

Concise Guide to Evaluation and Management of Sleep Disorders, Third Edition (American Psychiatric Publishing, Inc., 2002)

Sleep Disorders and Sleep Deprivation: An Unmet Public Health Problem (Institute of Medicine, 2006)

Sleep, Dreaming and Sleep Disorders (Rowman & Littlefield, 1993)

Overcoming Sleep Disorders Naturally (Basic Health Publications, 2005)

Sleep: The Complete Guide to Sleep Disorders and a Better Night's Sleep (Firefly Books, 2003)

Healthy Sleep Habits, Happy Child (Ballantine Books, 1999)

47

Stress Reduction/Relief Methods Chart

There are basically two ways to deal with stress in your relief: reduction and relief. They are two entirely different techniques. Stress reduction takes a look at exerting more control over the factors that are bothering you to the point of feeling stressed out and taking action. Stress relief is more inward looking and helps you develop methods of coping psychologically with the stressors in your life, knowing they will not go away, but there are methods available to handle their effects. Most of us will use a combination of techniques for stress reduction and stress relief, some of which can cross over.

The Challenge

When we complain about the stress in our lives to non-professionals we are often told to simply relax. But, what does that mean? Relaxing for some means pursuing a hobby, exercising, getting more sleep. For others it means taking active steps to change the situation that is stressing them out. For others it might include holistic approaches such as meditation, yoga or acupuncture. The main question we face is what methods we think we can use and how to institute them into our lives. These techniques are designed to reduce stress by lowering the stressors we deal with or relieve stress by helping develop behaviors and though patterns that make it easier to cope with the inevitable stress we all face. Sometimes the techniques can blur together. The challenge is to recognize the nature of our stress, whether we think we can have more success in reduction or relief or both, finding methods that work for us and being willing to change our approach if what we are doing is not working as well as we hoped. The simple charts here can help you identify and choose what is working for you and what might be worth trying. You have to acknowledge the stress in your life and deal with it actively to help ease the situations. Ignoring it and waiting for things to get better will not solve your problems and could just exacerbate the stress.

Stress Reduction Chart

The methods here can help you reduce the stress you are feeling in your life. Not all may be right for your situation, but most can apply to just about any stress event. The idea is to reduce the effect of the stressor by taking outside action. Some of these actions may be based on changing some of your habits and thought patterns. Check the ones you are currently using, the ones you might want to use and note the results you feel you are achieving.

STRESS REDUCTION TECHNIQUE	YES	NO	RESULTS
Get up 15 minutes earlier in the morning to help avoid common mistakes.			
Prepare for the morning the evening before by making lunch and setting out clothes to wear.			
Do not rely on your memory. Write down essential appointments or tasks.			
Make duplicates of all keys. Hide a secret house key outside and carry a duplicate car key in your wallet outside your key ring.			
Use preventive maintenance on your car or home appliances to avoid unpleasant surprises.			
Be prepared to wait for appointments. Spend the time reading a book or magazine.			
Avoid procrastination. Do today what you want to do tomorrow, if you need to do it today, do it now.			
Plan ahead. Keep your gas tank at lest one quarter full, keep an emergency stock at home.			
Do not put up with things that do not work. If something is a constant cause of aggravation, replace it.			
Give yourself 15 minutes of extra time to get to appointments and avoid the feeling of running late.			
Eliminate or restrict the amount of caffeine you intake.			
Use contingency plans in case your initial plan does not go as you expected.			
Relax your standards and realize the world will not end if you do not accomplish a planned chore.			
Count your blessings. For every one thing that goes wrong there are probably 50-100 that have gone well for you.			
Ask questions and take some time to repeat back directions you have received.			
Say no to work and personal requests you cannot handle and politely explain why you are refusing the request.			
Unplug your phone when you need quiet time. Turn your cell phone off as well.			

STRESS REDUCTION TECHNIQUE	YES	NO	RESULTS
Turn needs into preferences. There are things we need, such as food and water. The rest are preferences and can be adjusted.			
Simplify your work and life. Reduce your commitments.			
Make friends with positive people who are non-worriers.			
Get up and stretch periodically if your job requires you to sit for long periods.			
If you need to find quiet at home, use earplugs.			
Get enough sleep, but not too much.			
Organize your home and workplace so you lose the clutter and can place your hands easily on the things you need. You will be less likely to lose things.			
Use deep breathing throughout the day to help reduce stress, especially after a particularly stressful event.			
Keep a journal for your thoughts and feelings and review it periodically. Keep it private.			
Prepare yourself for a feared event through visualization of what the experience will be like and how you will feel about it. Visualize what you want the experience to be.			
Use a diversion—a voluntary change in activity and environment—to take the stress out of getting a job done.			
Discuss your problems with a family member or trusted friend and act on their help if you agree with it.			
Find a work environment and people who suit your needs and attitudes.			
Take it one day at a time and let the future take care of itself.			
Do something you really enjoy every day.			
Take a hot bath or shower to relieve tension.			
Help someone else in your life.			
Focus on understanding others rather than having to be understood.			
Take steps to improve your appearance such as a new hair style or makeover.			
Avoid the tendency to overschedule your day with back-to-back interviews.			

STRESS REDUCTION TECHNIQUE	YES	NO	RESULTS
Learn flexibility. Some things are fine to compromise on and do not necessarily have to be done perfectly.			
Eliminate destructive self talk using I cannot or I will not.			
Use your weekend for a change of pace from your regular week. Tackling and completing a job at home may make you feel better about not getting as much done at work as you would like.			
Avoid multitasking. Do one thing at a time and concentrate on each activity or meeting.			
Allow yourself some time every day for privacy, quiet and introspection.			
Do an unpleasant task early in the day and then move on.			
Learn how to delegate some of your responsibilities to trusted coworkers.			
Eat lunch or at least take a lunch break that gets you away from your desk.			
Develop a forgiving view of your family and coworkers. We all live in an imperfect world.			
Have an optimistic view of the world around you and realize most people are doing the best they can.			
Break large tasks into smaller and more doable goals.			

Stress Relief Chart

If you cannot influence the stressors around you to the extent necessary, you need to develop internal and external techniques to relieve the stress you are feeling. This type of relief will not solve the problems of your stress, but will help you deal with it in a productive way. Check off whether you are using or plan on using any of these techniques and the results you believe you have achieved.

STRESS RELIEF TECHNIQUE	YES	NO	RESULTS
Visualize yourself in a tranquil place.			
Gain control of your breathing using relaxed breathing or rapid breathing techniques.			
Get away from noise.			
Use your imagination to put yourself in a different place.			
See problems as opportunities.			
Do not take things personally.			
There are seldom any right answers.			
Be yourself and strive to control yourself, not others.			
Exercise, even if it is just walking.			
Use meditation.			
Take a nap.			
Get a massage.			
Practice yoga or tai chi.			
Listen to soothing music.			
Use guided imagery tapes.			
Use biofeedback or hypnotherapy.			
Stay away from the daily news for a while.			
Use aromatherapy through candles or scented oils.			
Maintain a healthy sense of humor and do not take yourself too seriously.			
Do progressive muscle relaxation, especially before you go to sleep.			
Do some easy physical labor around the house in a project that can be completed.			
Read a good book, especially a novel.			
Learn how to separate work from home, and avoid taking work home with you. If you work at home, have a dedicated space for your work.			
Develop a support system of friends and family you can bounce your stressors and relief ideas off of.			

The Solutions

Properly filling out and reading these charts can tell you what you are doing well and what you might want to try. There are no hard and fast rules for what stress reduction or relief techniques you can try, and you probably will not be able to do them all. Start with the most obvious and most easily done, chart the results, review them after three-six months and add to the techniques or change them if you believe it is necessary. These charts can provide an excellent road map to successfully navigating your way through a stressful life.

The Resources

The following Web sites offer more information about stress reduction and relief:

Stress EHow, *www.ehow.com*

Mayo Clinic, *www.mayoclinic.com/health/time-management*

Reduce Stress, *www.reduce.StressTips.org*

Franklin Institute, *www.fi.edu/brain/relieve*

Stress Busting, *www.stressbusting.co.uk*

All About Life Challenges, *www.allaboutlifechanges.org/stress-relief*

Holistic Med, *www.holisticmed.com/stress/free*

The following books offer more information on stress reduction and relief such as:

Reducing Stress (DK ADULT, 1999)

Learn to Relax: Proven Techniques for Reducing Stress, Tension, and Anxiety—and Promoting Peak Performance (John Wiley & Sons, 2001)

Walk Don't Run: Tips for Reducing Stress (Peter Pauper Press, 1998)

Break the Stress Cycle: 10 Steps for Reducing Stress for Women (Diane Pub Co, 1998)

1001 Ways to Relax: An Illustrated Guide to Reducing Stress (Amazon Remainders)

Transforming Stress: The Heartmath Solution For Relieving Worry, Fatigue, And Tension (New Harbinger Publications, 2005)

Smart Guide to Relieving Stress (Wiley, 1999)

The One-Minute Meditator: Relieving Stress and Finding Meaning in Everyday Life (De Capo, 2001)

48

Changing Yourself or the Situation Chart

Sometimes to relieve stress we have to make fundamental changes in ourselves and our situations at work and in our personal life. This is usually a last step to be done after we have tried other forms of stress relief and reduction. It carries the danger if making major alterations that may be harder to get back. We have to be open to looking honestly at what inside of us and outside of us is causing our stress and then being willing to make the changes necessary in both. Any discomfort is made up for by effectiveness in controlling our stress.

The Challenge

The philosopher Socrates once said The Unexamined Life is Not Worth Living. Many scholars believe he meant that people who stumble through life with little or no awareness of who they are and how they have lived have wasted their opportunity for a good life. The same might be said about our reaction to stress. Understanding ourselves and having a clear-eyed view of the situation we are in can be an important start in understanding our reaction to the various stressors in our lives. Once we have come to this realization, we can then decide to change how we think and act and what we choose to surround ourselves with. Sometimes this change is overt by finding a new job or ending a destructive relationship. Other times it might be more sub-conscious by coming to the realization that some things cannot be changed and have to be lived with. The challenge is to examine ourselves and the world around us, identify what the possible stressors are, find ways to change them and our outlook and learn from the changes we are willing to make. Living an examined life may mean some extra work for us, but is ultimately worth it. The charts here show you how to evaluate yourself and your situation and what techniques you can use to make needed changes to help alleviate stress.

Patterns of Behavior Chart

Here is a simple chart to help identify your patterns of behavior that may lead to how you experience stress. It is a good starting point to take a look at your behavior and the situations you find yourself occupying. Check yes or no to what you think is causing you stress in your approach and situation.

QUESTIONS ABOUT YOUR STRESS	YES	NO
Do I go with the flow or tend to get upset over any situation no matter how small?		
Do I cling to my anger and resentment and let it ruin my day?		
Do I take my work problems home with me?		
Do I take my personal life issues to work with me?		
Do I feel generally discontented with my life?		
Do I suffer from physical ailments due to stress, eating disorders, substance abuse or have trouble sleeping?		

The Four A's Chart

One of the methods to change yourself and your situation is to practice any or all of the four A's techniques. The four A's refer to Avoid, Alter, Accept or Adapt yourself or your situation to handle your stress. You can pick and choose from all four categories for whatever you are doing now or would like to do. Check off yes or no and note the results on the chart below for what you are currently doing and what you might want to do in the next six months.

AVOIDING TECHNIQUES	YES	NO	RESULTS
Take control of your surroundings. Leave early if traffic is a problem. Pack a lunch and eat at your desk.			
Avoid contact with people who bother you. Put physical distance between you and a troublesome coworker.			
Learn how to say no. Taking on too much does not make you a good person, just a stressed out one. Say no to things you cannot handle and explain why in a constructive way.			
Turn off the news. The world news is often uncontrollable by you and can only cause you stress. Substitute reading a relaxing book or listening to music.			
Prioritize your to-do list with A, B, C elements. For a hectic day forget the C elements.			

ALTERING TECHNIQUES	YES	NO	RESULTS
Respectfully and tactfully ask others to change their behaviors and be prepared to do the same yourself. Small problems can often create larger ones if they are unresolved.			
Communicate your feelings openly. Use I statements about what you think and feel.			

	YES	NO	RESULTS
Do not be afraid to take risks. Inaction can create stress. What have you got to lose?			
Practice better time management by organizing your day to group tasks together. Increased efficiency means extra time.			
Set limits in advance. Be proactive in what you can or cannot do and establish that as early as possible.			
If you are feeling the symptoms of chronic stress, such as headaches, stomach trouble, eating disorders, uncontrollable crying and sleep problems. Consult your physician or visit a therapist for professional help. There is no shame in asking an expert to help you identify stressors and change them.			

ACCEPTING TECHNIQUES	YES	NO	RESULTS
Talk with someone you trust to vent your feelings and look for advice.			
Forgive someone you believe has wronged you. It takes a lot less energy than holding a grudge.			
Smile even if you have to fake it. Smiles are contagious and may be reflected back at you.			
Practice positive self-talk. Replace negativity with what you do well.			
Learn from your mistakes. Teachable moments can be helpful rather than hurtful.			
View stress as an opportunity to focus on the task needed as long as you let it go when you are through with the task.			

ADAPTING TECHNIQUES	YES	NO	RESULTS
Adjust your standards. You probably do not need to clean up all the time or make a homemade meal every night.			
Practice thought-stopping Cease gloomy thoughts immediately and replace them with positive thoughts.			
Adapt a mantra with a simple saying like I Can Do This, you can repeat to yourself through a difficult task.			
Create an assets column. List the things you do well and change it as needed. Review it often to remind yourself you excel at many things.			

Use humor and imagination. Do not take yourself or the situation too seriously and learn how to laugh.			
Keep the big picture in mind. Most things you stress over will be small and, when placed in context, may not seem as daunting.			

The Solutions

Self-awareness leads to self-control and nothing is more calming than feeling we have control over ourselves and our situations. Chronic stress can have major effects on our physical condition and our relationships with others and it should not be taken lightly. Evaluate your responses carefully, change the charts over time and see how they affect you and your situation. You may not be able to eliminate the stressors, but you can make the changes you need to better cope with them. It can seem like a lot of effort, but all of these techniques are a matter of common sense and should not be viewed as a chore, but rather an opportunity.

The Resources

The following Web sites offer more information about changing yourself and response to stress:

Columbus Business First, *www.columbus.bizjournals.com*

Mayo Clinic, *www.mayoclinic.com/health/stress-relief*

Michigan State University, *www.healthed.msu.edu/fact/stress_response*

ADHD, *www.add_adhd-help-center.com/stress/response*

Arthritis California, *www.arthritis.ca*

Stress About, *www.stress.about.com*

Medical Moment, *www.medicalmoment.org*

The following books offer more information on changing yourself and responses to stress such as:

A *Clinical Guide to the Treatment of the Human Stress Response* (Springer, 2002)

Beyond the Relaxation Response (Berkley, 1985)

Stress Response Syndromes: Personality Styles and Interventions (Jason Aronson, 2001)

Exercise and Stress Response: The Role of Stress Proteins (Informa Healthcare, 2002)

Posttraumatic Stress Disorder: Acute and Long-Term Responses to Trauma and Disaster (American Psychiatric Publishing, 1997)

Treatment of Stress Response Syndromes (American Psychiatric Publishing, 2002)

Stress in Life and at Work (Sage Publications, 2001)

49

Managing Your Stress Level Chart

If you feel like you cannot adequately reduce or relieve your stress, you may have to face the prospect of accepting the stress in your life and finding ways to manage it. This means you cannot easily lessen the stress but you can find ways to cope with it. You need to enter this process understanding how it can work for you and finding methods that will help you manage your stress and carry on with your life.

The Challenge

You manage your money, you manage your family, you may even manage people on the job. You might consider yourself a good, empathetic manager. But, how well do you manage the stress in your life. Unmanaged stress can quickly become destructive to us. There are times when techniques for stress relief and reduction simply are not adequate and you are accepting the fact that the stressor is going to stay with you. Sometimes the presence of stressors can be beneficial and help motivate and focus our work and attention. But, long-term chronic stress is not usually helpful and can result in a variety of psychological and physical problems. You must learn methods of coping with stress that is going to be with you for a while, and to manage the stress in your life so you can keep moving forward even with stress taking a toll. There are several areas of stress that can be managed and a variety of techniques that can be used. The charts shown here can provide a checklist and tip sheet for how to manage the stress in your life. The challenge is when to recognize the presence of manageable stress, what areas of your life the stress impacts, finding methods to manage and cope with the stress and continually evaluating their effectiveness. As our lives change, our stressors will too and these charts should be continually studied and upgraded.

Different Areas of Stress

The areas of your life where you feel stressed will vary for each person and will change over time. However, in general the major stress areas that must be managed are:

- Job-related stress;
- financial stress'
- health and caregiving stress, especially as you grow older and
- personal stress in our home and social life.

Job-Related Stress Management

Most studies into stress find that job-related stress affects us more than any other. We feel less control of our situation on the job, and managing other people can represent its own type of stress. We have to work for a living and some type of job stress will just have to be managed. This chart gives you some ideas of what to do to manage job-related stress. Check off yes or no on what you are doing now or can do and the results you are achieving.

STRESS MANAGEMENT TECHNIQUES	YES	NO	RESULTS
Communicate with your boss or fellow workers to establish goals.			
Avoid taking the stressor personality. It is just a job.			
Make an effort to thoroughly understand what is expected of you.			
Say no if you are being asked to do more than you can handle.			
Learn how to delegate to other workers.			
Take breaks during the day and do some simple stretching or breathing exercises.			
Remove yourself from noise and distractions.			
Have comfortable furniture or work station			
Understand possible health and safety risks and communicate them to others.			
Try to take more charge of decision making.			
Do not fear a loss of a job or lay-off. You will survive it.			
Train thoroughly on new equipment and ask questions if you do not understand it.			
Avoid office politics and do not place yourself in co-worker's conflicts.			
Report any bullying or harassment and expect action.			
Do not live your life for work, but spend time with your family and for yourself.			
Get a job description and make sure you are staying with it. You should be given this before you agree to a new job and it can be negotiated.			
Get support, if needed, from your union or state and federal regulatory agencies.			

STRESS MANAGEMENT TECHNIQUES	YES	NO	RESULTS
Resist the urge for perfectionism. It will only hinder you from getting things done.			
Cultivate allies at work and talk over your stress-related problems with them Sometimes just sharing can work wonders.			

Financial Stress Management

We must have money to live and we often are not that good at managing our money. Through no overt fault of our own we find ourselves in financial trouble that can mean receiving debt collection activities, the loss of a car or appliances, having utilities turned off and even losing our homes. The stress involved in financial difficulties can be debilitating. The chart below gives you some simple ideas on dealing with the stress of your financial situation, not the situation itself. Just check each item yes or no that might apply to you and write down the results or expected results.

STRESS MANAGEMENT TECHNIQUES	YES	NO	RESULTS
Do not suffer alone. Share your concerns over financial matters with your spouse and immediate family and tell them what you hope to do about them.			
Avoid unhealthy coping behaviors such as drinking alcohol, taking drugs, smoking and overeating.			
Do not sacrifice health care for you and your family. This can be essential in managing your stress.			
Get as much sleep as possible and try to put the concerns away for the night.			
Do away with unhealthy emotions such as anger, anxiety, frustration and a growing sense of hopelessness.			
Take action to cut down on your debt and visit a reputable financial counselor.			
Be smart with your spending and avoid buyer's remorse.			
Clear out the clutter you do not need with a garage sale or by selling it on eBay or other online auction sites.			

Caregiver Stress Management

Taking care of someone else can present tremendous stress as can dealing with our own health issues. This is especially true as we grow older or have to care for the elderly with health concerns. This chart can help you manage the stress of caregiving. Check each item yes or no if you are doing it or want to do it and note the results.

STRESS MANAGEMENT TECHNIQUES	YES	NO	RESULTS
Eat nutritious meals regularly.			
Get plenty of sleep. If you have to be up during the night, try to take a nap.			
Exercise regularly even if it means finding someone else to be on hand while you are doing it.			
Take care of your health by not neglecting getting regular medical checkups and share with your physician any signs of caregiver stress.			
Get other friends or family members to help or just give you a break.			
Stay active in your social environment and try to keep in touch with friends, clubs and other activities for fun.			
Use community services and organizations to help you such as geriatric care manager, volunteers or staff from your church, respite care to give you some time off and adult day centers for the person you are providing care for.			
Talk to others about your stress and how you are trying to manage it.			
Deal constructively with negative feelings by coming up with positive ways to deal with natural anger and conflicting emotions.			

Personal Stress Management

Finally, you will have to deal with stress in a wide area of your personal lives from your partner to your family to you friends. These stressors may involve the people you love but occasionally get frustrated with. You can manage this stress by using the tips shown in this chart. Mark each item yes or no if you use and understand it or want to use and mark down the results.

MANAGEMENT TECHNIQUES	YES	NO	RESULTS
Take control of your situation. You are not powerless to control your stress.			
Give yourself time outs where you can be by yourself either in your home, working in your yard, shopping or seeing a movie.			
Reach out to others for help and do not retreat into your own world of stress.			
Watch your diet and exercise regularly.			
Use breathing and progressive muscle relaxation to let go of tension and stress.			
Be realistic of your own goals and objectives. Avoid setting yourself up for disappointment by setting unreachable goals.			
List your resources. Be aware of what you can use in your life to deal with stress.			
Stay flexible in what you can do and make changes to your approach to managing stress as needed.			
Avoid stress enhancers like excessive caffeine or stimulants.			
Get in touch by hugging your family and friends or hold your pet. Physical contact can be a terrific way to manage stress.			
Be aware of your needs, values and desires and listen to your body.			
Budget your time and energies to take care of the most important things first.			
Express your honest anger without going over the top or getting personal.			
Stop whatever you are doing that is causing stress, change the scene and take a short walk.			
Think about what the worst is that can happen and realize you will find a solution for the problem.			
Set priorities and multitask wisely. You cannot do everything at once.			

The Solutions

Know your stressors, classify them and come up with reasonable strategies to manage your stress. You cannot cure the condition but you can treat it wisely. At all times, share your concerns with others and ask for any advice they might have. You may be surprised at how many of your friends have suffered from similar stress. Misery may not love company, but knowing you are not alone in your feelings can help you get through your stressors. Then move on to handling the other elements in your life that are not stressing you out.

The Resources

The following Web sites offer more information about managing your stress level:

Help Guide, www.helguide.org/mental/work_stress_management

Cal Tech Counseling Center, www.counseling.caltech.edu/articles/managestress

Stress About.Com, www.stress.about.comod/financialstress

University of North Dakota Memorial Union, www.union.und.edu/involvement/leadership/handouts/manage_stress

CNN, www.cnn.com

Stanford University, www.hprc.stanford.edu

American Association of Retired Persons, www.aarp.org

The following books offer more information on managing your stress levels such as:

Performance Under Pressure: Managing Stress in the Workplace (HRD Press, Inc., 2003)

Good Stress, Bad Stress: An Indispensable Guide to Identifying and Managing Your Stress (Marlowe & Company, 2002)

The Complete Idiot's Guide to Managing Stress (Alpha, 1999)

Managing Stress (Problems in Practice) (Blackwell Publishing, 1989)

Managing Anxiety And Stress (Routledge, 1991)

50 Activities for Managing Stress (HRD Press, 1995)

Managing Your Stress: How to Relax and Enjoy (Happiness Unlimited Publications, 1982)

Part Ten:

Research and Resources

50

Latest Research on Stress Related Issues

If you are truly interested in identifying and managing your stress you should be aware of the latest research as well as respected stress research from past studies. This research can help point out methods of managing stress that you or your physician may not be readily aware of. The research is mostly available online and is mostly free, although some organizations may charge you a nominal amount to access a journal or newsletter. The research may also be available in hard copy at your local public library or your local medical libraries and you can copy what you need for future use.

The Challenge

For many people the idea of doing research is similar to getting a major operation. It may be necessary, but it will not be pleasant. This is usually based on our academic experience where we were forced to do research on topics that we were either not interested in or did not have any connection to our lives. This may not be true if you need to do research on a topic such as stress management. Most of us have a need to use management techniques to help with our stress, and the nature of the research has changed rapidly over the last few years, with the likelihood of it changing more. By using search engines and the sites shown here, you can gain access to specific pieces of new research or the searchable section of the actual Website. The emphasis here is on Websites, since they will usually contain the latest information long before a book is published. The challenge is to get comfortable with doing research, identifying what you are trying to find out to refine your search, evaluating the source and then using the research in a meaningful way. Done properly your research should not be an onerous task, but one that challenges you and leads you to exciting discoveries.

The Facts

Not all online research is created equally. Some of the information on the Internet is wrong or outdated. You need to carefully evaluate the research you are seeing to determine if it is worth your time and attention. The checklist below will give you a simple guideline on how to make that evaluation.

RESEARCH CREDENTIALS	SOURCE	URL	DATE	ACADEMIC	MEDICAL	RESEARCH ORG.	AUTHOR/ CREDENTIALS

Sampling of Latest Research on Stress

Warning Signs of Stress: When to See Your Doctor

Cleveland Clinic

http://www.clevelandclinic.org/health/health-info/docs/1400/1473.asp?index=6406

A quick, easy-to-read list of stress-related symptoms that might merit visiting your physician for an evaluation or a therapist.

How Can I Manage Stress?

American Heart Association

http://www.americanheart.org/downloadable/heart/110167971464923%20 HowCanIManageStress.pdf

Stress can cause more than physical discomfort. In the case of people already suffering from a heart condition such as arrhythmia, it can lead to stroke or heart attack. To manage a heart condition, you need to know how to manage your stress.

Relaxation Techniques: Learn Ways to Calm Your Stress

National Institute of Health

http:www.nim.nih.gov/medicineplus/stress.html

New techniques in stress relaxation are constantly being developed. This brief article gives you an overview of some of the newest ideas being circulated by health professionals.

Quitting Tobacco: Handling Stress... Without Smoking

National Cancer Institute

http://www.cancer.gov/templates/doc.aspx?viewid=A4C99D4E-FB79-49C2-967B-636B88E0ED7C

Nicotine is a stimulant and is one of the most abused drugs in the world. Smokers often increase their intake of nicotine when they feel stressed, which can lead to other conditions such as heart or lung disease. This article gives smokers some tips on substituting other relaxation techniques for that urge to light up.

Spirituality and Stress Relief: Make the Connection

Mayo Clinic Foundation

http://www.mayoclinic.com/print/stress-relief/SR00035/METHOD=print

Many of us live our lives without a strong spiritual base. This can be a formal religion or other belief systems. Relying and turning to spirituality and a higher power can help us keep our stress in balance and remind us of what is important and valued in our lives. This article gives some ideas and regaining spirituality.

Stress in the Workplace

American Psychological Association

http://www.apahelpcenter.org/articles/article.php?id=19

Modern workplace issues such as downsizing, outsourcing, new training and having to do more with less are causes of major stress. This article gives a look at what these new workplace issues are and how they have affected our current stress levels, as well as some ideas on how to reduce them.

When Stress Flares

Arthritis Foundation

http://ww2.arthritis.org/resources/arthritistoday/2005_archives/2005_05_06/2005_05_06_Stress_4.asp

The aches and pains we feel from stress may be symptoms of a more serious condition, such as arthritis. Unacknowledged until recently, stress can have a major effect on the severity and symptoms of arthritis and seriously limit our quality of life. This article links stress to arthritis and talks about how to avoid stress from worsening a difficult condition.

Childhood Stress

Kid's Health

http://kidshealth.org/parent/emotions/feelings/stress.html

Childhood is supposed to be a carefree time of play and discovering what life is all about. But, in many cases, childhood can be stressful. Children may be dealing with body issues, peer problems and stress in dealing with a family problem such as a divorce or death in the family. You cannot discount childhood stress and need to deal with it as the unique condition that it is. This site can help you better understand the newest research in childhood stress.

Helping Teenagers with Stress

American Academy of Child & Adolescent Psychiatry

http://www.aacap.org/page.ww?name=Helping+Teenagers+With+Stress&section =Facts+for+Families

Teenagers are prone to stress that adults feel but are also open to other stressors: dealing with peer pressure, the lure of drugs and alcohol, outside activities that can feel like more of a burden than a pleasure. This stress can cause teenagers to act out and withdraw from their families. They have difficulty in communicating their stress and may suffer from physical ailments such as sleep disorders. This site discusses the latest findings in teenage stress and the best ways to deal with it.

Stress and Your Health

Women's Health

http://womenshealth.gov/faq/stress.htm#7

Stress used to be considered a man's problem, especially in the days when men were the primary breadwinners. But, nowadays the problem of stress is shared by women who often have to balance a career or worklife with maintaining the home. This maintenance includes shopping, childhood care, providing a taxi service for busy children and cooking. Women's stress is just as difficult as men's and must be recognized for the differences. This article is a start in understanding the current research into women's stress and management techniques.

Stress at Work

National Institute of Occupational Safety and Health

http://www.cdc.gov/niosh/stresswk.html

The government organization for OSHA offers several publications on workplace safety including this excellent overview of the issue and consequences of stress at work.

Workplace stress can cause absenteeism based on physical ailments, breed discontent and result in workplace injuries because of burned-out and inattentive workers. This publication gives you some background in the latest findings of workplace stress, links to other work stress sites and ideas on how to help employees and managers with work stress issues.

New Research on Stress

Mental Health About.com

http://mentalhealth.about.com/b/a/222051.htm

About.com offers a variety of resources on a number of topics including mental health and stress. This article is an excellent summary of general and specific new research into the problems of stress. It also offers you a chance to apply to their newsletter for email updates. You can also post user reviews and communicate with the About.com editors on the material and how useful you found it.

Stress and the Cancer Community

Ohio State University Medical Center Stress and Immunity Cancer Projects

http://and.psy.ohio-state.edu/

Cancer causes a unique form of stress for the patient and their caregivers. The disease can cause great uncertainty in someone's life. However, life after cancer carries other stressful burdens that are just now being recognized. Post-cancer stress includes dealing with drugs, post-cancer treatments and the very real fears that the disease will return. Besides support groups and other literature, Ohio State University is providing new research into post-cancer stress and how to get through life after a life-threatening disease.

The Solutions

The sites shown here provide not only a sampling of the current research in stress, but give you some idea of the variety of information available. Notice the information comes from government agencies or medical organizations. These are your safest bets for good information, but you may still be able to find worthwhile material from other sites, including blogs. Evaluate what you are reading and, if you feel the information is conflicting or does not sound right, talk about it with your physician. You should never undertake an exercise regimen or over-the-counter drug treatments without talking to your physician. Even if you do not feel major stress at this point in your life, it is a good idea to be aware of what to expect and how you can survive the rigors of modern stress.

The Resources

The following Web sites offer more information about current stress research:

Medline, *www.ncbi.nlm.nih.gov/*

The Mayo Clinic, *www.mayoclinic.com*

Stress About.Com, *www.stress.about.com*

American Heart Association, *www.heart.org*

National Institute of Occupational and Safety Health, *www.niosh.gov*

American Association of Retired Persons, *www.aarp.org*

National Institute of Mental Health, *www.nimh.nih.gov*

The following books offer more information on current stress research such as:

Historical and Current Perspectives on Stress and Health (JAI Press, 2002)

Homan Stress: Current Selected Research (AMS Pr, Inc., 2007)

Stress and Mental Health: Contemporary Issues and Prospects for the Future (Springer, 1994)

Children's Stress and Coping: A Family Perspective (The Guilford Press, 1993)

Who Gets Ptsd?: Issues of Posttraumatic Stress Vulnerability (Charles C. Thomas Publisher, 2006)

Organizational Stress: A Review and Critique of Theory, Research, and Applications (Sage Publications, Inc., 2001)

51

Resources to Combat Stress

You do not have to sit immobilized by feelings of stress or suffer the very real mental and physical conditions that are caused by chronic or acute stress. There are resources you can use to recognize what type of stress you are feeling, how this stress is impacting your life and your family's life and what you can do to combat it. You need to take the time and effort to examine these resources and use them as you believe to be appropriate.

The Challenge

The best resource in fighting stress is knowledge and a good place to start with the search for the latest resources is online. You can also find magazine or journal articles, or books, but these may be more dated. Throughout this book we have included dozens of Websites and books that can help you with your stress, either as a resource by themselves or as a guide to further resources on the topic of stress. In addition to this information-based material, there are resources that take more of a hands-on approach to battling stress through relaxation techniques and other holistic therapies. In this chapter you will find some of the most useful Websites, books and other resources to combat stress, divided by the sections of this book. As with all material, you need to evaluate how current the information is and how reliable. Once you have located items that seem worthwhile, print them out or purchase them for future reference. Also, be sure to use the professional resources of a therapist or physician and the information resources of your support group of family and friends to help combat stress. The challenge is to choose a resource wisely and give it a fair chance to work in your life before moving on to something else. The process of combating stress is a lifelong commitment and must be taken seriously to help you.

Section 1: What Is Stress?

These resources will help you learn more about stress and recognize what types of stress you might be experiencing. They include resources on definitions, symptoms of stress, acute and chronic stress, health risks of stress and how men and women react differently to stress. The checklist below will give you a simple guideline on how to make that evaluation.

WEBSITE	URL
National Institute of Occupational of Safety and Health	www.niosh.gov
The Mayo Clinic	www.mayoclinic.com
Changing Minds	www.changingminds.org
Wellness Tips	www.wellnesstips.ca
Mental Health	www.mentalhealth.com
Science Daily	www.sciencedaily.com
American Psychological Association	www.helping.apa.org

BOOK TITLE	PUBLISHER	YEAR PUBLISHED
Measuring Stress: A Guide for Health and Social Scientists	Oxford University Press, USA	1997
The Complete Idiot's Guide to Managing Stress	Alpha	1999
Dr. Susan Lark's Anxiety & Stress Self Help Book: Effective Solutions for Nervous Tension Emotional Distress, Anxiety & Panic	Celestial Arts	1996
Acute Stress Disorder: A Handbook of Theory, Assessment and Treatment	American Psychological Association	2000
Coping with Chronic Stress	Springer	1997
Historical and Current Perspectives on Stress and Health	JAI Press	2002

Section 2: Causes of Stress

There are a variety of elements and environments that can cause stress from the actions of other people to the choices we make. These resources will help you understand the causes of stress and whether they are affecting your life. They include work and personal stress, stress of modern life, perfectionism and work/life balance.

WEBSITE	URL
Career Planning About	www.careerplanning.about.com
Quintessential Careers	www.quintcareers.com
Stress Directions	www.stressdirections.com
Making the Modern World	www.makingthemodernworld.net
Shrink Stress	www.shrinkstress.com
The Health Center	www.thehealthcenter.info/emotions/perfectionism/causes
Work Life Balance	www.worklifebalance.com

BOOK TITLE	PUBLISHER	YEAR PUBLISHED
Measuring Stress: A Guide for Health and Social Scientists	*Oxford University Press, USA*	*1997*
Surviving Stress at Work: Understand It, Overcome It	*Trafford Publishing*	*2006*
Stress at Work: Management and Prevention	*Butterworth-Heinemann*	*2005*
Your Personal Stress Profile and Activity Workbook	*McGraw Hill Humanities/ Sciences/Languages*	*2005*
Personal Stress and Well-Being Assessment (HRD Press, Inc., 2002)	*HRD Press, Inc.*	*2002*
No Time: Stress and the Crisis of Modern Life	*Douglas and McIntyre*	*2005*
When Perfect Isn't Good Enough: Strategies for Coping with Perfectionism	*New Harbinger Publications*	*1998*
Perfectionism: What's Bad About Being Too Good	*Free Spirit Publishing*	*1999*
Harvard Business Review on Work and Life Balance	*Harvard Business School Press*	*2000*
Work-Life Balance (Overcoming Common Problems)	*Sheldon Press*	*2003*

Section 3: Assessing Your Personal Stress Level

You will need a variety of tools to find out what type and to what extent personal stress is affecting you. This is the first step in determining how to cope with these stressors. The chart below lists some of the resources for assessing your personal stress such as stress intake, a simple quiz, major life changes, coping strategies and job burnout.

WEBSITE	URL
Health Scout	*www.healthscout.com*
Pew Organization	*www.pewinternet.org*
Family.Org,	*www.family.org/lifechallenges*
American Institute of Stress	*www.stress.org*
My Prime Time	*www.myprimetime.com/health/burnout/ burnout*

BOOK TITLE	PUBLISHER	YEAR PUBLISHED
Principles and Practice of Stress Management, Second Edition	The Guilford Press	1993
Family Stress	Ballantine Books	2004
Making Crucial Choices and Major Life Changes	Media Psychology Associates	2006
In Transition: Navigating Major Life Changes	Morehouse Publishing	2002
Families and Change: Coping With Stressful Events and Transitions	Sage Publications, In.	2005
Coping: The Psychology of What Works	Oxford University Press, USA	1999
Overcoming Job Burnout: How to Renew Enthusiasm for Work	Ronin Publishing	2005
Beating Job Burnout: How to Transform Work Pressure into Productivity	Ronin Publishing	1993

Section 4: The Basic Methods to Deal With Stress

There are many ways to deal with stress, but most of them fall under certain basics you can employ immediately to help with your stress. These basics are explained in the resources here and include reducing stress, relieving stress, coping mechanisms and how to let go.

WEBSITE	URL
Reduce Stress	www.reduce.StressTips.org
Franklin Institute	www.fi.edu/brain/relieve
Stress Busting	www.stressbusting.co.uk
Health Resource Network	www.stresscure.org
Positive Health	www.positivehealth.com
Stress Doctor	www.stressdoc.com

BOOK TITLE	PUBLISHER	YEAR PUBLISHED
Reducing Stress	DK ADULT	1999
Learn to Relax: Proven Techniques for Reducing Stress, Tension, and Anxiety— and Promoting Peak Performance	John Wiley & Sons	2001
Smart Guide to Relieving Stress	Wiley	1999

BOOK TITLE	PUBLISHER	YEAR PUBLISHED
The Big Book of Stress Relief Games: Quick, Fun Activities for Feeling Better	*McGraw-Hill*	*2000*
Families and Change: Coping With Stressful Events and Transitions	*Sage Publications, Inc.*	*2005*
Coping: The Psychology of What Works	*Oxford University Press, USA*	*1999*
Secret of Letting Go	*Llewellyn Publications*	*2002*
The Language of Letting Go	*MJF Books*	*1998*

Section 5: Dealing With Workplace Stress

One of the most common settings for stress is the workplace. We may face the difficult boss, impossible working conditions, long hours, lack of resources and demands to do more than we were hired for. This chart gives you some resources in dealing with a difficult work place and its stress and includes the intergenerational workplace, the bad boss, the impossible schedule and limited resources.

WEBSITE	URL
Bad Bossology	*www.badbossology.com*
Working America	*www.workingamerica.org*
Rothman Management Development	*www.jrothman.com*
Able Work Schedule	*www.uos.harvard.edu*
iVillage	*www.quiz.ivillage.com/cgi-bin/ goodhousekeeping/tests/perfectionist*
All the Tests	*www.allthetests.com*
Small Business Association	*www.sba.gov*

BOOK TITLE	PUBLISHER	YEAR PUBLISHED
A Survival Guide for Working With Bad Bosses: Dealing with Bullies, Idiots, Back stabbers, And Other Managers from Hell	*AMACOM, American Management Association, 2005*	*2005*
Alternative Work Schedules	*Allyn & Bacon*	*1998*
The Impact of Work Schedules on the Family	*Institute for Social Research*	*1983*
Making Collaboration Work: Lessons from Innovation in Natural Resource Management	*Island Press*	*2000*

Section 6: Dealing With Personal Stress

The other aspect of stress in our lives revolves around our personal lives. This can include our family, aging issues, being a caregiver and growing up and growing old. Dealing with personal stress may seem easier than dealing with business stress, but it represents an entirely different type of challenge. These resources help you identify your personal stress and how to alleviate it. They include the family, relationships and intimacy, the single life, children, teens, seniors and being a caregiver.

WEBSITE	URL
American Family Physician	www.aafp.org
Life Positive	www.lifepositive.com/Mind/psychology/stress/social-anxiety
Emotional Wellness	www.emotionalwellness.com/intimacy
Stress and the Single Mom	www.stressandthesinglemom.com
Living Single Again	www.livingsingle.com
American Academy of Child and Adolescent Psychiatry	www.aacap.org
Teen Matters	www.teen-matters.com
American Association of Retired Persons	www.aarp.org
Caregiver Stress	www.caregiverstress.com

BOOK TITLE	PUBLISHER	YEAR PUBLISHED
Family Stress Management	Sage Publications, Inc.	2001
Handbook of Stress, Trauma, and the Family	Taylor and Francis	2004
Naked Intimacy: How to Increase True Openness in Your Relationship	McGraw-Hill	2002
The Courage to Trust: A Guide To Building Deep and Lasting Relationships	New Harbinger Publications	2005
Single and Loving It: Living Life to the Fullest	Harrison House	2003
The Handbook for Helping Kids With Anxiety and Stress	Youthlight, Inc.	2003
The Handbook for Helping Teens With Anxiety and Stress	Youthlight, Inc.	2003
The Emotional Survival Guide for Caregivers: Looking After Yourself and Your Family While Helping and Aging Parent	The Guilford Press	2006

Section 7: Tips for Reducing Overall Stress

Reducing stress means finding resources outside your inner life and actions you can take to affect the stressors that are bothering you. It means recognizing the type of stress outside your own feelings and what you can do to cope with them. Here are resources on some tips for reducing stress including managing your time better, saying no, taking care of yourself, asking for help, changing yourself and response to stress and changing the situation.

WEBSITE	URL
Get More Done	www.getmoredone.com/tips1
Self Growth,	www.selfgrowth.com
Self Help Magazine	www.selfhelpmagazine.com
Caring to the End	www.caringtothend.ca
Medical Moment	www.medicalmoment.org
Crisis Center	www.crisiscenter.com/dstress
Stress Hardy	www.stresshardy.com

BOOK TITLE	PUBLISHER	YEAR PUBLISHED
Time Management	McGraw-Hill	2003
The Time Trap: The Classic Book on Time Management	MJF Books	2002
Saying No: A User's Manual	The Virtual Press	2003
Taking Care of Yourself: Strategies for Eating Well, Staying Fit and Living in Balance	Sounds True	2002
Mayday!: Asking for Help in Times of Need	Brett-Koehler Publishers	2007
Stress Response Syndromes: Personality Styles and Interventions	Jason Aronson	2001
Changing for Good: A Revolutionary Six-Stage Program for Overcoming Bad Habits and Moving Forward	Collins	1995

Section 8: Tips for Relieving Overall Stress

Relieving stress involves looking inwards and finding personal methods to achieve a more relaxed life. It involves hobbies, recreational activities and relaxation techniques that do not change the stressors, but change your response to stress. The tips include exercising, writing, letting feelings out, hobbies, volunteering and relaxing your mind and body.

WEBSITE	URL
How to Be Fit	www.howtobefit.com/exercise-to-relax
Relishing Life	www.relishinglife.com/71/turn-to-writing-for-stress-relief/
Growing Aware	www.growingaware.com.au
Deal With Stress	www.dealwithstress.com/Hobbies-As-Stress-Relief
Volunteer Match,	www.volunteermatch.org
Mindtools	www.mindtools.com/stress/RelaxationTechniques/PhysicalTechniques
Stress Vacation	www.stress-vacation.com/relaxation

BOOK TITLE	PUBLISHER	YEAR PUBLISHED
Turn Stress into Bliss: The Proven 8-Week Program for Health, Relaxation, Stress Relief	Fair Winds Press	2005
Writing to Heal: A Guided Journal for Recovering from Trauma and Emotional Upheaval	New Harbinger Publications	2004
Leading Out Loud: Inspiring Change Through Authentic Communications	Jossey-Bass	2003
Get a Hobby: 101 All-Consuming Diversions for Any Lifestyle	Collins	2007
Volunteering: The Selfish Benefits: Achieve Deep-Down Satisfaction and Create That Desire in Others	Committee Communications	2001
Instant Calm: Over 100 Easy-to-Use Techniques for Relaxing Mind and Body	Plume	1995
Ageless Body, Timeless Mind: The Quantum Alternative to Growing Old	Harmony	1994
Body Mind Balancing: Using Your Mind to Heal Your Body	St. Martin's Griffin	2005

Section 9: Stress Reduction/Relief Worksheets

You need a plan to reduce or relief stress and part of making that plan is using paperwork to note the techniques you are using or can use and what their results might be. These charts will help you focus your thinking and concentrate on what can work for you. The charts include stress levels, sleep levels, stress reduction/relief methods, changing yourself or the situation and managing your overall stress level.

WEBSITE	URL
World Room	www.worldroom.com/pages/womensworld/stress
National Sleep Foundation	www.sleepfoundation.org
Stress EHow	www.ehow.com
ADHD	www.add_adhd-help-center.com/stress/response
Stress About.Com	www.stress.about.comod/stress

BOOK TITLE	PUBLISHER	YEAR PUBLISHED
The Stress Management Handbook	McGraw-Hill	1999
Concise Guide to Evaluation and Management of Sleep Disorders, Third Edition	American Psychiatric Publishing, Inc.	2002
Smart Guide to Relieving Stress	Wiley	1999
Walk Don't Run: Tips for Reducing Stress	Peter Pauper Press	1998
Treatment of Stress Response Syndromes	American Psychiatric Publishing	2002
Good Stress, Bad Stress: An Indispensable Guide to Identifying and Managing Your Stress	Marlowe & Company	2002
The Complete Idiot's Guide to Managing Stress	Alpha	1999

Alternative Methods for Dealing With Stress

Besides traditional clinical methods for stress reduction and relief there are other techniques and products available that provide a holistic or homeopathic solution. You should be careful about using these techniques and carefully evaluate their good and bad effects. Here are quick resources on some of the most common techniques.

Massage

www.healing.about.com/od/massagetips/Massage_Therapy_Tips.htm

Acupuncture

Aroma Therapy

www.joellessacredgrove.com/Herbs/aroma.html

Biofeedback

www.whfhhc.com/Biofeedback/

Hypnotherapy

www.hypnosishealthcare.com/forum/hypnosis/index.html

Yoga

www.yogatohealth.com/

Dietary Supplements

www.energywave.com/rssfeed.xml

The Solutions

These resources are just a starting point for learning more about the nature of modern stress among people of all ages and how stress can be treated. You should use online search engines such as Google or Yahoo, your library and book store and your physician or therapist to find additional resources. Keep your mind open to new ideas, there is new research constantly entering the market on stress. The key is to know what to acknowledge and what to ignore as you work to improve your life.